O9-ABE-236

FLASHBACK

FLASHBACK

POSTTRAUMATIC STRESS DISORDER, SUICIDE, AND THE LESSONS OF WAR

PENNY COLEMAN

BEACON PRESS
BOSTON

BEACON PRESS
25 Beacon Street
Boston, Massachusetts 02108-2892
www.beacon.org

Beacon Press books
are published under the auspices of
the Unitarian Universalist Association of Congregations.

Printed in the United States of America

09 08 07 06 8 7 6 5 4 3 2 1

This book is printed on acid-free paper that meets the uncoated paper
ANSI/NISO specifications for permanence as revised in 1992.

Design and composition by Wilsted & Taylor Publishing Services

Library of Congress Cataloging-in-Publication Data
Flashback : posttraumatic stress disorder, suicide,
and the lessons of war / Penny Coleman.— 1st ed.
p. cm.
Includes bibliographical references and index.
ISBN 0-8070-5040-7 (hardcover : alk. paper)
1. Post-traumatic stress disorder—United States.
2. Vietnamese conflict, 1961–1975—Veterans—Mental health.
3. Vietnamese conflict, 1961–1975—Psychological aspects.
4. Veterans—Mental health—United States.
5. Soldiers—Mental health—United States.
6. War neuroses—United States—History.
7. War—Psychological aspects.
8. Suicide. I. Coleman, Penny.

RC552.P67F58 2006
616.85′21—dc22 2005030606

For Daniel

CONTENTS

FOREWORD

JONATHAN SHAY, M.D., PH.D.

TO SPEAK OF JOY in connection with this book, which contains so much pain, could make anyone uneasy. But joy is what I felt when I encountered the purity of Penny Coleman's writing, thinking, scholarship, and, most of all, compassionate understanding. I literally stayed up most of the night reading the publisher's proof.

Joy is also my uninvited reaction to learning something new that I feel I ought to have known. But after all, learning something new is one of the three core meanings of the Greek word *katharsis,* which Aristotle used to explain the audience's pleasure in Athenian tragedy: what clarifies understanding,[1] the pleasure of seeing clearly after being in the dark. There *is* tragedy in *Flashback.*

I have worked for eighteen years with Vietnam combat veterans like Daniel O'Donnell, Coleman's late husband. With the exception of a half-dozen combat veterans from other wars, Vietnam veterans have been my only patients. They have taught me most of what I know about psychological injury. These veterans are an extremely varied and contentious group in every respect you can think of, save one: they are totally unified on the subject of protecting the young men and women whom we, the American people, through our elected representatives, send into harm's way. They are the source of my "missionary work" to the armed forces. They are particularly fierce on the subject of suicide prevention among those currently serving, and on keeping each other alive in the community of veterans in our treatment program. Because of the strength of this community, there has been only one suicide among the veterans who belong to it.[2]

I want to point out a couple eye-openers in this book, and then I'll turn to the One Big Thing that snapped me awake.

First is the famous stoic silence of WWII veterans about any chronically endured pain they carried—from what they saw, what they did and failed to do, who was mourned, and who was heaped with honors, despite culpable military malpractice that got people killed. Here is a WWII example of the latter:

> The replacements paid the price for a criminally wasteful Replacement System that chose to put quantity ahead of quality.... It was paying lives but getting no return. It was just pure waste and the commanders should have done something about it.
>
> Example: in January 1945, Capt. Belton Cooper of the 3rd Armored Division got thirty-five [untrained] replacements to help crew the seventeen new tanks the division had received [without getting to know each other or train *together* on the tanks]....
>
> The previous night, the thirty-five replacements had been in Antwerp. At 1500 they lumbered off in a convoy of seventeen tanks headed for the front. Two hours later, fifteen of the 17 were knocked out by German panzers.[3]

After the war the survivors probably kept mum. To be sure, the cultural prestige of American folk stoicism reached its zenith in that era and stiffened many a veteran's upper lip. But I have long believed —and have twisted many a historian's arm to look into it—that the largest still-untold story of the U.S. in WWII lies in the huge, three- to five-thousand-bed "neuropsychiatric" hospitals built in that period. We know very little about what the staffs of these hospitals actually thought was wrong with the veterans or what they were doing for the veterans and why. We know even less of what the veterans who were hospitalized thought was being done for them or to them. And we know nothing about the silent warning taken by veterans who never came within hospital walls.

In my imagination I hear a WWII combat veteran after the war saying to himself, "If anybody knew what goes on in my nightmares or what I think about, they'd toss me in _____ [fill in the name of your local VA hospital here] and lose the key." Which brings me to *Flashback:* In Chapter 2, Penny Coleman describes the "reign of terror" of the "ice pick lobotomies" performed by the thousands, mainly on women and veterans, in U.S. hospitals until Thorazine was released for general use in 1952. Bingo! A jaw-dropper! I was describing *Flashback* to my revered colleague and teacher, Dr. Lisa Fisher, a clinical psychologist, and she said, "I currently have a WWII patient who says he was *terrified* of being lobotomized." The experience of my own patients—almost all of whom, as I said earlier, have been Vietnam veterans—of being called "whiners" by WWII veterans is part of why I found this so eye-opening. The emotionally raw Vietnam veterans knew nothing about the fear, years earlier, behind the WWII veterans' silence—now turned to scornful bravado.

Second, suicide is the dog that didn't bark in the *National Vietnam Veterans Readjustment Study*—known as the *NVVRS*. The word simply does not occur in either the three-hundred-plus-page executive summary of this landmark, Congress-funded epidemiological study, nor in the fat companion volume, *Tables of Findings and Technical Appendices,* which is a gold mine of rigorously gathered data. What we scientifically "know" about veterans' lives and fates is profoundly influenced by the direction of our gaze. We get no answers to questions we don't ask. Veteran suicides are *important,* not just to the surviving spouses, children, parents, and comrades of the dead veterans, but to all of us. I see no hidden agendas to the *NVVRS,* for which I have great esteem and which I have quoted from many times. But its silence on suicide or even attempted suicide (about which *NVVRS* collected data but did not report them) is suddenly very noticeable —*Flashback* brought it to my attention.

Ever since the first modern social science on suicide by Emile Durkheim we have known that measuring the rate of suicides is maddeningly difficult. Is a motorcycle crash a suicide or an accident? A death in a bar brawl? A shoot-out with police? A drug overdose? Do we have in place the kind of public health surveillance of returning veterans that would permit us to spot increased mortality from *all* sources? We do not. As we know from the Mental Health Assessment Team reports on the current Iraq and Afghanistan theaters, soldier/veteran suicides are very much a current concern. One staff officer on a military base recently described the rate of deaths by motorcycle among recently returned current theater service members as "a holocaust." How many of these are counted as suicides? How many should be?

Finally, *Flashback* shook me awake to something that I have said publicly so many times that I have stopped hearing it myself—that war itself causes psychological injury that is sometimes lethal, and that we *can* end the human practice of war.

For the last ten or so years I have engaged in preventive psychiatry advocacy to the U.S. and other NATO forces. My pitch is simple: I am a missionary from the veterans I serve. They don't want other young kids wrecked the way they were wrecked, and here are the things to change in military policy, practice, and culture that will at least partially prevent psychological and moral injury . . .[4] I explain that in public health terms this is secondary prevention of combat trauma, and that *primary* prevention is to end war, which I tell them is entirely possible. Having said this to many uniformed audiences, I can report that they don't snicker. In fact I have yet to meet anyone in uniform who has actually been in war and personally tasted its hideousness who is militarist. (I have unfortunately met plenty of civilian warmongers who seem to imagine that war exists to give them a feeling of excited uplift.)

I am not talking about ending evil or ending all violence. These are beyond our capacity. But war is a state-sponsored activity, and this, I believe, we *can* end. An end to war is the work of generations, like the centuries-long task of ending public, legal, chattel slavery.[5] Exactly the same arguments against practical efforts to end war today were made to the Quakers, who called for an end to slavery more than three hundred years ago: It has been with us since time began, people said, part of human nature, everywhere in the world. They were told not to waste their breath because it would never happen. But here we are.

How can war be ended? The answer is both boringly familiar and dismal in the contemplation of such long, hard labor: we must create trustworthy structures of collective security, within which citizens of *every* state would have a well-founded confidence in their security from attack by another country—backed up by the reliable expectation of prompt, effective, and massively multilateral armed intervention.[6] This was essentially Emmanuel Kant's conjecture two centuries ago in *Perpetual Peace.* He saw international peace as domestic peace writ large. Just as the work of the police officer is still needed inside a peaceful country, the work of the soldier is still needed in a peaceful world, especially during the centuries it will probably take to get there. But like the generations of anti-slavery abolitionists, we must pass this to our children as a heritage.

Some readers will understandably see "trustworthy collective security" as just more war, war to end war, war for peace ... (George Orwell, call your answering service!) During the Cold War, "peace through [military] strength" was one of the main slogans, meant to justify ever more expenditure on acquisition of ever more expensive military equipment. While in my experience, U.S. military professionals are not militarists, I cannot say the same about U.S. military industries and their most enthusiastic civilian allies in politics and the media.[7]

Ending war is the primary means of preventing combat trauma. *Flashback* has recalled me to its urgency.

Jonathan Shay, M.D., Ph.D., is a staff psychiatrist at the Department of Veterans Affairs Outpatient Clinic in Boston. He has been the chair of Ethics, Leadership, and Personnel Policy in the Office of the U.S. Army Deputy Chief of Staff for Personnel. He was a visiting scholar-at-large at the U.S. Naval War College and he performed the Commandant of the Marine Corps Trust Study. *Shay is the author of* Achilles in Vietnam: Combat Trauma and the Undoing of Character *and* Odysseus in America: Combat Trauma and the Trials of Homecoming.

INTRODUCTION

This book is not about heroes. English poetry is not yet fit
to speak of them.
Nor is it about deeds or lands, not anything about glory,
honor, might, majesty,
Dominion, or power, except War.
Above all I am not concerned with poetry.
My subject is War, and the pity of War.
The Poetry is in the pity.
Yet these elegies are to this generation in no sense consolatory.
They may be to the next.
All a poet can do today is warn. That is why the true
Poets must be truthful.

—WILFRED OWEN, *The Collected Poems*

FOR ONE WHO HAS SPENT the past five years researching the relationships among military service in Vietnam, posttraumatic stress disorder (PTSD), and suicide, the news reports that have been coming out of Iraq since the fall of 2003 have a particular sadness. In August 2003, a string of soldier suicides and daunting psychiatric casualties provoked the army to send a team of mental health experts to Iraq. Their report confirmed a suicide rate three times greater than what is statistically normal for the armed forces. It acknowledged that fully one-third of the evacuated psychiatric casualties "departed theater with suicide-related behaviors as part of their clinical presentation." Yet in spite of the daunting numbers and ominous implications for the future, the report concludes that "suicide among OIF [Operation Iraqi Freedom] deployed Soldiers is occurring for the same reasons typically found among Soldier-suicides": namely insufficient or underdeveloped life coping skills; marital, legal, or financial problems; chronic substance abuse; and mood disorders.[1]

It is baffling, if not astonishing, that these military psychiatrists, supposed experts in combat-related stress, have so normalized war that it is overlooked as the source of the disease they have been sent to diagnose, that its horror can be thus discounted and its psychic effects rendered invisible. A separate section of the report, intended to assess the general health and well-being of soldiers in Iraq, lists as the most often reported combat stressors "seeing dead bodies or human remains, being attacked or ambushed, and knowing someone who was seriously injured or killed."[2] But the report considers none of these factors in its analysis of the etiology of soldier suicides.

As this introduction is being written, young American and British soldiers are being told that Iraqi children playing in the road are being used by insurgents to slow down their convoys, rendering them more vulnerable to attack. In such situations, they have been ordered to run the children down.[3] What this means for those children and their families speaks for itself, and I do not mean to suggest for a moment that the most horrific implication of such a policy is its effect on the troops. But when those young soldiers subsequently find it difficult to sleep, or love, or perhaps even justify their own continued existence, and that is dismissed as underdeveloped coping skills, we are either witnessing a terrifying disconnect or a truly monstrous agenda.

The past hundred years have tragically afforded scientists, doctors, and the military an ongoing supply of combat-traumatized soldiers to study. The overwhelming evidence proves beyond a doubt that war is a disease that kills and maims, not just by tearing apart soldiers' bodies, but also by ravaging their minds. In every war American soldiers have fought in the past century, the chances of becoming a psychiatric casualty were greater than the chances of being killed by enemy fire.[4] Surprise is at best a disingenuous response to what is happening yet again.

I begin this book by tracing the history of combat-related stress from the "irritable heart" of the American Civil War through the "shell shock" of WWI and the "battle fatigue" of WWII to what is now known as "posttraumatic stress disorder." It is a fascinating history that goes chest-to-chest with the romance and glory of war and outshouts all the great old movies. It is an unpleasant and insistent declaration that, on top of the bodily wounds, war inevitably causes mental wounds that sicken not just our veterans, but our civilian citizens and our society.

The war in Vietnam was a very different kind of war than other twentieth-century American military ventures, so it is worth exploring the ways in which the structure, organization, and fundamental culture of the American military machine contributed to the trauma suffered by veterans. For example, as Americans, we have largely managed to forget the GI movement's effective sabotage of America's forces in Vietnam. Most Americans believe that the fierce nationalism of the Vietnamese and the tenacity of the antiwar movement at home were responsible for bringing our troops home. Most Americans have forgotten—or never fully absorbed—the import of the GIs who incapacitated first the army and then the navy and air force from within, leaving Nixon no choice but to withdraw. This reconstruction serves two purposes for me. First, it is an example of how inconvenient versions of history get overwritten as political environments change. And second, it is a way to bring up a question I cannot answer, but still feel compelled to raise: namely, whether, and in what ways, resistance or refusal in the face of moral outrage serves to protect an individual psyche from the effects of an overwhelming traumatic experience.

In a discussion about the war in Vietnam and PTSD, we must also address a separate aspect of postwar amnesia: the relationship between PTSD and suicide in combat veterans. Once again, in history we find the origins of American attitudes toward suicide, which help explain the silence and shame that surround the act, silence and shame that have colluded in the official denial of the relationship of suicide to PTSD, thereby allowing an epidemic of self-inflicted deaths to go unseen.

One of the most characteristic symptoms of a posttraumatic stress disorder, according to psychiatrist Judith Herman, is the "oscillating rhythm . . . between the two contradictory responses of intrusion and constriction."[5] In the most basic terms, intrusions, or flashbacks, are spontaneous reenactments of the traumatic event—the mind's attempt to integrate an intolerable memory and establish a kind of psychic equilibrium. Constrictions are a state of numbing or avoidance that are a self-protective reflex when attempts at integration fail. What Herman calls a "dialectic of trauma" is established when intolerable memories provoke imperfect psychic defenses, which are, in turn, equally vulnerable to penetration. It is impossible, short of death, to defend against anything that might trigger a traumatic memory, but it is equally impossible to find an acceptable way to live with that memory in the frenzied back-and-forth between two equally repellent states of being. Nothing gets interrogated, nothing gets healed, no equilibrium is found, and the dialectic becomes a potentially self-perpetuating cycle.

In the pages that follow, I will argue that what Herman says about individuals can be usefully applied to societies as well. Specifically, American social history in the aftermath of the war in Vietnam is fraught both with flashbacks and episodic amnesia on the part of the government, the public, the military, and the psychiatric profession. It is a history of lessons hard learned and then forgotten, a history that offered opportunities for change, chances to think creatively—to try on different beliefs and behaviors—that were lost because of the fundamental assumptions they challenged and the upheavals they implied.

There is one way in which the communal analogy to Herman's "oscillating rhythm" sadly fails. The amnesia suffered by a traumatized individual is involuntary; it is itself an aspect of mental illness. Manipulation of the communal memory and the conscious creation of episodic amnesia cannot be so excused. In the conclusion, I discuss the ways in which the current American administration has responded with denial and spin to the suicides of American soldiers serving in or recently returned from Afghanistan and Iraq. Such manipulation is a conscious and deliberate betrayal of public trust and has generously served some while others have borne the cost.

In between the chapters of this book are edited interviews with women whose husbands—or in some cases sons or fathers—came back from Vietnam so devastated by their experience there that they chose to end their own lives. Their stories directly engage what it means to bear the cost. They are women's history, and women's history has always been dismissed or erased because it is too personal, too private, too emotional. But if there ever was an example of the personal being political, this is it. For too many people, war has become permissible because it has become distant. The voices of these women, the immediacy of their loss and their pain, defy that complacency and offer us a measure for our own humanity.

It is only recently that I have begun to think of myself as a Vietnam War widow. In the '70s, when Daniel and I met, we were just two young photographers, trying to make a go of a difficult marriage. Daniel had recently returned from Vietnam. He told funny stories about hijinks during R&R, but he refused to talk about anything more serious. He slept too much, drank too much, smoked too much marijuana, and held me much too close. He was hurt in ways I couldn't fix. When I tried to distance myself, he tried to kill himself. When I found him and called the paramedics, he screamed at me from his hospital bed that he would try again as soon as he was released. I left him, headed home to New York, and was already married to someone else when his sister called to tell me that he had taken his own life. Living with a PTSD vet is its own traumatic experience. I have no memory of what I felt. I suppose I was numb. I didn't go to the funeral.

It never occurred to me to blame the war for what had happened to us. I tried to blame him, but ended up blaming myself. If only I had been kinder, more patient, less self-absorbed, quicker to notice and identify trouble. I can find more compassion for us both from this distance. I can see now that he was just a kid who tried to stay alive in a situation that exploded all the rules he had ever lived by, and that he was too sorry and too ashamed to start over. And I can see now that I, too, was in over my head in a situation I neither understood nor controlled. But at the time I believed his death was my fault, and I crept into a psychic lair to lick my wounds in private.

We know that denial is often a first response to traumatic events. Numbing is another. I submerged myself in my new life and never spoke about that piece of my past. But the guilt, the shame, and the fear that what had happened once might happen again continued to infect my life and my relationships. It was not until the late '80s, when I encountered the literature on PTSD and learned the extent to which veterans of the Vietnam conflict had been affected, that the absolute shell began to crack. The PTSD symptomology sounded eerily familiar, and in the suggestion that perhaps it had not all been my fault, I found some room to breathe. Finding my way to the surface has been a long and slow process. It would be dishonest to suggest that the process is complete, but writing this book has surely moved it along.

In many ways, my life since Daniel died has been the life we planned together. I worked as a photographer. I had two children and began to teach photography at a university. I have photographed and told stories of milestones and outrage and celebration, of cultural difference, political aspiration, and individual achievement. I have experienced the power of photographs and text to create community, to bring individuals together, to open doors through which might be glimpsed hidden suffering, courage, shared history, and commonalities of interest. Now I have finally opened a door I myself closed years ago. After twenty-five years, and in light of what I have learned about posttraumatic stress disorder, I have explored, with other women, the parameters of a grief that many of us suffered in silence, shame, and isolation.

When Daniel made his first suicide attempt, posttraumatic stress was not even a recognized category of illness. He had not come home from Vietnam with a manual for care. There was no public discussion or awareness of what he was going through, and there was no place to turn for help. In the stories told by other widows, some of which I've included in the following pages, I heard over and over how veterans and their families blamed themselves and each other for the bizarre and painful turns their lives were taking. Age-old judgments about what kind of men fell apart in combat made it difficult for families and individuals to ask for help. The Veterans

Administration (VA) was at first surprised, then ill-equipped to deal with the magnitude of the problem. Many veterans were left feeling that their pain was being exploited to inflate the budget of a bureaucracy that was heartlessly resistant to their legitimate claims for help. Lack of understanding and compassion among the ranks of the helping professions exacerbated the veterans' difficulty, and they were left to cope as best they could. Many of their coping mechanisms proved to be counterproductive, antisocial, and self-destructive.

There are some 58,000 names on the Wall. By the late 1980s, the *mainstream* media were reporting that the number of Vietnam veteran suicides had exceeded the number of combat deaths.[6] This number includes those who never left a note, who simply drove the family car into a tree, or who died of an overdose, the deaths that families prefer to call "accidents." Those reports have been the subject of heated dispute. But whether or not they were accurate, and I believe they were, it was of little comfort to those of us whose lives had been shattered. We were communities of one then, and little has changed for us since.

In repeating my own and the stories of the other women in this book, I hope to bear witness to one of the true costs of war, one that is rarely considered when passions are hot and patriotism becomes a code word for uncritical support of government policy—namely, collateral damage. The U.S. military defines collateral damage as "unintentional or incidental damage" occurring as a result of military actions.[7]

Such damage not only can occur; it inevitably does. I am not now talking about the civilian casualties that occurred in Vietnam during what they call the American War. The four million Vietnamese *civilian* deaths in the war were neither "unintentional" nor "incidental," but part of an articulated strategy to win the war through attrition.[8] The magnitude of that loss is beyond comprehension, but it has its place in the official histories. The collateral damage I am talking about is here, in this country, and it has been effectively hidden from sight. It consists of those soldiers whose names are not included on the lists of MIAs or WIAs or KIAs, though they are in a very real sense missing, wounded, or dead, even if by their own hands. And it includes those of us they abandoned when they chose not to go on. Together we became collateral damage when they brought their wounded bodies and minds home to us.

Many widows of post-Vietnam suicides still don't understand how sick their husbands were. They still don't understand that it was the war, and not a personal failure, that determined the tragic events of their lives. At the very least, they and the families of future soldiers have a right to know what to expect and a right to appropriate services and support. We didn't know, and the shame, the guilt, and the isolation made our grieving, our healing, our survival far more difficult.

The pain that continues to cycle excruciatingly through the lives of veterans and the lives of those they call home needs to be included in a cost/benefit analysis of every war. War is a disease that continues to kill long after the treaties are signed. After twenty-two years of chaos and destructive misery, Maryallyn Fisher's husband, Dennis, took his own life. We should all listen well when she says, "This war isn't over. It's 1999, and my husband just died from the Vietnam War."

In presenting these stories, I want to acknowledge a major gap. I had hoped to find women who would address different aspects of the war and the postwar experience. I was committed to writing a book that would represent the broadest possible spectrum of those who fought in Vietnam and returned emotionally broken, and what this had meant for their families and communities. Though African Americans served in Vietnam in disproportionate numbers, which I explain in my history of this era, there is no African American widow in this book. In my own defense, I wrote letters, published articles, attended conferences of African American organizations, put outreach appeals on innumerable Web sites, hung requests on VA bulletin boards in Black neighborhoods . . . all for naught. I have been unable to make contact with a single African American widow who would speak with me. I have thought long and hard about why that might be: bitterness in the Black community about the war in Vietnam, attitudes in the Black community toward suicide, culturally loaded definitions of the terms "widow" and "suicide"?[9]

Donna Barnes teaches suicide risk management in Howard University's Department of Psychiatry. She is also one of the founders of the National Organization of People of Color Against Suicide (NOPCAS) and a survivor of her son's suicide. When I initially contacted her about help with my outreach efforts, she said she supported what I was trying to do, but felt that I should write about what I know. "Let us tell our own story," she advised. After that initial contact, Dr. Barnes was deeply generous with advice and help, but her outreach in my behalf was equally fruitless.

I have since thought that maybe she was right in the first place. Maybe the way those young men came back from Vietnam is yet another reason Black America rages at white America. Maybe letting a white woman tell that story now would feel like just another level of betrayal.

The story of the Vietnam war widows discussed in this book is a hidden piece of the women's history of my generation. It is, or rather it should be, a part of the official history of the Vietnam era, of twentieth-century America. Its invisibility stems in part from the ways in which women's history and family history are commonly erased in the "official" versions of events. It stems in part from the temptation to turn away from veterans and their needs when they come home, to distance ourselves from the brute behaviors they carry out in our name and avoid assuming the burden of responsibility for their care. It stems from a centuries-old fear and loathing that has stigmatized not just the suicide, but, however irrationally, the family as well. And it also stems from the misguided, stubborn attempt to forget America's first military defeat and ignore the rich opportunity to reexamine our communal beliefs and our national mythologies.

This book, then, is about memory and denial as much as it is about combat stress, suicide, and Vietnam. It is about the "oscillating rhythm" of repetition and reflection that has compromised every segment of our society and makes it far more likely that we will again find ourselves in the same traumatic situations, equally unprepared, ill-equipped, and vulnerable. The emotional wounds and suicides among soldiers are neither an anomaly nor an aberration. They are inevitable. They are old news. As will become clear, much has been learned about the nature of combat-related stress responses. Techniques have been developed that alleviate symptoms, to some extent, for some sufferers, but the long-range cure for war-related trauma must be prevention of the contexts within which traumatic stress occurs, because, to date, no cure short of abstinence from war has proven to be reliable.

In the years since the war came to an end, historians, psychiatrists, politicians, journalists, citizens, veterans, and the military establishment itself have all weighed in on what went so terribly wrong. Much of the focus has been on why we lost the war, whether and how it could have been won, and the morality of our presence there. Far too little attention has been focused on the havoc wrought on Vietnamese society. I in no way want to discount the importance of such a focus, even as I argue that the incidence of PTSD among American forces cannot be separated from the brutality and immorality of what was done to the Vietnamese, their culture, and their country. My focus, however, will be on the experience of the American combat forces, why that experience was so damaging, and why that damage continues so many years later.

Certainly the war in Vietnam was extraordinarily devastating for me and for other widows, some of whom tell their stories in the pages that follow. That is in part because for us it was, and continues to be, so very immediate and personal. We know what it is like to live with a PTSD vet, to love him and to be unable to touch his pain and his despair. We survived the suicides of the men we loved and intimately understand how shame and guilt get in the way of open grief. We also know how those self-inflicted deaths have infected our other relationships with the fear of suffering that same awesome loss again.

That said, we do not claim any special right to sorrow. There is enough to go around for each of us as individuals, as members of kinship groups as small as our families and as large as the world community. We ask that you listen to our stories not as a kind of penance, and not because we will all share in some kind of cheap absolution. We ask that you to listen because the personal is also profoundly political. Nothing we say or do as individuals or as a nation will bring back the ones we loved and lost. We will never be able to take back those moments in which we did not have the resources or the wisdom to help, those moments in which we behaved badly, ineffectually, offered too little or too late—those moments of which we are ashamed. We will continue to feel our guilt and our grief, because to let them go is to let go of memory. Memory makes us who we are. We can choose to forget, but that would be just another kind of death, a dangerous excision of a part of our individual and communal selves that would make what we lived meaningless. We owe something more than that to those we lost.

Choosing to remember embraces the possibility of doing better next time, making better choices, being a better person, a better partner. But it is not just as individuals that we must remember; it is also as citizens. If we, as citizens, act on what we have learned, perhaps we can avoid repeating the mistakes we made in Vietnam; perhaps we can snatch something meaningful from the horror. I began writing this book in an attempt to acknowledge Vietnam war widows whose loved ones' names are not inscribed on the Wall, whose loved ones were those other, more hidden deaths. The chapters that follow trace the relationship among military service, what we now call PTSD, and suicide. The stories that alternate with those chapters are about the women left behind, what they told their children, and where they found comfort. In transcribing and editing these stories, I have tried to listen well, with sadness for what we didn't know, for the help we were never offered, for the trauma and the horror and the heroism it took to survive. I hope they will provide some healing, both in the telling and in the hearing, for all of us. But perhaps even more to the point, they are a cautionary tale, offered in a spirit of warning, remedy, and prophylaxis.

If preventing war in the first place is beyond our collective imaginations at this time—and I do not for a moment concede that it is —we are looking at a future that will include inevitable casualties, wounds of both bodies and minds. American soldiers who are now in Iraq will certainly come home changed. Many will come home damaged. Aside from physical wounds, they will suffer from PTSD, and their families will suffer with them. If past experience is a predictor, many will die in desperation by their own hands. I began writing this book as history. Would that it had remained so.

LINDA ROBIDEAU

One day he just broke. He didn't make any sense. He was in the living room sharpening knives. I said, "What are you doing?" He said, "I'm getting ready." I said, "Getting ready for what?"

I called the police. I didn't know what else to do. But he put up a barricade, right in the hallway. He told them, "Ever seen a pig bleed to death?" So they backed off. Then he took his shirt off and said, "I have to let the pain out." He took the knife, and he made a big X on his belly.

Every year he talked about killing himself—and always around May and June. It was the anniversary of when all his friends died. Sometimes he tried. He would take the car and get liquored up and deliberately drive to hit a tree. Overdoses of medication, lots of times. He just never readjusted to civilian life. He didn't like a lot of things that we have to be tolerant of. He didn't like to be in crowds. He didn't like the smell of diesel. If a car backfired, this is the first guy who goes down on the floor. He didn't like it when it rained in May or in June.

Any Asian, he didn't like. We had a neighbor who was Oriental, and one night when I came home from work my husband Don was sitting in the window and he's scoping this guy out with a gun. I said, "You can't shoot him just cause you don't like him." In the end he did not harm anyone but himself.

By 1984, we ended up at the VA hospital. He started having dreams and he'd wake up fighting me. They told him his records were lost. "There's nothing in your folder, so there's nothing we can do but medicate you." A whole slew of psychiatric medicines followed. Things would get better for a while, but then we'd be back again to May and everything would fall apart.

The day before Father's Day, June 16, 1996, Don barricaded himself in the bedroom by putting shutters over the windows and locking the door. He had put camouflage paint on his face, and he put on his medals and a camouflage shirt. He never did that, so I knew I was in big trouble. He came out and he said, "I'm going to do it. I'm sick of this life. I'm sick of the pain. I'm sick of the fucking neighbors. I'm sick of everything. I don't need no doctors or social workers or police. I just want to stop the pain." I got on my hands and knees and I begged him. I said, "Please, please don't kill yourself, because your pain will be over, but mine will just begin. I can't live without you." So he said, "Okay then, I'll take you with me and then you don't have to worry."

That night I called the shelter in Boston for Vietnam veterans. They came, but they wanted to take him to the "bunker"—I guess that's a place they bring someone in crisis—and he wouldn't go. I couldn't convince him. When they left he said, "I'll fix it in the morning. Fuck them."

I kept trying to talk to him, but if he saw or heard me is beyond me. So I went to bed. But when he laid down, I had to think, was I ready to die? I really wanted to be with him because we loved each other so much and we'd been through so much. But I thought about my sons. I called up the vets again the next day, and they said, "It's time for you to take care of yourself. You have to leave."

I went to Worcester, and the next day I had the vets call him and say, "Linda will come home if you just calm down." But he couldn't. He said he was going to cap himself at noon. He told the vets that, and then he tore the phone out of the wall.

I just could not come home. I was paralyzed with fear. I called the police, but I was afraid if I went home, I'd get there before them, and that he would kill me and kill himself, or kill himself in front of me. My heart wanted to go home, and then I didn't. Whether I bit the bullet or helped him, I should have stayed. I always stayed before. I finally called the police again, and they said I could come home now. He had shot himself, close range with a .45, on the front lawn.

He left me a long suicide note. He said he didn't want me to be mad at him, that he loved me, and he didn't know how I put up with him all those years. He didn't want to hurt no one. And he kept saying, "Help me, help me, somebody help me, I'm going to cap myself."

I carry a struggle that says that my husband was really not a hero because he killed himself. Last year, on the TV on Veterans Day, one of the Crosby, Stills, and Nash dedicated a song to the men who took their own lives also. When I heard that, it was one of the biggest reliefs I ever had. What Don did at the end, whether it was wrong or right, doesn't take away from what he did before. And I thought that there was no one else like me in the United States. It's not comforting, but at least now I know I'm not the only one.

But there's something else I got to say. It's awful, but when he died, I felt relief. Just for a second. It's the truth. I said, "Oh jeepers, he's finally at peace, he's free from the nightmares and the problems and the pain." I felt so guilty. He held me close for thirteen years. He held me every night. Thirteen years wasn't long enough. I will never forget Don. He's always in my eyes.

PAULA ELVICK

My dad was a real GI Joe. He wore his fatigues around the house all the time, and he had a military strictness. You didn't obey the rules, you got put in the brig. He was a lifer, a patriot, and we were brought up to "love your country."

I don't think he would have chosen to go to Vietnam. He was a veteran of the war in Korea. He was thirty-nine, an old guy, when they told him to go to Vietnam. He went where they told him to go. He spoke a little Vietnamese and lived in a Vietnamese home, so he got to know some of them pretty well. I remember he wrote that he was sorry to be there in such a hard time because it was such a beautiful country and such a beautiful culture. Those are the kinds of things he wrote about. I think he was trying to protect us from the rest.

When he came home, in 1968, we were stationed at Travis Air Force Base in California. Everybody could see he'd changed. He was going through—I'm sure they were stress attacks, but I don't know. They were like nightmares. He would wake everybody up screaming. One of them was really scary. I found him crawling in the hall. He was talking to me in another language, I guess Vietnamese. At first I wasn't frightened, just curious what he was doing. I thought he was awake. But then I realized that he wasn't, and I got my mother.

He started going out to bars a lot around that time. It was extremely stressful for all of us to see a person who used to be outgoing, boastful—you know, happy—come back withdrawn, negative, mean, abusive, with us never understanding why. It came to a point where I hated him and I absolutely blamed the war.

When I was twenty-eight, I moved to New York to go to law school. My father called me the night he shot himself. He told me he missed me. He wanted to drive to New York and get me. I told him I'd be coming home at the end of the summer. To this day, I look back at the conversation. I didn't hear desperation. If I had known anything about suicide at that time, I would probably have caught some

of the things he was talking about. "Did you know," he said, "that when you were a baby I took out an insurance policy for you and your brother?" That was as clear as could be, but I didn't hear it. Then I got a phone call at five in the morning saying that he was dead.

When my dad died, my mother was very ill. I had to pull the funeral together. I went to the VA to ask for help to bury him. I took my father's briefcase full of his commendations and his medals and stuff like that, but when I told them he died from a self-inflicted gunshot wound, they said, "The VA won't pay for that." I was so devastated. I had to go to a private funeral home. The day of the burial, the VA called me and said they'd made a terrible mistake. They offered to bury him in a military cemetery with a color guard, which is the twenty-one-gun salute and the flag and all that. I said it was too late, I'd already paid for the plot. But I took the color guard because I wanted him to have a military funeral.

The VA didn't give us anything. They told me that when he killed himself, his pension died with him. It's been a hard thing for me to forgive. My baby brother wasn't even fifteen.

I finished my law degree, but then I got suspended. That's a different story, but I drank myself out of it. I knew I was in real trouble. My middle brother, Pete, said he was going to be away and I could have his place in Mendocino while he was gone to work things out. I went home to pack my things and was all ready to come, when I got another five-in-the-morning phone call. Pete had driven his car off a cliff. I didn't see it coming at all. He had a daughter and a son, and he loved his kids so much.

I hit bottom about two months after that, and finally got some help. I still go to AA meetings at the VA. My brothers and sister are all sober now too—well, except one. He's the baby. We're working on him. Sometimes when I get together with my sister and brothers, we go through old pictures and try to figure out when things changed, when things started. We try to understand what he went through, and why it was so bad that he had to take himself away from us. And then, what happened to us?

Vietnam—that's what happened. Before that we were a family. When my father came back, everything fell apart.

CHAPTER ONE

FROM IRRITABLE HEART TO SHELL SHOCK

DURING THE AMERICAN CIVIL WAR, it was called "irritable heart" or "nostalgia." In the First World War, it became "shell shock," "hysteria," or "neurasthenia." During World War II and the war in Korea, it was "war neurosis," "battle fatigue," or simply "exhaustion." When veterans started coming home from Vietnam, it was at first called "Post-Vietnam syndrome." Then, in 1980, with the publication of the third edition of the American Psychiatric Association's *Diagnostic and Statistical Manual of Mental Disorders* (DSM-III), "posttraumatic stress disorder" (PTSD) entered the official lexicon. The names have changed over time, but the phenomenon they describe has remained distressingly constant: war causes mental illness that is life-altering and, in far too many cases, fatal.

Bullets and bombs are destructive to human beings in fairly predictable and immediately apparent ways. Terror and horror work more mysteriously, but the psychic wounds they inflict are no less real or incapacitating. Such wounds are more difficult to see, to categorize, or to measure. They have been less well understood and so have been more vulnerable to prejudice and superstition. Jonathan Shay, who has written two of the most important books about combat-induced trauma, champions the idea that PTSD *is* a legitimate war wound and that the veterans who suffer its injury "[carry] the burdens of sacrifice for the rest of us as surely as the amputees, the burned, the blind, and the paralyzed carry them."[1]

Over time, perhaps the most intractable prejudice has been that those who fall victim to the mental illness caused by war are somehow inherently weak in body or character. That belief has had, and continues to have, many adherents, in spite of evidence that some of the most famous and admired heroes of war, from Ulysses to Audie Murphy, have suffered from symptoms that meet the diagnostic criteria of PTSD. The parallel misconception, that a warrior's success is ensured if his body is strong and his character firm, has likewise plagued and inconvenienced military organizations. If such ideal warriors could be reliably identified, it would certainly make the maintenance of armies more straightforward and the subsequent cost of disability pensions less daunting. Not for lack of trying, no such correlation has been discovered. After 150 years of study, there are still no reliable predictors for who will be affected by their combat experience and under what circumstances. Once affected, there is still no cure. All that is really known is that war is a disease that affects the minds of many who get close to its horrors. The disease can be so painful and debilitating that those afflicted often lose their health, their sanity, their dreams, their families, and often their lives.

The most recent DSM, the fourth edition, published in 1994, describes the circumstances in which PTSD is likely to occur as "a traumatic event in which . . . the person experienced, witnessed, or was confronted with an event or events that involved actual or threatened death or serious injury, or a threat to the physical integrity of self or others, [and] the person's response involved intense fear, helplessness, or horror."[2]

That description pointedly includes traumatic situations that might occur in either civilian or military contexts. It reflects the priorities of the two groups most instrumental in agitating for the official recognition and inclusion of PTSD in the DSM—and perhaps most affected by that recognition. Those two groups were the returning Vietnam veterans and the resurgent or second-wave women's movement. The posttrauma symptoms experienced by veterans eerily mirrored those experienced by victims of sexual abuse. In the early '70s, the women's movement had made violent crimes against women a central issue of its activist agenda and, as veterans and women came to recognize the commonality of their cause, they joined forces to lobby for official recognition of the disease from the medical community. It is poignant to note that since the original inclusion of PTSD in the DSM-III in 1980, the criteria have changed. In the original, the traumatic event was described as falling "outside the range of usual human experience." That criterion was dropped in later editions. As Judith Herman so appropriately points out in *Trauma and Recovery*, "Rape, battery, and other forms of sexual and domestic violence are so common a part of women's lives that they can hardly be described as outside the range of ordinary experience. And in view of the number of people killed in war over the past century, military trauma, too, must be considered a common part of human experience; only the fortunate find it unusual."[3]

The symptoms that are typically manifested following such a trauma can be divided into three clusters. The first, the intrusive cluster, includes recurrent, uncontrollable recollections of the traumatic event, such as frightening dreams or flashbacks. Those flashbacks are often so convincingly "real" that the sufferer behaves as though he or she were actually in the remembered moment. The experience can be both terrifying and dangerous, not just for the one who experiences the intrusion, but for anyone else who happens to be present. The second, the avoidance cluster, includes attempts to avoid circumstances that might trigger such recollections or flashbacks. To that end, many sufferers withdraw from social contact. They experience a protective emotional numbing and a restricted range of emotions that suck the joy from life and the vitality from relationships. The third, or hyper-arousal cluster, involves difficulty sleeping, violent outbursts, and an exaggerated startle response. Individuals affected by this set of symptoms act as though they were still in immediate danger, leading to inappropriate, socially unacceptable behaviors. To officially fall within the diagnostic guidelines, the symptoms must last for at least a month. A duration of less than three months is considered "acute," three months or more is considered "chronic," and "delayed" refers to an onset of symptoms at least six months after the traumatic experience.

THE EARLY HISTORY OF PTSD

Official recognition of PTSD may be relatively new, but the history of combat-related distress is an old one. Jonathan Shay is both a psychiatrist who treats Vietnam combat veterans and a classics scholar. He believes that Achilles, as described in *The Iliad,* would almost certainly be diagnosed as having PTSD today. In his book *Achilles in Vietnam,* Shay parallels the behaviors and symptoms of the Greek hero in Homer's 2,700-year-old story with those of American veterans of the war in Vietnam, and finds them to be strikingly similar. The vulnerability of Achilles' heel is a symbol for the vulnerability of his mind.[4] His grief and rage at the death of his friend Patroclus, and his sense of betrayal at the hands of his commander, Agamemnon, are such that he suffers a breakdown and has to be restrained so he cannot harm himself. He then directs his pain outward, committing atrocities against the living and the dead until the gods and even the ghost of Patroclus are appalled and intervene.

Agamemnon's betrayal of Achilles[5] may seem tame to a modern audience, when compared to the systemic leadership betrayals suffered by American soldiers who fought in Vietnam, but it is from that betrayal, Shay argues, that "the catastrophic operational failure that the Greek army suffered in the first fifteen books of the Iliad" directly flowed. And, he adds, it was that betrayal from leadership, coupled with the death of Patroclus, that was responsible for Achilles' personal collapse. Shay uses the term *thémis,* a word he translates from the Greek as "what's right" to describe the "trustworthy structure" that *should* characterize a soldier's relationships within the military. The horizontal, or peer, relationships, the vertical relationships along the chain of command, and the personal relationships that soldiers have with their branch of the service all must be grounded in the belief that they have been appropriately trained and supplied.[6] In the absence of such a trustworthy structure, soldiers are exposed to the combination of moral grievance and combat stress. Shay believes it is that combination that is central to lasting psychological injury. "Veterans can usually recover from horror, fear, and grief once they return to civilian life, so long as 'what's right' has not been violated."[7]

PTSD AND THE AMERICAN CIVIL WAR

George Washington's Continental Army, which became the U.S. Army, was plagued with mental health disorders that are recognizably similar to those seen today. Labels of "melancholia" and "insanity" were loosely applied to the most extreme cases, the psychoses, the paralyses, or to those who suffered from invasive flashbacks. "Nostalgia" referred to chronic situational depressions, which were thought to stem primarily from homesickness. "Drunkenness," according to Joseph Lovell (surgeon general, 1817–1828), was responsible for half of the deaths in the U.S. Army during the period of his tenure. Lovell was a temperance advocate who succeeded in abolishing the daily rum ration, which probably makes him a questionable primary source, but it does seem likely that some of the excess consumption, not unlike the self-medication so frequently noted among today's vets, was an attempt to keep demons at bay.[8]

The psychic distress of soldiers was a serious but relatively uncomplicated issue for nineteenth-century commanders. During the years of the American Civil War, it was assumed by commanders on both sides that men of strength and character would maintain a "manly" attitude in battle. There was little sympathy in either army for those who did not. Both armies made discharge for psychiatric complaints virtually impossible. If a soldier was beyond masking his traumatic symptoms, he had few options. If he tried to desert and was caught, his comrades would be forced to stand at attention to witness his execution. He would be buried where he fell, and the ground smoothed over his unmarked grave to symbolically erase his existence.[9] He otherwise might apply for a psychiatric discharge and, in some cases, a sympathetic commanding officer would reassign him to light duty.[10] But in applying for relief, he risked calling attention to his distress. If his application was rejected and he could not manage to mask his symptoms, he would be officially labeled a coward or a malingerer. The penalty for cowardice or malingering was the same as that for desertion. He might just as well have run off in the first place. Executions were intended both to eliminate the contagion of weakness and to terrify the ranks into obedience. Such severe consequences must have discouraged many from seeking help. They certainly encouraged many others to resort to flight.

At the outset, the social and economic issues over which the war was fought had inspired passion on both sides. Romantic notions of heroism, glory, and honor fed a short-lived frenzy of voluntarism in both the North and the South. By 1862, however, as word of battlefield carnage, rampant disease, and intense hardships became known, the enthusiastic rush to enlist was seriously slowed. The Confederate army was forced to pass a draft law in 1862. The Union followed suit the next year. The laws were unpopular, unwieldy, and patently unfair. They exempted most professionals, and included commutation and substitution clauses, which allowed a draftee to buy his way out of service altogether or pay to send someone else in his place. Pundits North and South began calling it "a rich man's war and a poor man's fight." Shay would have called it a betrayal of what's right. The injustice of the draft provoked draft riots in several cities, most notably in New York.

Whether drafted or enlisted, though, the soldiers who fought for the North or for the South were certainly exposed to "events that involved actual or threatened death or serious injury, or a threat to the physical integrity of self or others," and there was adequate cause for a response that "involved intense fear, helplessness, or horror." It is impossible to know how many of the almost 400,000 deserters (about 10 percent of both armies) were running from personal demons, but it was the only recourse, short of execution or suicide, available to those most acutely afflicted.[11]

Against that background, Dr. Jacob Mendes DaCosta is credited with conducting the first scientific study of combat-related stress. He called the array of symptoms he identified "the irritable heart of a soldier" because so many of his patients complained of shortness of breath, palpitations, anxiety, and chest pain. But generally, soldiers' complaints varied widely, and so did the diagnoses. William Hammond, who was Lincoln's surgeon general, appropriately called the state of nineteenth-century American medicine "the end of the medical Middle Ages." Unlike their European counterparts, who were becoming familiar with the work of Koch and Pasteur, and who were adopting scientific methodologies to investigate disease, American doctors who served in both armies had virtually no practical training or clinical experience. Their understanding of a soldier's symptoms was therefore based largely on superstition, custom, and a good measure of imagination and the supernatural. What DaCosta diagnosed as irritable heart, another doctor might have called insanity or sunstroke. "Nostalgia," which was a popular diagnostic category at the beginning of the war, implied a weakness of character neither army chose to indulge. After the early years, the diagnosis was firmly discouraged: 5,200 soldiers were hospitalized with "nostalgia" before 1853, but between 1853 and 1865 not a single case was reported. There were, however, 145,000 hospitalizations for constipation, 66,000 for headache, and 58,000 for neuralgia.[12]

The title of Eric Dean's book about the traumatic effects of combat on American Civil War veterans, *Shook over Hell,* is taken from the medical records of one Jason Roberts, a Union soldier who used this expression when describing his symptoms to doctors. Doctors described Roberts as "sometimes . . . raving and excited, at others melancholy. . . . Very peculiar and eccentric, flying from one Subject to another, and talking incoherently on all Subjects. . . . The subject of religion and his experiences in the army being paramount in his mind."[13] The core of Dean's book is an analysis of the case histories of 291 Civil War veterans who, between 1861 and 1920, were committed to the Indiana Hospital for the Insane. Using medical records, letters, memoirs, newspaper articles, and pension files, Dean concludes that, whatever nineteenth-century doctors chose to call it, these inmates all suffered from symptoms that would today be diagnosed as PTSD. "Many of these men," Dean writes, "continued to suffer from the aftereffects of the war and, along with their families, often lived in a kind of private hell involving physical pain, the torment of fear, and memories of killing and death."[14]

A tradition of support for disabled veterans dates back to the original colonies. The laws of the Plymouth Colony in 1636 promised soldiers that "if any that shall goe returne maymed [and] hurt he shalbe mayntayned competently by the Colony duringe his life."[15] In 1776, the Continental Congress pensioned veterans who had been disabled in the Revolution. After the Civil War, however, activist veterans organized and lobbied for a pension system that would cover not only those who had been disabled, but all Union Army veterans and their dependents. (Veterans of the Confederate army were not eligible for any federal benefits and had to rely on relatively modest state entitlement programs.[16]) By 1891, fully one-third of the federal budget went to military pensions, and eventually, more money was paid out in pensions than the $8 billion spent on prosecuting the war itself.[17]

In the midst of all that generosity, those who suffered from "irritable heart" or "nostalgia" found it virtually impossible to qualify for support of any kind. The Pension Bureau required proof that symptoms had originated in service, especially if, as was often the case, the onset of symptoms was delayed.[18] Proof was hard to come by. If, after years of intolerable battlefield nightmares, a disturbed veteran turned to drink, he was held responsible for his "vicious habits" and rejected. If he used drugs to quell his violent outbursts, he would likewise be rejected. Vicious habits, to the Victorian mind, were an indication of moral laxity. They were considered indicators of intemperance, and intemperance was believed to upset the delicate systemic balance on which sanity rests. Acknowledgment of any form of "self-pollution" rendered the claimant morally unworthy of official support. As in the aftermath of future wars, those who had been psychically damaged, those whose wounds did not show, those who were least able to advocate for themselves, were afforded the least support and compassion.

CHARCOT, JANET, AND FREUD

The growing veneration of science, and medicine as science, that characterized the nineteenth century energized efforts to move away from moralistic or superstitious approaches to diseases of the mind or the soul. In the 1870s and 1880s, at his Salpêtrière clinic in France, the neurologist Jean-Martin Charcot undertook a revelatory study of the malady then called hysteria, a mental disorder with physical manifestations of unknown origin. Before Charcot's experiments, patients whose symptoms included localized paralyses, stutters, or muteness had been dismissed by doctors as malingerers—who, coincidentally, exhibited many of the same symptoms as DaCosta's traumatized veterans of the Civil War. Charcot demonstrated that he could both induce and relieve these symptoms through use of hypnosis, thereby proving that the complaints, though not physical in origin, were both genuine and psychological.[19] Charcot was more interested in identifying and categorizing his patients' symptoms than in identifying the root causes of their distress. That work he left to two of his students: Pierre Janet and Sigmund Freud.

Within a decade of Charcot's original work on hysteria, both Janet and Freud had arrived at a shared conclusion that trauma was at the root of all hysterical symptoms. Both believed that the symptoms masked unbearable memories, and both believed that if the traumatic memories could be accessed, the symptoms would ease. They both also believed that the way to access those buried memories was through talk, but at that point their ideas diverged. Janet was convinced that traumatic symptoms were a direct response to a devastating experience that had overwhelmed the psyche. The experience was too frightening, too horrible, too unacceptable for the mind to absorb. He theorized that, in the face of such an extreme assault, the personality split into conscious and subconscious aspects, a process he called *dissociation*. It was the demons buried in the subconscious mind that Janet held responsible for traumatic symptoms.

Freud, on the other hand, insisted that a premature sexual encounter was always to blame. In 1896, in *The Aetiology of Hysteria,* he "put forward the thesis that at the bottom of every case of hysteria there *are one or more occurrences of premature sexual experience,* occurrences that belong to the earliest years of childhood, but which can be re-produced through the work of psychoanalysis in spite of the intervening decades" (my emphasis).[20] If such an occurrence was not uncovered in the process of analysis, the analyst simply hadn't looked hard enough or in the right place.

A year after the publication of *The Aetiology of Hysteria,* Freud backed away from his insistence that the origins of all trauma were an *actual* premature sexual encounter. Instead, he proposed that traumatic symptoms might also be the result of repressed sexual fantasies, desires, and instincts that had been thwarted by societal prohibitions. In other words, the traumatic sexual experience might only have been imagined, "fantasies which my patients had made up."[21]

There is continuing debate concerning the reasons for Freud's retreat from his original thesis, but the complex relationship of Freudian theory to women was one important factor in changing his mind. Many of Freud's patients were the wives and daughters of the Viennese bourgeoisie with whom he socialized. When these women presented him with histories that included sexual abuse, he must have found it very difficult to accept the memories as real.[22] Freud's jargon, moreover, famously associates mental instability with women; "hysteria" derives from the Greek word for womb, while "neurasthenia" simply means "weak nerves." The feminization of psychological illness had—and continues to have—implications for the treatment of war-related trauma. The association of mental imbalance with hormonally compromised females contributes to a prejudicial judgment about the character of a soldier, calling into question his strength of body or mind, if not his manliness. Furthermore, the elevation of a repressed childhood event, either real or imagined, over the devastation of a more recent concrete trauma had profound treatment implications both for veterans and for the victims of sexual abuse. Instead of addressing a soldier's horror at having witnessed the evisceration of a comrade or the unbearable betrayal felt by a woman who had been raped by a relative, Freudian doctors encouraged their traumatized patients to dig beneath the most obvious and recent violence to search for some hidden, specifically sexual, event that lay buried in their subconscious past. More immediate atrocities were dismissed as irrelevant or, at most, catalytic.

Janet found that premise absurd. In 1892, in "The Mental State of Hystericals," he challenged "the justification for pushing this method of sexual interpretation to an extreme.... The main defect of psychoanalysis is that it does... invariably set to work in order to discover traumatic memory, with the a priori conviction that it is there to be discovered—like a detective who has a fixed idea where the culprit is to be found. The worst of it is that such detectives will always run their culprit to earth in the end. So, too, will the psychoanalysts; owing to the nature of their methods, they can invariably find what they seek."[23] Janet's prescient ideas and research were effectively sidetracked for the better part of a century by the intellectually fashionable Freudians. His *L'automatisme psychologique,* first published in 1889, but not translated into English until 1965, forms a broad framework on which much of today's understanding of PTSD has developed. That was far too late, however, for the traumatized soldiers of WWI.

SHELL SHOCK AND WORLD WAR I

At the outbreak of the First World War, the horrors of trench warfare produced psychiatric casualties in shocking numbers. Men in the trenches were trapped below ground level, often for weeks at a time, in a world bounded by cold, mud, rats, lice, dysentery, and the shrieks of both deadly incoming artillery and dying comrades. They were immobile, helpless, and passive witnesses to what those arbitrary shells did to the men around them, imagining what the next might do to them. The 1,906 British cases of "behavior disorder without physical cause" admitted to hospitals in 1914 grew to 20,327 in 1915, or 9 percent of battle casualties.[24] Then on July 1, 1916, the very first day of the horrific battle fought in the Somme Valley, 60,000 of the 110,000 British troops who attacked a mere six German divisions were either killed or wounded.[25] Historian Paul Fussell gives full credit for the slaughter that became known among the troops as the "Great Fuck Up" to Sir Douglas Haig, commander of the British forces. According to Fussell, Haig believed that his working-class army was "too simple and too animal to cross the space between the opposing trenches in any way except in full daylight and aligned in rows or 'waves.'"[26] For the next four months, Haig held to his plan until freezing mud put an end to the massacre. By that time, the Somme had claimed another half-million British casualties.[27]

It is hardly surprising that such madness would take a toll not just of bodies, but of minds. At times, more than 50 percent of the evacuated casualties were psychiatric. The response of the director-general of medical services was that "wastage" was simply not to be evacuated "unless there are definite lesions and symptoms which require prolonged hospital treatment."[28] Initially, the British psychiatrists who saw some of those first psychiatric casualties, specifically Dr. Charles Myers, looked for a physical explanation, hypothesizing that the constant and random concussion of bursting shells caused actual lesions in the brain. Myers called it "shell shock." The name stuck, in spite of the fact that subsequent autopsy results failed to bear out his theory.

With the idea of brain lesions discredited, doctors once again sought explanations for traumatic symptoms in the moral character of the individual. Instead of prescribing psychotherapy to discover the underlying sexual trauma, which was in any event too time-intensive to conform with military priorities, the authorities dusted off the terms "malingerer" and "coward" and used them to justify court-martial or dishonorable discharge. As during the American Civil War, many who broke down were summarily shot.[29] Denis Winter, in *Death's Men,* quotes one hard-boiled division commander who insisted that there was no fear in his division because, at the first symptoms, he tied the coward to the front-line barbed wire for thirty seconds "with most effective results."[30] Thirty seconds was generally adequate time for a sniper from the other side to shift what might have been a psychiatric casualty statistic into the medical, if not the mortality, column—killing, as it were, two birds with one stone. It was finally, just "a matter of luck," as one military psychiatrist put it, whether a distressed soldier was hospitalized for shell shock or shot for cowardice.[31]

The callous attitudes that shaped extreme military discipline in the field were mirrored behind the lines in the treatment centers of "traditionalist" military psychiatrists. Clovis Vincent in France and Lewis Yealland in England were particularly infamous. Both practiced a form of faradic stimulation, or electric shock, applied to whichever part of the body was refusing to cooperate. Used in combination with threats and humiliation, the treatment was patently cruel, exquisitely painful, and finally unreliable.[32] It was also rarely practiced on officers. "Torpillage" (literally "torpedoing"), as it was known in France, was discredited after a patient, fearing he was about to be electrocuted, struck Vincent in the face. The patient was convicted of assault by a military tribunal, but the conviction was reported in the popular press. Public revulsion resulted in the sentence being overturned, and the barbarous practice fell out of favor.[33]

Between the ultimate discipline of the military hard-liners, the punitive practices of the psychiatric traditionalists, and the narrow Freudian construction, there gradually emerged a more moderate group of "shell shock" doctors looking to develop a theory of practice that acknowledged compassion and reason, but within the bounds of efficacy demanded by the military. Myers, no longer believing in a physical explanation, and by then consulting psychiatrist to the British Army, instituted a new policy to deal with combat-related stress: prompt, forward, and simplified treatment.[34]

If men were not to be evacuated, they would have to be treated close to the front. That necessity fortuitously conflated with Myers's conviction that time and distance tend to dim a soldier's group loyalty and identification. If, as Myers believed, loyalty to one's comrades was central to a soldier's capacity to withstand horror, terror, and death, then separation from those comrades, be it in distance or time, would lessen those bonds. Evacuation to a safe and comfortable rear hospital, he reasoned, would allow individuality to reassert itself. Self-preservation would drown out loyalty.[35]

Myers's insistence on a "simplified" or short-term treatment was only partly dictated by logistics. He had also observed the tendency of soldiers to use lengthy analytical exploration to convince themselves that they had good reason for having reached the limits of their endurance. Under Myers's tenure, doctors were taught never to use the words "shell shock" when speaking with their patients. The validation implicit in a clinical-sounding diagnosis seemed to encourage, rather than ease, their symptoms. Prompt, forward, simplified treatment amounted to a good night's rest, a hot meal, and some positive morale boosting, all with the emphatically expressed assumption that the soldier would soon return to the lines. The goal of treatment was therefore the restoration of psychic defenses for the purpose of return to combat duty. Whether or not such repressive or suppressive therapy was in the interest of the soldier, it was certainly successful by military standards—in the short term.[36] Sigmund Freud is said to have likened the role of the military psychiatrist to that "of a machine gun behind the front line, that of driving back those who fled."[37]

The possibility that Americans might find themselves involved in this war prompted the first formal training in psychiatry for regular army medical officers. By 1915, that training consisted of four clinical sessions at the Government Hospital and lectures in military law and malingering, demanding a total investment of twenty-four hours of an officer's time.[38] A further measure of the respect accorded psychiatry in the U.S. army when the Americans joined the war in 1917 is that the man who was put in charge of the soldiers' mental health, Thomas Salmon, was a bacteriologist by training who had acquired what he knew about psychiatry screening immigrants arriving at Ellis Island.[39] By the time the Americans joined the war in 1917, the British and French experience with the efficacy of brief forward treatment had been demonstrated, and it was instituted in the American army with gratifying success. There were echelons of treatment centers, providing progressively longer and more intensive care at increasing distance from the front. Rest, warmth, food, and encouragement were the curatives of choice. Staff were ordered to use the British label "N.Y.D.N."—not yet diagnosed (nervous)—instead of dramatic labels like "shell shock," to avoid the frightening suggestion of a brain injury. They were, furthermore, instructed to emphasize the glorious traditions of the military, the opportunity to claim the honors and rewards of victory, and a place in the "family" unit. Evacuation meant separation from the paternal officer and brother soldier, and finally becoming that most unhappy of mortals, the lone casualty. It was in a sense a desertion, since it left comrades to carry on alone.[40] Regardless of whether we consider that script emotional blackmail, it was certainly effective. Seventy percent returned to their units in less than five days, and over half of the remaining 30 percent, within two weeks.[41]

WILLIAM H. R. RIVERS AND SIEGFRIED SASSOON

Of all the psychiatrists serving in the First World War, Dr. William H. R. Rivers is perhaps the best remembered. His thoughtful and innovative attempts to navigate humanely between the needs of his patients and the needs of the military earned him the directorship of the British hospital for psychiatric casualties at Craiglockhart in 1915.[42] Prior to the war, Rivers had been a general practitioner and a lecturer in psychology at Cambridge University. He was also an avid anthropologist and had spent the years immediately preceding the war studying the kinship patterns and social customs of Melanesian islanders. In his anthropological interviews, Rivers had learned both to question and to listen carefully. The experience would serve him well at Craiglockhart.

Rivers agreed with the Freudians that "talking over his painful experience... usually gives [a patient] immediate relief and may be followed by great improvement or even rapid disappearance of his chief symptoms."[43] He found Freud's techniques of dream analysis to be extremely useful as a means of uncovering what was troubling his patients, but he was unimpressed with Freud's contention that trauma symptoms were the result of repressed sexual memories. He wrote, with some evident bemusement, that "Since the army at the present time would seem to be fairly representative of the whole male population of the country, this failure to discover to any great extent the cases with which the literature of the Freudian school abounds might well be regarded as significant."[44]

Few among Rivers's patients seemed particularly distressed by the sexual aspects of their early lives. What distressed them instead was what they had experienced at the front. "The terrifying dreams, the sudden gusts of depression or restlessness, the cases of altered personality amounting often to definite fugues, which are among the most characteristic results of the present war, receive by far their most natural explanation as the result of war experience...."[45]

Rivers believed that Freud's hypotheses would ultimately prove useful "to stimulate inquiry and help us in our practice, while we are groping our way towards the truth." He was convinced, however, that those hypotheses should be seen as only a "partial truth," and he found the Freudian insistence on the centrality of sexual issues to be a distortion that would be risible, were it not so tragic. The Freudians, he chided, "and to a large extent Freud himself, have become so engrossed with the cruder side of sexual life that their works might often be taken for contributions to pornography rather than to medicine."[46]

Rivers was not denying that individual experience, sexual history, and even heredity might play a part in the onset of war neurosis; rather, he questioned their centrality. The neurotic symptoms he observed in his patients appeared to be more democratic than the Freudians suggested, attaching equally to those who had suffered childhood sexual abuse and to those who had not, to the apparently well adjusted and to those who were not so, to those who had been recognized for bravery and heroism and to those who had not.[47] "Certainly, if results are any guide," he wrote, "the morbid states disappear without any such complexes having been brought to the surface, while in other cases the morbid states persist in spite of the discovery of definite complexes, sexual or otherwise, going back to times long before the war."[48] The central problem, he concluded, seemed not to be coming from the men themselves, their heredities and their histories, but from the horrors they had experienced. Perhaps, as Janet had suggested, the real sickness was war.

In 1917, a very public incident drew attention to Rivers, his theories, and his methods. The poet Siegfried Sassoon was assigned to his care at Craiglockhart. Sassoon had enthusiastically enlisted at the outbreak of the war, and was quickly promoted to officer and posted to the western front in France. He was renownedly, even recklessly, brave, winning for himself the nickname "Mad Jack." In 1916, he was awarded the Military Cross for rescuing wounded comrades under heavy fire, but after being wounded himself in 1917, Sassoon was sent back to England.

His physical wounds, however, were the least of Sassoon's troubles. He had been emotionally devastated by his war experiences and was suffering from hallucinations and horrific nightmares. He had also become profoundly disillusioned by the prosecution of the war. In July of 1917, he wrote a letter of protest to his commanding officer. That letter, "A Soldier's Declaration," referred to England's aims as "evil and unjust." It attacked the "political errors and insincerities for which the fighting men are being sacrificed," and asserted that "the war is being deliberately prolonged by those who have the power to end it." The letter was published in the London *Times* and read out in the House of Commons.

The 1914 Official Secrets Act specifically forbade contact with the press by a member of the armed forces.[49] Sassoon had reason to believe that his "Declaration" would provoke a court-martial—in fact, he invited just such a response, to give his protest a higher public profile, but his friend and fellow poet, Robert Graves, intervened on his behalf. Graves convinced the authorities that the public trial of a celebrity hero was not in their interest, and that it would be best for all concerned if the letter were treated as a medical matter, a symptom of Sassoon's "shell-shock." Sassoon was too ill to protest further. It was decided that he would be sent to Rivers at Craiglockhart for treatment.

A SOLDIER'S DECLARATION

I am making this statement as an act of wilful defiance of military authority, because I believe the war is being deliberately prolonged by those who have the power to end it.

I am a soldier, convinced that I am acting on behalf of soldiers. I believe that this war, upon which I entered as a war of defense and liberation, has now become a war of aggression and conquest. I believe the purposes for which I and my fellow-soldiers entered upon this war should have been so clearly stated as to have made it impossible to change them, and that, had this been done, the objects which actuated us would now be attainable by negotiation.

I have seen and endured the suffering of the troops, and I can no longer be a party to prolong these sufferings for ends which I believe to be evil and unjust.

> I am not protesting against the conduct of the war, but against the political errors and insincerities for which the fighting men are being sacrificed.
>
> On behalf of those who are suffering now I make this protest against the deception which is being practiced on them; also I believe that I may help to destroy the callous complacency with which the majority of those at home regard the continuance of sufferings which they do not share, and which they have not sufficient imagination to realize.
>
> S. Sassoon, July 1917[50]

Under Rivers's care, Sassoon's nightmares receded, but with the improvement of his health, his commitment to his fellow soldiers, if not to the war effort, reasserted itself. He felt he had abandoned his comrades and began to pressure Rivers to recommend that he be returned to the front.

Rivers, like many wartime psychiatrists, suffered a conflict of professional loyalties. On one hand, it was his responsibility as an army officer to "cure" Sassoon of his nervous distress as quickly as possible and return him to duty. On the other, it was his responsibility as a doctor to protect his patient from a recurrence of the very illness he was treating. In Rivers's case, this conflict was made more difficult by his own pacifist leanings and the personal affection he had developed for Sassoon. Finally, in the face of Sassoon's persistent determination to resume his command, Rivers agreed to recommend his release from Craiglockhart, but the ethical, moral, and personal cost was too high, and he left the hospital soon after Sassoon's release. Sassoon managed to survive the war, but spent the rest of his life reliving and writing about those experiences, haunted by memories of the unspeakable horrors he had witnessed.

Aside from the issue of whether or not it is treasonous to criticize your own in wartime, Sassoon's breakdown and reenlistment highlighted two important lessons from WW I military psychiatry. The first challenged the prejudice that a man's strength and strength of character could be used to predict his success as a soldier. By those calculations, Sassoon's heroism, his patriotism, and, for many, his membership in the exclusive ranks of a fine old fox-hunting upper-class family should have rendered him immune to the stress of battle. Not so. And second, loyalty was a powerful motivating factor for a soldier, available to military institutions, but not always used by them to their advantage. Sassoon *chose* to return to the front; he *chose* to risk provoking a recurrence of his frightful illness out of a sense of loyalty to the men with whom he had served. As Herbert Speigel, a front-line psychiatrist, would write at the beginning of the next war, choosing words that sound strangely at odds with the traditional vocabulary of war, "What enabled them to attack and attack, week after week in mud, rain, dust and heat? It seemed that the answer lay not in any negative drive but in a positive one. It was love more than hate that propelled these men."[51] They seemed to be fighting for somebody rather than against somebody.

Prompt, forward, and simplified treatment, as instituted in World War I, worked for the military by dramatically reducing the number of evacuees and thereby preserving manpower levels. It rejected the punitive barbarities of the medical materialists in favor of a more psychogenic approach, one that acknowledged the role of psychic shock, terror, and horror in trauma reactions. Psychology, as a science, had won a new legitimacy and authority that would carry over into postwar civilian populations. Unfortunately, many of the psychologists' postwar civilian patients would be veterans, and many of those veterans would present unexpected problems. The army had dared to imagine that suppressed wartime neuroses would disappear with the cessation of the conflict. What actually happened was far more complex and ominous.

MARYALLYN FISHER

Ugly men could not have gotten away with what Dennis got away with. That's the truth—I would never have taken it, none of his women would have, and he had a lot of women. I was Mrs. Fisher the third. I've never seen such a handsome man in my whole entire life. He used to take my breath away.

There was never a doubt in my mind that he loved me, but there was the really good Dennis and then there was the really bad Dennis. He would go out on these binges and he would write bad checks. I would say, "Okay, don't worry about the bad checks; I'll go down in the morning and pay for them. Oh, you stole from your mother? I'll go down and deal with your mother and, yes, I'll make sure that she doesn't call the police. Here's something to eat." I mean, I just took care of everything, and nothing I was doing was working. When I took care of all the problems for him, that didn't work. When I threw him out, that didn't work. Screaming and going to therapy, that didn't work. When I let him take the medication in the house, that didn't work; he just abused the medication. Nothing I was doing was working, but I didn't think it was his destiny to die. I thought that God had a different plan or he would've been dead a long time ago. Dennis was a dope fiend. You don't use dope the way Dennis used dope and stay alive, so I always thought that he was going to stop, that he was going to get clean. I just believed that in my heart, that it wasn't his destiny; that it wasn't our daughter Jean-Marie's or my destiny either. I didn't know what it was going to take, but something was going to have to happen, and then he was going to get better and we were going to be okay.

So what was he doing? Drinking. He worked as a carpenter, and at an oil refinery, but those were short stretches, like two-three months. He was never able to hold a long-term job. Authority issues, for sure. And his anxiety level was too high. He would go into rages over nothing. He wouldn't sleep for like three days, and then he would be crazy. The holidays were a nightmare; planes, helicopters, everything was a nightmare. He couldn't handle anything. I didn't know what his problem was, but I wanted that shit to stop. I was the one that was starting to lose it, because he was doing weird stuff that nobody else would understand. Nobody else does understand unless they're married to a PTSD vet.

Dennis didn't talk about Vietnam at all, so I don't know all the details. But I know he got blown up over in Vietnam. He was in something like a tank, and there were, I think, six of them, and a hand grenade flew in there. They all died except for Dennis. I know that that was one of the traumas. There was a little girl that he befriended that one of the officers raped, and that upset him. Also, he was in a helicopter, and the guy who had the machine gun got shot to death, and Dennis had to move him and take over the machine gun. Shrapnel went through his shoulder and through his neck, about an inch away from the base of his spine. His disability was 110 percent. They only gave him 10 percent for the PTSD.

We didn't even talk about PTSD until we had been married for a few years, Jean-Marie had been born, and he was in therapy. He'd been living with symptoms for years, but nobody knew what it was. A diagnosis of posttraumatic stress? From the V.A.? Forget it! We had to fight for that. This was the '80s and nobody I talked to had any understanding of PTSD. They just wanted to get him out. They came to my house every night with a big padded envelope of medications, all types: Vicodin, Methodone cocktail, Paxil. Take this, go away. Towards the end when he got really bad, he would go to bed in November and wouldn't get out of bed until March. And that's the truth.

It was a big thing in therapy when we finally understood that it was PTSD. It took six months, just working on that one thing. He would be screaming and telling me it was all me, and I would say, "Dennis, it's your PTSD," and instead of saying, "No it's not, you fucking bitch, it's you!" he would finally say, "Okay, I'll think about that," and he would go out to the garage and do it. We had gotten to that point, but he just couldn't go through to the other side. He'd have to hit the bar.

I gave up the last two years. Actually, I should have left two or three years before I did. Nothing was working. He didn't need to go out and drink, he didn't need to do cocaine. We had a whole cabinet filled with different types of medication from the V.A. He just started abusing the medication like he did the other drugs.

There were some good people running the support groups at the Vet Center in Bellingham, Washington. I was going to the Partners of Vets with PTSD. I had been in groups before with women who were exactly like me—they couldn't get out either. I would listen to them talk about their lives and think, "Are you out of your mind? You're crazy!" Then I'd look around, and I'm in the circle with them. That's when I really felt isolated, because I wasn't going anywhere. But the women's group at the Bellingham center helped me tremendously. These women got it, and they helped me decide that I would not go into my forties being this crazy. And it was that crazy. Jean-Marie was cutting herself because she was that messed up. There was no way I could keep her there. I turned forty in September, stalled until February, and then put everything I could into the car and grabbed the kid. Certain things I couldn't take, like my jewelry box that had my charm bracelet in it, charms my parents had given me. I couldn't take them because if I took them it meant I wasn't coming back.

I had been gone a year and a half when I got the phone call. It was the Everson police, and I thought, okay, now what did he do? But the cop said Dennis had shot himself. I wouldn't let them take him off the life support until we got there. Because if only his heart was beating, I had to get there before. I kept calling the hospital, saying keep him going until—just don't let his heart stop until we get there.

They had a white cloth over him and his eyes were open and I could see his green eyes. He was still warm and his heart was still beating. I was there when his heart went down from 64 to 32 to 19 to 6 to 2. I had my arms around him, I had my head on his chest, and I heard his heart stop beating. I'm really grateful for that.

I let the nuns come in to pray around Dennis, but I wanted to say no. I was enraged that this had happened. This was not right. I did everything I was supposed to do. So why did my husband have to leave the world like that? Why? Why did God allow this to happen?

Why does Jean-Marie have to go through this? I kept trying to figure it out, trying to figure out what I could do to undo it. After about three months it started dawning that this was permanent. There was nothing I could do, that this just was, that he was dead.

I couldn't talk to Jean-Marie. I didn't have anything to give her. But she had no outlet. She was talking to people, and I just wanted her to stop. I didn't want anybody to know that he died like that. It was the shame—on top of everything else, it was the shame. When something like this happens, you are so wide open and vulnerable, you have absolutely no defenses. I didn't want my husband's suicide being discussed over coffee at the diner. I didn't want a lot of people knowing, because I couldn't stand to have his death treated casually. And I couldn't defend him because I had nothing. I was just totally, completely an open wound.

It was Jean's idea to go to Sons and Daughters in Touch.[52] The meeting was on Father's Day. You don't know how bad it was on Father's Day because that was the day he shot himself. But we went down there, and we felt welcomed. We were around other people who understood—these people got it. We were standing in line for coffee, and all of a sudden I started crying and I couldn't stop, and I couldn't stop telling people, "My husband shot himself in the head." Jean did the same too, and that's when she really cried. Everyone looked at us with empathy and let us finish. Nobody went, "Oh my God!" They understood. That was such a relief. I was having a hard time getting everything out, and I was falling and choking over what I was saying: "This isn't over, this isn't over. It's 1999, and my husband just died from the Vietnam War."

JEAN-MARIE FISHER

My dad was awesome. Maybe I do put him on a pedestal, but I think that's where he deserves to be. We spent a lot of time together. He used to always buy stuff for me, just because. He bought me lots of wish dolls from South America. You put them underneath your pillow and you make a wish. My nose ring was a birthday present from my dad when I turned thirteen. None of the kids my age had them. I liked that. He let me dye my hair, and one time he drove me up to Canada for ice cream because nothing in our town was open. Sometimes he would just talk to me. He told me about how he couldn't sleep. That's why he stayed up a lot, because of his nightmares. He would just be dreaming, but it wasn't really a dream. He was awake, only he couldn't move, he couldn't scream. I remember, when Daddy died, I think I went a little crazy. I would be sitting in class and I would just be thinking of him and I would see him with the gun to his head. I would close my eyes and the image wouldn't go away. I would open them and it'd still be there. So I think I understand.

But I remember being scared a lot, too. He was so unpredictable. There were times when he was really weird. I remember one time he was sitting out in the garage with a BB gun. He was shooting at mice that weren't there. I was scared out of my mind. That's why I didn't want kids coming over to my house. He used to build stuff, like racing cars and want me to play with him, but I couldn't ever stay too long. After a while, he would just get aggravated. I would do something wrong and he would go crazy. He would start screaming at me, and I'd go into the house crying. Once we even had to have a separate house for him in Bellingham, which is like eighteen miles away. It was very small and dark and it always smelled like incense. Dad loved incense. I think that he was on a lot of drugs then. I figured it out because once when we went over to his apartment he was lying there crying. He wanted to go find something and my mom kept saying it wasn't there. I figured out that they were talking about drugs. It was really awful to see my dad cry.

I didn't talk to my dad for two years after my mom took me to live in New Jersey. I thought he'd ruined my life. But I felt bad, too, because I knew that he wouldn't be able to deal with us leaving. What's he going to do? He stays up all night, he doesn't eat right. He was already so messed up. My mom would always tell me that he really loved me, but I would tell her to stop saying that because it just made it worse.

I said goodbye to him when he was still on life support. At first, Mom just kept saying it wasn't suicide, it was an accident, and I wasn't allowed to tell anyone. It pissed me off that I wasn't allowed to talk about it. I kept thinking that if it was suicide, we shouldn't have left; we should've stayed there. Maybe he would've quit the drugs. But I don't really think that he would've. Mom says that if we had stayed, it would have been just as hard. I think I do kind of understand it. Nothing was making him happy. My dad was a drug addict, but what else was there for him? If he wasn't on drugs, he would have those nightmares. I don't want that for my dad.

When he died, at first I handled it in a really bad way. This girl used to bring a water bottle filled with vodka to school, and we would get drunk every day. I went to classes stoned and I had really bad grades. I thought it should've been me, it should've been me, and so I used to cut myself a lot. I cut myself to make my life messed up so that I could feel okay. I was so used to living a really messed-up life that when I wasn't crying I felt weird. That's what I'm used to. Real pain. So I would cut myself, and then I would cry, and then I'd think, "What have I done? I'm such a messed-up person." But lately I've been pretty good. I quit drinking and smoking, and I don't even think about cutting myself anymore. I just now realize that I don't think about it anymore. I think that's so great.

My biggest interest right now is everything that has to do with the Vietnam War. I'm reading a lot of war books. I watched *Full Metal Jacket* and *Platoon*. It makes me see what my dad went through, and I think, wow, no wonder he was weird. And no wonder he was an atheist because a lot of people gave up on God with what they saw. My dad actually killed people. He was trained to kill people. You're trained to kill people, you get shot a lot, and then you come home to a regular family. How weird is that?

CHAPTER TWO

PTSD AND MODERN WARFARE

> On a tour of this country... I have visited 18 governmental hospitals for veterans. In them are a total of about 50,000 destroyed men... men who were the pick of the nation 18 years ago. Boys with a normal viewpoint were taken out of the fields and offices and factories and classrooms and put into the ranks. There they were remolded; they were made over; they were made to "about face;" to regard murder as the order of the day. They were put shoulder to shoulder and, through mass psychology, they were entirely changed. We used them for a couple of years and trained them to think nothing at all about killing or being killed. Then, suddenly, we discharged them and told them to make another "about face!" We didn't need them anymore.
>
> —MAJOR GENERAL SMEDLEY BUTLER, United States Marine Corps, two-time recipient of the Congressional Medal of Honor, from a letter written in 1936 and excerpted in *The VVA Veteran,* April 1995

THE LEAD-UP TO WORLD WAR II

FOR WORLD WAR I VETERANS returning home with disabling injuries, there was no healthcare system specifically dedicated to their needs. The Public Health Service was theoretically charged with their care, but by 1921, they were treating eight times as many patients as before the war, and in the same prewar facilities.[1] Many disabled veterans found themselves sleeping on cots—or even on floors—in the halls of America's overwhelmed hospitals. Many just gave up the struggle, and sat on street corners with tin cups and signs reading: "Help Me. I'm a Disabled Veteran."[2] Further, the expectation that psychiatric casualties would ease once soldiers returned home proved to be optimistic. Even veterans who had performed well in combat, and others who had responded positively to treatment in the war zone, began to complain of debilitating symptoms once they came home. It was only the luckiest and the most resourceful who managed to navigate the overwhelmed and overwhelmingly complicated system of government health services.

Colonel Albert Glass, a military psychiatrist who studied frontline psychiatry in World War I, practiced it in World War II, and was responsible for its implementation in Korea, later articulated what doctors discovered in years following World War I. "The fluid reversible acute psychiatric states (of newly traumatized soldiers) were replaced by chronic neurotic syndromes that either represented a continuation of the combat breakdown, were a recurrence of a wartime neurosis, or arose in individuals who had no record of previous nervous disability during the war. The neurotic war veterans, separated from the dynamic elements of the combat situation seemed to have combined or integrated battle trauma with the neurotic elements of personality to form a fixed psychological disorder which reacted to usual difficulties as if they were battle stimuli. In effect, they fought the battle of civil life with the wartime symptoms of tension, noise, sensitivity, explosive outbursts of rage, helplessness, and battle nightmares."[3]

What Glass was describing was a second and previously unrecognized aspect of combat-related stress reaction: the delayed response. In effect, psychiatrists had figured out how to efficiently return many distressed men to the front by suppressing their feelings and their symptoms, but they did not know how to address the prolonged and chronic damage such suppression would cause to their psyches. Combat stress was now understood to be intractable, unpredictable in its onset, and, perhaps most disturbing of all, it was often irreparable. Of the 300,000 disabled World War I veterans, some 50,000 were still hospitalized twenty years later for psychiatric illnesses.[4]

Caring for those veterans whose symptoms persisted in spite of front-line interventions and those whose symptoms developed after their return home cost American taxpayers almost a billion dollars between the two world wars.[5] Harry Sullivan, who would become the first psychiatric adviser to the new Selective Service System (1940), was very concerned about the potential cost of psychiatric casualties in any coming war. "The taxpayers of the United States have spent on neuropsychiatric disabilities related to the conscription and war of 1917–8, 946-odd million dollars. The cost is still going up. Everything else has gone down . . . but the neuropsychiatric load goes up steadily, in its magnitude, year by year."[6]

It was not surprising that, given the politics and atmosphere of the time, those in positions of military and political authority would look to "science" for a more perfect (and cheaper) answer. The "science" was eugenics, which had been gaining intellectual and political influence in the United States since the late nineteenth century, when large numbers of Southern and Eastern Europeans immigrated to the United States. Their presence had changed the complexion of American society. The economic depressions that occurred about every ten years, from the 1870s leading up to the Great Depression, resulted in unemployment, worker exploitation, and the rise of militant labor unions. Rather than blame economic and social institutions for the disruption and unrest, eugenicists found a convenient scapegoat in the immigrant populations. Simultaneously, reconstruction in the South was adding large numbers of recently freed Black slaves to the industrial labor pool, exacerbating a xenophobic frenzy. The American gene pool, it was claimed, was becoming contaminated, its essence diluted. The defectives (specifically Blacks, Jews, Southern Europeans and Slavs) would have to be culled like inferior livestock. The emigration restrictions of the '20s were an attempt to improve American society through social engineering, excluding the weaker elements and encouraging the ablest and the fittest to breed.

Though the values and beliefs espoused by the eugenicists were less than rational, their overtly racist message resonated with traditional military culture. Some men were weaker and therefore predisposed to break down in combat. Mental deficiencies were assumed to be hereditary, and, in the future, it was posited, such weak links could be identified "scientifically" and weeded out before they ever put on a uniform, thereby eliminating a corrosive element in the army and saving the American taxpayers millions of dollars in disability pensions.[7] Addressing an audience of distinguished psychiatrists attending the annual meeting of the American Medical Association in 1921, in an address that was respectfully published in the next *Journal of the American Medical Association*, G. H. Benton attacked those veterans of the First World War who, in his opinion, suffered from "pension neurosis." Pension neurosis, or "Italianitis," is a "particular condition (that) occurs among foreigners, especially Italians, Greeks, Austrians and Poles. It is most pronounced in Italians. . . . One of the fundamentals of the condition seems to arise from the general belief that the United States is a very wealthy country and that its government is due and destined to provide for them for the rest of their lives."[8]

By the late '30s, when German Jews began their flight from increasingly terrifying Nazi rhetoric, there was a vigorous national debate in the United States about whether or not the American frontiers should be opened to receive them. General George Van Horne Moseley, who served as deputy chief of staff of the army under General Douglas MacArthur, told a gathering of medical reservists at Tulane University in 1938 that, in his judgment, America should protect itself from the contamination of people who have been thrown out of other countries as "undesirables." Refugees, he opined, should only be accepted "with the distinct understanding that they all be sterilized before being permitted to embark. Only that way can we properly protect our future."[9]

Though Moseley's speech was controversial, it hardly positioned him on the hysterical margins. When he retired later the same year, his close friend and confidant George C. Marshall wrote to him, "I know you will leave behind a host of younger men who have a loyal devotion to you for what you have stood for. I am one of that company, and it makes me very sad to think that I cannot serve with you and under you again."[10]

By the time a second world war appeared inevitable, eugenics was deeply embedded in American popular culture, and with it the belief that it was science that would, could, and should solve the problems of humanity. Thomas Salmon, who learned psychiatry while screening immigrants at Ellis Island before overseeing the psychic health of soldiers in World War I, and who is revered to this day in military psychiatric circles, was a leading proponent of the eugenics movement. His influence is unmistakable in the disastrous plan the U.S. Army instituted to engineer a fighting force that would be both fierce and invulnerable, if not to physical at least to psychiatric injury.

That plan was predicated on the accepted (and wholly unscientific) belief in military circles that some ethnic groups were, by virtue of their genetic heritage, predisposed to developing war neuroses. So, in spite of everything that had been learned from previous conflicts, on the eve of the Second World War, the American army chose to revert to the entrenched idea that a successful warrior could be predicted, and thus selected. Good character, manly strength, and intelligence would be identified in preinduction screenings that would make front-line psychiatry obsolete—and the postwar pension bill far less daunting. It is ironic and profoundly sad that the "good" war, against a fascist ideology of eugenics and racial purity, was so essentially tainted by our own homegrown version of Social Darwinism and ethnic nationalism. The Selective Service Act of 1940 abandoned the known in favor of a wholly untried and deeply morally compromised program. It proved a very expensive gamble.

Eugenics promised that such screenings would "scientifically" select the best and the brightest who would make insuperable warriors, and weed out those whose psychological makeup predisposed them to be a danger to themselves or to their comrades. Screening would keep them out of the army in the first place. Journalist Nicholas Lemann tells a wonderful story about the results of the early IQ tests administered by the army:

> Intelligence tests have always produced a kind of photograph of the existing class structure, in which the better-off economic and ethnic groups are found to be more intelligent and the

worse-off are found to be less so. In his book analyzing the results of the intelligence tests that the Army had given recruits during the First World War, for example, Carl Brigham, an early psychometrician and the father of ETS's leading test, the Scholastic Aptitude Test, reported that the highest-scoring identifiable group was Princeton students—this at a time when, by today's standards, Princeton was a den of carousing rich boys.[11]

Nonetheless, the screening approach proved irresistibly seductive. It justified segregated army units and an essentially all-white officer corps. It conveniently—for some—masqueraded as science assumptions that were mere racism, misogyny, homophobia, xenophobia, and a rash of other prejudices. It affirmed the myth of the good warrior as supremely and identifiably a white male of Northern European ancestry.

Perhaps the most obvious shortcoming of this novel approach was that no reliable set of criteria had been developed for identifying those most desirable and those most at risk. As a result, about 1.6 million draftees discovered that they were "defective." In the course of a three-minute interview, they had somehow exposed themselves as idiots or psychotics, nail-biters, bed wetters, or masturbators, and, as such, had been judged unfit for the *new* U.S. Army.[12] The process would have been farcical if it wasn't so painful for those who were mystified by their less than flattering classifications. Ben Shephard tells of a group of Harvard doctors who thought they could assess a potential warrior on the basis of body type: "normal, masculine, men had flat, angular bodies, narrow hips and pubic hair running towards the navel, whereas cowards had soft bodies, wider hips, and pubic hair that spread laterally."[13] Not surprisingly, the results of screenings based on such criteria proved next to worthless.

WORLD WAR II

World War II is not associated with combat-related stress in the popular imagination. While images of World War I shell shock and

Vietnam flashbacks both have a place in public memory, World War II is remembered as the "good war" whose soldiers defeated an unequivocal evil and returned with Gene Kelly optimism. Flush with GI benefits in housing and education, the story goes, the "Greatest Generation" assumed the perquisites and responsibilities of a superpower, and passed on their stories of righteous heroism to the baby boom they spawned in their victor's enthusiasm. Yet, at least at the outset, the troops who made it through the induction screenings fared far worse in combat than had soldiers in the Great War. In 1942, U.S. psychiatric casualties were more than five times those of the previous war.[14] In the absence of front-line psychiatric treatment centers, soldiers affected with "neurotic" symptoms were labeled "ineffective" and sent home—shamed, devastated, and untreated. By 1943, the number of psychiatric discharges exceeded the number of new enlistees.[15]

Clearly, someone had blundered. The army's initial war plans had included no resource allocation for old-school forward treatment centers. Consequently, there were few trained psychiatrists to staff them. Belatedly and hurriedly, the lessons of the last war were unpacked, and military psychiatry was rediscovered. The assignment of two psychiatrists to the front-line evacuation centers in North Africa in 1943 made an impressive point: In four days they managed to return 50 percent of the psychiatric evacuees to combat.[16] Food, showers, and especially sleep, both natural and drug-induced,[17] were the first line of defense.

Over the next year, as quickly trained psychiatric recruits were rushed to the front, the evacuation rate for psychiatric casualties fell dramatically.[18] The recruits were instructed to emphasize cheerleading over therapy, and cautioned never to mention "war neurosis." Instead, they were to talk about a man's responsibility to his comrades and his country, and to offer firm reassurances that with a little rest he would soon be ready and willing to rejoin his unit. These new guidelines reflected the newly accepted idea that, given adequate stress, a trauma response was inevitable and universal. Roy Grinker and John Speigel, whose *War Neuroses in North Africa* (1943) became a sort of bible for new military psychiatrists, put it this way: "The psychological deficiency resulting from combat stress is of the greatest practical concern because no one is immune. If the stress is severe enough, it strikes an exposed 'Achilles' heel' and if the exposure to it is sufficiently prolonged, adverse psychological symptoms may develop in anyone."[19] That observation marked one of the central paradigm shifts of World War II military psychiatry.

The doctors, however, were far more open to change than the generals. In 1942, the commander in chief of British forces in the Middle East, General Sir Claude Auchinleck, strongly urged a reintroduction of the death penalty for cowardice and desertion.[20] Auchinleck was perhaps extreme, but the same year, Churchill had this to say about psychiatric casualties:

> I am sure it would be sensible to restrict as much as possible the work of these gentlemen, who are capable of doing an immense amount of harm with what may very easily degenerate into charlatanry. The tightest hand should be kept over them, and they should not be allowed to quarter themselves in large numbers upon the Fighting Services at the public expense. There are, no doubt, easily recognizable cases which may benefit from treatment of this kind, but it is very wrong to disturb large numbers of healthy, normal men and women by asking the kind of odd questions in which the psychiatrists specialise. There are quite enough hangers-on and camp followers already.[21]

In 1943, frustrated with the limited success of the psychiatrists and their inability to agree on protocols, the U.S. Army officially decreed that henceforth all psychiatric cases would initially be diagnosed as "exhaustion" and treated accordingly.[22] The shift revealed both the disgust and distrust of the military brass toward psychiatric casualties, psychiatrists, and psychiatry in general. Their antagonism was memorably exposed in what became known as the "slapping incidents." Lieutenant General George S. Patton was visiting wounded troops in Sicily. Standing at the bedside of a young man with no visible wounds, Patton decided that the soldier was a psychiatric casualty. In fact, he had malaria and a fever of 103 degrees, but Patton hadn't bothered to ask. He slapped the boy across the face with his gloves and called him a "goddamned coward." A week later, he slapped another boy, brandished his pistol, and threatened him with a firing squad if the boy did not immediately return to the front. "Your nerves, hell; you are just a Goddamned coward, you yellow son of a bitch. . . . You're going back to the front lines and you may get shot and killed, but you're going to fight. If you don't, I'll stand you up against a wall and have a firing squad kill you on purpose. In fact, I ought to shoot you myself, you Goddamned whimpering coward."[23]

The story made the news. General Eisenhower, fearful that the Germans would use the story as propaganda, forced Patton to publicly apologize. Ultimately, Patton lost his command over the incidents. "Old Blood and Guts," however, was not alone in his feelings. To the military mind, a military doctor's first allegiance was to the institution. Patton's contempt for the young men he slapped and for the doctors who "coddled" them reverberated with many of the brass. On the other hand, doctors trained to give priority to the health of their patients experienced their roles as inherently conflicted. And, for all the tough talk about courage and responsibility, there was no arguing with the fact that a soldier who couldn't remember his own name, or use his paralyzed legs, or keep from weeping was, at best, not an asset to his comrades—and, at worst, he was a threat to their safety.

In sum, there were important lessons made available to military psychiatrists in World War II. First, preinduction screenings had not proven to be some kind of magic, modern solution. Then there was the understanding that every man has a breaking point. "Each moment of combat imposes a strain so great that men will break down in direct relation to the intensity and duration of their exposure," reported the *Journal of the American Medical Association* in 1946. "Thus psychiatric casualties are as inevitable as gunshot and shrapnel wounds in warfare."[24] That understanding had gained a lasting foothold among military psychiatrists, if not among the generals, and would affect military policy in future wars. And finally, there was a lesson that the generals would find equally hard to accept, that group identification and cohesion were critical in fending off psychiatric problems. The experience of prolonged danger leads soldiers to develop extreme emotional dependency upon their peer group and leaders, and it is the morale and leadership of the small fighting unit that offers the strongest protection against psychological breakdown. That dependence is what Herbert Speigel called "love."[25]

Beyond those understandings, which could be used to protect soldiers from psychiatric breakdown, military psychiatrists had also identified a variety of ways to gain access to the traumatic memories that incapacitated soldiers. Hypnosis, "narcosynthesis" (drug therapy), and "talking cures" had all been used to get at least some soldiers back to their fighting units. But, as Grinker and Speigel warned, the effect of combat "is not like the writing on a slate that can be erased, leaving the slate as it was before. Combat leaves a lasting impression on men's minds."[26] What happened to soldiers after their "successful" forward treatments, what happened to them after they returned to their units or after they returned home, was of little interest or concern to those responsible for military policy.[27]

By the late 1940s, the psychiatric casualties of WWII, combined with those left over from the previous war, had swelled the asylum and hospital populations in the United States. According to the V.A., its 102,000 hospital beds were filled, and 20,700 patients were waiting for admission.[28] Fully 60 percent of the postwar V.A. patients were psychiatric.[29] Limited funds and limited space opened the door for one of medical history's most obscene experiments: the ice pick lobotomy.

Walter Freeman, a neurology professor at George Washington University, believed that he had isolated the nerve connections responsible for certain psychoses. He hypothesized that he could effect a cure by severing those connections. Under local anesthesia, Freeman used a hammer to tap a modified ice pick through the patient's eye socket and into the prefrontal lobe, which was then severed from the rest of the brain. The economic arguments for such a procedure were compelling. A lobotomy could be performed for $250, while it could cost upwards of $35,000 a year to maintain a patient in a hospital.[30] The curative arguments were less compelling. There was never *any* convincing evidence that the procedure worked. Lobotomized patients were certainly less aggressive, but most were reduced to listless, dull-eyed shadows of their former selves.

Nonetheless, Walter Freeman was elected president of the American Board of Psychiatry and Neurology in 1948. As many as fifty thousand of his signature procedures were performed in the United States throughout the 1940s before the introduction of the antipsychotic drug chlorpromazine (trade name Thorazine) in 1952 marked the end of Walter Freeman's reign of terror.[31] Once again, the implicit equation of hysterical women and traumatized soldiers influenced both theory and treatment. The vast majority of lobotomized patients were women, the main exception being the thousands of returning veterans.[32]

KOREA

Oscar Wilde once said that losing one husband was a tragedy; losing two was simply carelessness. After the tragic mistakes of the Second World War, the decision by the army to do without psychiatrists at the beginning of the war in Korea seems careless at best. Frustrated by and disdainful of the "shrinks'" failure to stem the flow of "wastage," it once again became military policy that American boys would fight, or else.[33]

Once again, the results were predictably and immediately alarming. Psychiatric casualties were seven times higher in the first year than in World War II.[34] Albert Glass, who had served in WWII and written extensively about combat trauma, was recruited to undo the mess. Glass brought with him the forgotten and ignored lessons of previous wars, specifically the convincing correlation between combat stress and the lack of unit cohesion and effective leadership. Glass was convinced that there was far less to be gained from focusing on the weakness of the individual than on the weakness of the group, for "These group or relationship phenomena explained marked differences in the psychiatric casualty rates of various units who were exposed to a similar intensity of battle stress."[35]

To protect unit cohesion, he quickly reintroduced prompt, forward treatment, but with two important modifications. First, he made certain that psychiatrists themselves were immersed in the realities of front-line warfare. They lived and socialized with the fighting men who were their charges. Glass also made certain that their training specifically addressed the conflicting loyalties of a military doctor to both the patient and to the institution. Their training stressed Glass's belief that not only was it in the best interests of the unit to have its psychiatric casualties quickly reintegrated, but it was "in the best interests of the individual to rejoin his combat unit, for in no other way can the individual regain confidence and mastery of the situation and prevent chronic tension and guilt."[36] It was instilled in the front-line counselors that evacuation would not only irreparably damage a soldier's self-respect, but would also leave him chronically disabled by guilt and shame. Therefore, counselors need not feel their loyalty to the army to be in conflict with their loyalty to the soldier.

Glass's second modification was in response to his belief that psychiatric casualties were inevitable and universal, given adequate stress. The rotation system he proposed to protect soldiers from becoming psychiatric casualties was based on a point system.[37] This system attached a certain value to the duration of exposure and the intensity of individual combat experiences. For example, infantrymen rated four points a month, artillerymen three, and rear-echelon forces, two. When a soldier had accumulated thirty-six points, he was rotated home, regardless of how the war was progressing. It was an attempt to both anticipate breakdown and to intervene before it happened.

The World War II statistics of 23 percent psychiatric casualties dropped to 6 percent after Glass took over, and Korea was ultimately considered a success for military psychiatrists.[38] Glass attributed the success to prompt, forward treatment, as well as to the new point system, but as we will see in Chapter Three, that point system, as it was "refined" and implemented in Vietnam, was to cause major problems.

What was expected as America became mired in Vietnam was patterns of battlefield breakdown similar to those of Korea. What was seen, at least initially, was figures that were even lower: only slightly more than 1 percent of combatants had to be evacuated as psychiatric casualties.[39] An age-old problem appeared to have been solved, but any celebration was to prove premature. It soon became clear that the demonic pathogens were not so easily beaten. They had only mutated, modified their assault. Their new manifestations, during, but especially after, the war in Vietnam, would prove to be every bit as virulent and lethal as anything that had come before. While it was still largely a mystery why some soldiers were affected while others were not, it was becoming clear—to anyone who chose to notice—that war was a disease that had no cure.

JUDY JAMES

Suicide is a selfish act, and Ben was not a selfish person. What finally put him over the edge twenty-six years after he came home from Vietnam, I will never know. He probably didn't even know himself. Ben was my best friend. We had an almost psychic connection. We always seemed to know what the other one was thinking. But this time it failed me. Sometimes I'm afraid he thought I knew what he was planning and that I was condoning it because of my silence. If I have any guilt, it is that I should have known. We both knew what his problem was and that suicide was a possibility. But he was under the care of professionals, and he had a good marriage and a well-paying job. We were doing everything right. So I let my guard down. You can never let your guard down.

Ben enlisted in the army after he graduated from high school. He wanted to serve his country. He arrived in Vietnam with the 101st Airborne in December 1967. His letters home contained descriptions of the countryside and the conditions, but very seldom his experiences. The one exception was a letter dated February 18, 1968:

> We're still in Quang Tri Province. . . . The NVA is blowing up the roads and bridges as fast as the Sea Bees rebuild them. We're the only ones that get anything done permanently. We kill people.
>
> Good-bye,
> Ben

Ben was shot in the arm and sent home in April 1968. He avoided the V.A. and threw his Air Medal and his Purple Heart in the trash. He started classes at Whittier College, dropped out, went through two brief marriages, and had a problem with alcohol and drugs.

He had never heard of Posttraumatic Stress; he just thought he was going crazy. In the early '80s, he got involved with the Vet Center in Sacramento, a volunteer organization staffed by combat veterans. When he found out there were so many others who shared his symptoms, he told me that knowledge literally saved his life. He had a C & P exam (compensation and pension) for his PTSD, and was granted a 10 percent disability in March 1983.

Everything was pretty good for a while after we married in 1985, but about a year later, Ben began to feel depressed, sad, and tearful for no apparent reason. In his room, he had to orient the desk so that he was facing the door, and in public places, he always had to have his back to the wall. He stockpiled food and survival gear and guns. He was having combat nightmares and told his doctor he felt quite certain that he would have killed himself if it had not been for my support.

Ben was put on medication for the first time, and his PTSD rating was increased to 30 percent. We learned everything we could about the condition, and discovered that his symptoms were pretty typical. He began to talk a little about his survivor's guilt. He told his doctor that of the 350 men who underwent jungle training with him and went to Vietnam together as a unit, only 18 of them came back alive.

Four or five times a year, he would have what I called a "spell." It was like he would turn into another person. He would get this edge to his voice, and nothing my daughter, Aubree, or I did would be right. Finally, he would retreat to his room upstairs, slamming the door. I just left him alone. After a time, he would come out and be very apologetic. He knew I would still be there for him when he "came down."

In January 1993, he spent a month in the PTSD unit at the V.A. Medical Center in San Francisco. I found a note he had written in the hospital that said, "To survive my part of the Vietnam War, I detached myself entirely from what I saw, and completely forgot the battles and the names and the faces of the men I had served with.... I have come to understand that this type of detachment is not something stepped into and out of easily. It takes time and effort."

In July 1994, I went with some old friends to a family cabin we have on the upper Sacramento River. Ben could not go because of his work schedule. I talked to him on the phone Sunday. He sounded fine. Aubree called me after she got home from work on Wednesday and, when I asked about Ben, she said that the same "Do Not Disturb" sign had been taped to the bedroom door for two days. I asked her to look to make sure everything was all right. She came back to the phone frantic. Ben was on the bed not moving, and there was a bottle of pills and booze on the bedside table. Ben had not had a drink in twelve years. I told her to call 911. Ben knew that Aubree would find his body. I am finding it very hard to forgive him for that.

I don't know when Ben made his fatal decision, but it wasn't spur of the moment. He had gone through financial files and left things in order on his desk. He left me a short but not very revealing note. "Judy, There should be close to $xxxxxx. I'd like to have left you more. I'm at the end of my rope. I love you forever. Ben"

It has been tremendously hard bringing up things that I have been trying to put behind me, but I want people to know about posttraumatic stress. I want people to know that there are ways to deal with it, to make it better, but there are no guarantees. We can't guard them twenty-four hours a day. I want to tell survivors that all their "should haves" probably wouldn't have changed a thing. Ben had a privileged upbringing, a good job, and a loving, happy, stable marriage. He had beaten his addictions. We knew about PTSD. He was under psychiatric care and on medication, and I was in constant contact with his medical providers. I thought we were doing everything right. I thought we had everything under control. And still he killed himself.

JOYCE GARCIA

Bobby used to tell me stories about his days in Vietnam and I didn't understand. He was a paratrooper and saw a lot of the war from the air. I knew it was hard for him to tell me about the killing. All he told me was that he hated guns and didn't ever want one in the house. Bobby never looked at me when he told me these things. He became stiff and stared off into who knows where. I learned not to ask many questions because he seemed to hate himself for telling me.

Bobby was not a man who wore combat boots to prove a point. He wore his because he was trying to show he was not ashamed of his fellow veterans. He was appalled at the behavior of the public toward the soldiers. It made him mad, and it brought tears to his eyes when he saw fellows missing an arm or a leg out in public. I learned that he was one of those who felt some guilt that he still had his limbs and his life while others didn't. He began to feel like nothing was ever going to help him stop hearing the grenades go off in his dreams. He said he could still smell burning flesh. I just grimaced. It was not easy for him. I wanted to enjoy life, and he was feeling guilty that he had one.

He began to come home late from work, and he started to ask me what I did all the living day long. I began to think I was married to a stranger. I believe he was finally coming to the realization that the Vietnam War was not going to leave him just because he left it. By the time he died we were separated and I was working at a large inner-city department store and beginning to discover that the world was much larger than I ever imagined. I had friends that made Bobby cringe. I met people he didn't understand.

He was only twenty-five years old when he died by clamping the hose of our vacuum cleaner to the exhaust pipe of our red and white pickup truck and then securing it by tape and cardboard to the window of our car. He sat there alone and died. It was February 13. We had a date for the next day, for Valentine's Day, and it must have been just too painful for him to have to plan a date with his wife who was living away from him. I had been gone from him for just over three months, and we had been talking about trying again. He must not have thought the date was going to do any good. Was he remembering that I was beginning to be afraid of him because he could not sleep and was cranky every day? Was he thinking I was getting too aware of his drinking? I had started to ask questions: Why was he always either sleeping heavily or so awake he was almost manic? Why did he drive the car like a fool and put us all in danger? Why and why and why?

It is nearing the anniversary of his death, and I always feel it coming on. The rest of the year I can be strong and can feel the distance, but February always feels so sad to me.

He didn't die in honor with a bullet through his body shot by the enemy, but was taken from all his loved ones just as surely as if he were shot on the field of war. He never had one night's peaceful sleep since he came back from Vietnam.

I was twenty-one when my husband died, and I'm fifty now. I did not lose my love for Bobby when he died. I did not lose my faith in him when he disappeared. I lost me. I have spent the last twenty-nine years striving to live a life Bobby would have been happy to share with me. I am getting more bewildered by his death as the years go on. Right now I am having some real issues with why the hell didn't he take into consideration that I might need him even more as the years passed? And his daughter, it's much harder for her. I at least knew him. I knew he was a good man. All she knows is that he left her behind.

Bobby gave up his life, not years later all alone in that truck. He really gave it up when he went to war, when he put on a uniform and learned to jump out of a plane. Bobby was an honorable man. He never sought help from the army for the demons who chased him in his sleep and made him jump out of his skin when he heard a car backfire. He didn't know there was help. It was the early days and no one knew there was help to be had for posttraumatic stress disorder. He just thought he was going nuts, and before he went over the edge by accident, and maybe took his family with him, he decided to do it quietly. He even made sure he did all his laundry beforehand so I wouldn't have to come back to the house to do it for him. He even made the bed. There was not one thing left for me to tidy up when I went back to the house. There was no note either. He did not say goodbye. He just went quietly away.

CHAPTER THREE

(WHY) WAS VIETNAM DIFFERENT?

> All of us, like all nations, are tested twice in the moral realm: first by what we do, then by what we make of what we do. A condition of guilt, a sense of one's own guilt, denotes a kind of second chance; we are, as if by a kind of grace, given a chance to repay to the living what it is we find ourselves owing to the dead.
>
> —PETER MARIN, *Freedom and Its Discontents*

BETWEEN 1962, WHEN THE FIRST Marine Corps squadrons arrived, and 1973, when American troops scrambled to evacuate Saigon,[1] approximately three million Americans served in the armed forces in Vietnam. Of those, according to the findings of the congressionally mandated *National Vietnam Veterans Readjustment Study*, 30.9 percent, or about one million men, were projected to have a lifetime prevalence of PTSD.[2] What was it about this war that made it so extraordinarily—and lastingly—devastating for those Americans who fought?

In order to begin to understand the reasons, it is important to remember precisely who fought in Vietnam. Some American soldiers had indeed enlisted out of idealism; others enlisted because job opportunities were limited and recruiters promised special training and choice assignments.[3] In the early years of the war, the armed forces managed quite efficiently to fill their ranks with volunteers, but as the war dragged on, as public attitudes became increasingly conflicted, and as information about the horror and brutality became readily available, fewer men went voluntarily. By 1967, almost half of the enlisted men were draftees. By 1969, draftees constituted 88 percent of the infantry.[4]

The Vietnam era draft, unlike that of previous wars, was far from "blind." Lewis Hershey, who had served as director of selective services since 1941, is said to have regretted the "fine" people who died in World War II. A generation of professionals, in particular engineers and scientists, had been lost in that war. The draft he designed for the Vietnam years sought to correct that talent drain by calling up for service those he believed society could most easily manage without, and leaving those "fortunate sons"—to quote the bitter 1970 Creedence Clearwater Revival song—to carry on with their lives. In the national interest, he designed a system of deferments for college students, most of whom were middle- and upper-class whites who were being educated for the future benefit of the nation. The working class, the undereducated, and the poor were channeled into the most dangerous service.[5] Hershey's draft was, at best, heavy-handed social engineering; at worst, it was eugenics. By the mid-sixties the racial and class inequities of the American army in Vietnam were obscene. According to military historian General S. L. A. Marshall, "In the average rifle company the strength was 50 percent composed of Negros, Southwestern Mexicans, Puerto Ricans, Guamanians, Nisei and so on. But a real cross-section of American youth? Almost never."[6]

By mid-1966, there were 362,000 American soldiers serving in Vietnam.[7] The generals were calling for an additional 200,000. President Johnson, who was fearful that abolishing student deferments would fuel the antiwar protests, signed on to a plan proposed by his defense secretary, Robert McNamara. McNamara's plan promised to swell the ranks of recruits with a minimum of political pain. Between 1966 and 1972, "Project 100,000" recruited more than 350,000 young men previously considered ineligible for the military because of their low test scores. McNamara and the army advertised Project 100,000 as a Great Society program, part of Johnson's "War on Poverty." It was disingenuously billed as an opportunity for the subterranean poor to serve their country and be trained in areas that would enhance both their military careers and their later civilian lives. *Washington Post* reporter Myra McPherson referred to this program as "one of [McNamara's] most heinous acts as the chief architect of the war."[8]

The military relied on tests to determine eligibility and job assignments. Functional educational environments provided the means to perform well on those tests. In a society where access to such educational environments was restricted on the basis of race and class, it is hardly surprising—though no less offensive—that 80 percent of those inducted through Project 100,000 had dropped out of high school, and 40 percent could read at less than a sixth-grade level. They were nicknamed "the Moron Corps" by their fellow soldiers, and were used primarily to augment combat infantry units.[9] They were put directly into combat, and their casualty rates were twice as high as those of other entry-level categories.[10]

White combat infantrymen were more inclined to believe that it was class, not race, that determined a soldier's service assignment, and by inference, his expendability. Demographics support their suspicions. Historian Christian Appy estimates that the enlisted ranks in Vietnam "were comprised of about 25 percent poor, 55 percent working class, and 20 percent middle class, with a statistically negligible number of wealthy."[11] Harvard's class of 1970, for example, sent 2 out of 1,200 graduates to Vietnam.[12] As journalist Walter Lippman pointed out, none of the senior or even junior members of the Johnson administration resigned to take up arms in Vietnam.[13]

Whatever biases were built into the draft itself, there was an overtly racist component in service assignments. The buildup of troops to be sent to Vietnam coincided with an epidemic of inner-city riots. Between 1965 and 1968, two hundred American cities experienced ghetto uprisings.[14] Hershey's draft effectively sucked up many angry, poor, and recently radicalized Black youths from inner-city streets, trained them, armed them, and fed them in disproportionate numbers into the most dangerous combat infantry positions. The government attempts to justify the overrepresentation of Black soldiers in American combat troops are typified by Senator Daniel Patrick Moynihan's rationalization that "Given the strains of disordered and matriarchal family life in which so many Negro youth come of age, the armed forces are a dramatic and desperately needed change, a world away from women, a world run by strong men and unquestioned authority, where discipline, if harsh, is nonetheless orderly and predictable, and where rewards, if limited, are granted on the basis of performance."[15]

Aside from the racial and class inequities, there is another significant statistic that characterized the American army in Vietnam: the *average* age of the U.S. combat soldier in Vietnam was nineteen. They were infant-ry in the truest sense of the word. In World War II, it had been twenty-six. Over 60 percent of those who died in Vietnam were between the ages of seventeen and twenty-one, and age certainly contributed to the depth of the survivors' psychic wounds.[16]

Author, psychiatrist, and classics scholar Jonathan Shay calls himself a "missionary from psychologically injured veterans." One of the most important things he claims to have learned from his patients is that a betrayal of thémis, or "what's right," is at the root of much of the psychic pain suffered by America's Vietnam veterans. He describes three broad categories of experience in which thémis was betrayed for American soldiers who fought in Vietnam, three broad categories of institutional failure that resulted in profound and widespread psychiatric damage. Those categories were appropriate training and equipment, unit cohesion, and competent, ethical, properly supported leadership. "Military psychiatrists have been telling us at least since World War I," Shay argues, "that these three things can prevent some (not all) of the life-long symptoms that can follow prolonged heavy combat."[18] He believes that it is the "ethical duty" of those in a position to decide how other people are sent into danger to make certain that every possible protective mechanism is in place. That was not done in Vietnam.

In the following pages, I will identify the specific ways in which the military failed to implement those three requisites, thereby combining the inevitable trauma of war and the dubious nature of America's mission in Vietnam with explicit policies that jeopardized and undermined the psychiatric health of American soldiers.

TRAINING AND EQUIPMENT

Modern military basic training is a relatively new phenomenon. While basic training for Americans in previous wars consisted largely of drilling and the practice of military skills, by the Vietnam era that had been changed to include the inculcation of new attitudes and reflexes, which I will discuss later. First though, I think it is useful to outline briefly the traditional organizing principles of boot camp.

At the beginning, the recruit is separated from his family and friends. He is stripped, first of his clothes, then of his hair—both emblematic of his civilian individuality. His ego is then systematically undermined by an abusive and omnipotent drill instructor who scorns his ability to think for himself and mocks his civilian values and beliefs. Psychologist and professor of military science Lieutenant Colonel David Grossman writes that twenty years have not dimmed the memory of his first encounter with a drill instructor in basic training: "From this time on *I* will be your *mother*, your *father*, your *sister*, and your *brother*. *I* will be your best friend and your worst enemy. *I* will be there to *wake* you up in the morning, and *I* will be there to *tuck* you in at night. You will *jump* when I say '*frog*' and when I tell you to *s*—— your only question will be '*What color.*' IS THAT CLEAR?"[19] It was, and still remains, the drill instructor's job to teach that "physical aggression is the essence of manhood" and that "violence is an effective and desirable solution for the problems that the soldier will face on the battlefield." Above all, the instructor must teach unquestioned obedience.[20]

Canadian journalist and military analyst Gwynne Dyer describes this process as "a conversion experience in an almost religious sense."[21] The kind of conversion phenomenon experienced by military recruits is more complete and more devastating in a nineteen-year-old than in a twenty-six-year-old. The loneliness of isolation from family and friends; the disorientation of unfamiliar surroundings, clothes, and appearance; the overwhelming, often abusive, challenges of basic training—all are deliberately exploited to fragment the recruits' identity. The pieces will then be reassembled around a new set of values and a new primary community. Psychiatrist Peter Bourne describes basic training as having "evolved in the guise of a masculine initiation rite that often has particular appeal to the late adolescent struggling to establish a masculine identity for himself in society."[22] The tragedy is that in a training situation specifically designed to produce soldiers, not civilians, the elements of masculine identity that are overwhelmingly emphasized are aggression and obedience.

Nineteen-year-olds are children in transition to adulthood. They are, according to psychologist Erik Erikson, in the process of trying to identify a single integrated identity, an "I" that is consistent with the many new roles their expanding independence presents.[23] Aside from their agility and strength, that state of transition, or flux, is one of the main reasons the military prefers young recruits: they have not yet had time or opportunity to decide what kind of an "I" they will be. They are vulnerable, impressionable, malleable—all desirable qualities if the objective is to replace whatever preexisted with a new and overriding set of attitudes and reflexes. "It's easier if you catch them young," says Dyer. "You can train older men to be soldiers . . . but you can never get them to believe that they like it. There are other reasons too, of course, like the physical fitness, lack of dependents, and economic dispensability of teenagers, that make armies prefer them, but the most important qualities teenagers bring to basic training are enthusiasm and naiveté."[24] The marines appropriately call this process "forming," and Dyer quotes a marine captain who candidly informs his new recruits: "We're going to give you the blueprints, and we're going to show you how to build a Marine. You've got to build a Marine."[25]

The young soldiers built to fight in Vietnam were accidents waiting to happen; they were what psychiatrist Robert Jay Lifton calls "an atrocity-producing situation" and what Sartre called "inevitably genocidal."[26] They had been drilled to think of the enemy as an inferior life form, as gooks. Their commanding general, William Westmoreland, had separate toilet facilities built for Americans and Vietnamese at his headquarters.[27] "Orientals don't place the same value on human life as we do," he told his staff. In Peter Davis's Oscar-winning documentary *Hearts and Minds,* the footage of Westmoreland proclaiming this opinion about "Orientals" is juxtaposed with footage of a Vietnamese woman, desperate with grief, trying to throw herself into her husband's grave. It is an iconic moment, versions of which American soldiers encountered on a regular basis. Having been led to expect an inhuman enemy whom they could kill with impunity, they were instead confronted with a society of human beings who bled and wept just like the folks back home. Soldiers were left with a terrible choice: to accept what they had been trained to believe, or to believe the evidence they could see with their own eyes, or feel with their hearts.

Senator Bob Kerrey, whose contested version of what happened one night in the village of Thang Phong became the subject of brief public debate in 2001, claimed that American soldiers in Vietnam were never trained in the laws of war. He only learned of the U.S. Army's *Field Manual 27-10, The Law of Land Warfare,* which specifically prohibits the killing of civilians, long after the war ended.[28] It was such profound betrayals of command responsibility that left many soldiers tragically unsure of what behaviors were permissible. "They lost their innocence with an M-16 in their hands and a license to use it," says Veterans Administration psychologist Eric Gerdeman.[29] The massacre at the village of Song My (called My Lai 4 on the soldiers' maps) of hundreds of unarmed Vietnamese civilians, mostly women and children, on March 16, 1968, by American soldiers was only one well-publicized example of inevitable genocide. Compounding the example set by those soldiers, the young Major Colin Powell, who had been charged with investigating rumors of the atrocity, assured his superiors that, "In direct refutation of this portrayal is the fact that relations between American soldiers and the Vietnamese people are excellent." It would be more than a year and a half before the story was leaked to Seymour Hersh and he made it public. It would be another two years before platoon leader William Calley was court-martialed, found guilty of murder, and then officially pardoned by Nixon. Whatever portion of that story was available to soldiers in the field, it cannot but have convinced them that protecting the lives of Vietnamese civilians was not an official priority—or even a particular concern.

In addition to their young age and the physical and psychic abuse of basic training, there is another difference in the way soldiers were "built" to fight in Vietnam: namely, the focus on "operant conditioning." That difference is in some ways the most problematic because, by military standards, it has been so unarguably effective. Operant conditioning means that American soldiers kill more often and more efficiently.

During World War II, an official army historian, U.S. Army Brigadier General S. L. A. Marshall, conducted a study of the firing rates of soldiers. After thousands of postcombat interviews, he concluded that, even when their lives or the lives of their comrades were immediately threatened, *75 to 80 percent of soldiers were not firing their weapons.* "The average and normal healthy individual," Marshall concluded, "the man who can endure the mental and physical stresses of combat—still has such an inner and usually unrealized resistance toward killing a fellow man that he will not of his own volition take life if it is possible to turn away from that responsibility.... At the vital point, he becomes a conscientious objector."[30] Needless to say, since the publication of Marshall's revelatory study, the military has been searching for effective mechanisms for overcoming this resistance of soldiers to killing their fellow human beings. Military leaders have been searching for ways to take off the safety catch and turn those conscientious objectors into conditioned, reflexive killers. And they have been finding them.

When most people think of "operant conditioning," they probably think of B. F. Skinner's rats learning to push bars for food pellets. Operant conditioning posits that organisms, including human beings, move through their environment rather haphazardly until they encounter a reinforcing *stimulus.* The experience of that stimulus becomes associated in memory with the *behavior* that immediately preceded it. In other words, a behavior is followed by a *consequence,* and the nature of the consequence, reward or punishment, modifies the organism's tendency to repeat the behavior.

Since World War II, the principles of operant conditioning have transformed the nature of military training exercises. For example, marksmanship in the World War II era was taught with bull's-eye targets. Soldiers were simply required to see how often and how accurately they could place a shot at the center of a target. Vietnam-era recruits, on the other hand, learned to shoot under conditions that more realistically mirrored combat situations. They were dressed in full combat gear and positioned in foxholes, while their targets, which popped up randomly, looked like men and convincingly "died" when hit. In behavioral terms, the man-shaped target was the stimulus; the instantaneous response to the target was the behavior; and positive reinforcement was given in the form of immediate feedback when the target was hit and dropped. Another layer of reinforcement was added when "hits" were exchanged for marksmanship badges that could be exchanged for additional privileges or rewards (three-day passes, praise, recognition, and the like). Soldiers were not, however, encouraged to think of the targets as human beings, but as targets that happened to look like human beings, and that were to be "engaged" and "attrited." Along with traditional marksmanship, soldiers were taught the skill of "massing fire," blanketing an area with bullets rather than squeezing off single, carefully placed rounds, on the assumption that it is easier to shoot at a "thing," a field or a riverbank, than at another human being, even if that human being is wearing the uniform of an enemy soldier.[31] Shooting thereby becomes disconnected from killing. If the goal of such training was to reprogram the human software by disconnecting the internalized conscientious objector, it would seem that it was successful. Compared to the 20 percent firing rate of World War II, the firing rate in Vietnam was between 90 and 95 percent. The downside of that disconnect was that more firing leads to more killing, and soldiers who kill, or believe that they have killed, are more likely to suffer PTSD.[32]

War Psychiatry, the army's five-hundred-page Medical Corps textbook on combat trauma, talks about "the aversion most mammals have to killing conspecifics (members of their own species)," but notes that "pseudospeciation, the ability of humans and some other primates to classify certain members of their own species as 'other,' can neutralize the threshold of inhibition so they can kill conspecifics."[33] In other words, the systematic dehumanization of the enemy is another way in which modern military training intentionally seeks to disconnect a soldier's action from its moral, ethical, spiritual, or social implications. For example, PFC Reginald Edwards recalled that when he first arrived at Camp Pendleton in 1963, the marines were "doing Cuba stuff. Cuba was the aggressor. It was easy to do Cuba stuff because you had a lot of Mexicans. You could always let them be Castro. We even had Cuban targets. Targets you shoot at. So then they changed the silhouettes to Vietnamese. Everything to Vietnam. Getting people ready for the little gooks. And, of course, if there were any Hawaiians and Asian Americans in the unit, they played the roles of aggressors in the war games.... The only thing they told us about the Viet Cong was they were gooks. They were to be killed. Nobody sits around and gives you their historical and cultural background. They're the enemy."[34]

It goes without saying that when it has been drummed into a frightened young soldier that gooks, dinks, slopes, or Commies are all blurred subcategories of the subhuman, the "other," it becomes virtually inevitable that he will blur the distinctions between North Vietnamese, South Vietnamese, Viet Cong, or civilian.

Grossman calls this form of training "psychological warfare, [but] psychological warfare conducted not upon the enemy, but upon one's own troops."[35] Every aspect of battlefield behavior is rehearsed until response becomes reflexive. As soldiers become more conditioned, as their training ensures that they will be more likely to fire their weapons and more likely to mass their fire, it also becomes more likely that they will kill. Grossman calls the development of this reflex to kill "killology."

A dramatic example of the effectiveness of modern military training on American soldiers was the 1993 Battle in Mogadishu, the event on which Mark Bowden based his bestseller *Black Hawk Down*. In a seventeen-hour fight, 160 American soldiers battled thousands of Somalis in fierce, urban combat. Eighteen Americans died, but they killed an estimated one thousand Somalis. The Americans had been trained using modern methods. The Somalis had not. Major Peter Kilner, an active-duty officer who, among other things, taught philosophy at West Point, attributes this "extraordinary casualty ratio" to their conditioning. "Soldiers are conditioned to act without considering the moral repercussions of their actions; they kill without making the conscious decision to do so," he explains. "Soldiers who kill reflexively in combat will likely one day reconsider their actions reflectively. If they are unable to justify to themselves that they killed another human being, they will likely, and understandably, suffer enormous guilt. This guilt manifests itself as post-traumatic stress disorder (PTSD), and it has damaged the lives of thousands of men who performed their duty in combat."[36]

Training soldiers to believe that there is a credible moral justification for killing in combat, Kilner argues, would help to alleviate guilt and therefore subsequent trauma. Elaborating on what that training might entail, Kilner provides a revealing insight into the lessons the military establishment took from the Vietnam experience. Kilner's idea of a "moral justification" is based on an assumption that is both astonishing and, in our current political context, deeply disturbing. He does not mean that soldiers should be given a moral justification specific to the circumstances in which they will be challenged—a historical or political or social context that explains why, for example, they might be asked to fight Vietnamese, or Serbs, or Iraqis at some specific point in time. What he does mean is that every soldier has made the choice to enlist: "They had other options, however unpleasant they may have been." Having made that choice, it becomes the responsibility of leadership to embed in their training the unquestioning faith that America and its leaders will always and only go to war for moral reasons: "Because the moral responsibility for going to war lies with political authorities and because the political authorities' intentions are often opaque, soldiers should be largely immune from judgments about the just ends of a war." It seems a soldier's training should somehow manage to cauterize doubt, anesthetize the questioning mind, and substitute blind trust, so that, like "religious crusaders, they would fight with the assurance of moral rightness."[37] Grossman even has a term for such assurance: "a bulletproof mind."

Bulletproof minds have not yet been perfected, though films such as *Bladerunner* and *The Matrix* have tried to imagine what they might be like and how they might change society. A recent article in the *New York Times* reported on the optimism of some in the military robotics field that robots would solve this problem, but there is still the question of how "remote" the controller need be to avoid the guilt of agency.[38] So bulletproof minds on wheels remain for now a disturbing fantasy.

The American soldiers sent to Vietnam were certainly not so equipped. They knew they had been sent to defend Freedom. They had been warned that if they failed in their mission, not only Vietnam, but other Southeast Asian nations (and beyond) would fall like "dominos" before expansionist Communism, leaving the Pacific a "Red" sea. The situation they were dropped into was far more complex.

As a nation, we are still debating whether or not Vietnam's importance to American interests was genuinely, if unwisely, overestimated; whether the Vietnamese resistance forces took merely aid or their marching orders from the Soviet Union and/or China; and whether or not United States involvement was the logical extension of arrogance, entitlement, and greed. Be that as it may, by the mid-1960s it was enough for Lyndon Johnson, and then for Richard Nixon, that the United States had laid its prestige, credibility, and, by extension, its power on the line. Withdrawal was perceived as humiliation. America would not be bested by what Johnson called "some fourth-rate, raggedy-ass little country."[39] In the name of freedom and democracy, we dropped four million tons of bombs *on our allies* in the South, and another million tons on the North.[40] More than eighty million liters of dioxin-based defoliants were sprayed, again primarily on the South.[41] Four million *civilians* were killed—on top of 1.5 million soldier casualties.[42] As the statistics mounted, it became harder to camouflage the war as a reasonable policy that might in any way be construed as beneficial to the Vietnamese, much less the Americans. In 1968, standing amid the wreckage of Ben Tre, a city leveled by the American response to the Tet Offensive, a U.S. major told Associated Press correspondent Peter Arnett: "It became necessary to destroy the town to save it."[43]

The Vietnamese, however, were fighting a different war. For centuries, they had been besieged by other nations—China, France, Japan, France again, and only then the United States. Vietnam had been an occupied country for over one hundred years. The Vietnamese were fighting for independence from colonialist oppression and for the right to call themselves Vietnamese. In 1919, when Woodrow Wilson promised self-determination for all peoples at Versailles, the Vietnamese were bitterly disappointed to discover that, for some reason, they were not included. Again, in 1945, having fought on the side of the Americans against the Japanese, there had been a moment of optimism. In the square where he is now buried, Ho Chi Minh, founder and president of the Democratic Republic of Vietnam, proclaimed the independence of Vietnam in the words of the American Declaration of Independence, making certain that the crowds he addressed understood the origin of his words. But the French were unwilling to leave, and the Americans were unwilling to intervene. "It was patriotism, not communism, that inspired me," Ho explained. But when, in 1946, he cautioned the French, "You can kill 10 of my men for every one I kill of yours, yet even at those odds, you will lose and I will win," the French chose not to listen.[44] So, later, did the Americans.

To whatever extent the American soldiers who began to arrive in 1964 were aware of that history, their training had certainly led them to expect the vanguard of oppressive, totalitarian, international Communism. Instead they found themselves embroiled in the bitterest of combinations: a civil war and a war for independence. The Americans were not embraced or even supported by a grateful populace. They were not perceived as liberators, but as the latest gang of colonialist thugs. The local populace often risked their lives to sabotage American efforts. It was troubling for many GIs to realize that the "enemy" did not fight like the dupes of totalitarian oppressors.

Their dedication and discipline were unmistakable, and they fought as though they had a genuine sense of purpose. As the "Communists" morphed into nationalists, the villagers, for whose freedom the GIs were supposed to be fighting, looked, acted like, in fact often were the enemy. "Charlie has a philosophy," is the way one disillusioned GI put it. "I would wonder what provoked a woman or a little kid to get out there and fight like this unless they honest to God felt that their beliefs were right. It was scary to me, waking me up, making me ask what I was doing there. I mean, what WERE we doing there?"[45]

Those Americans who had enlisted often had done so out of a belief that their country had always stood for freedom and justice. Looking back on his arrival in Saigon at the age of twenty-two, Ambassador Richard C. Holbrooke, who worked with the U.S. Embassy in Vietnam in the 1960s, bitterly remembers his trust in the U.S. government as naïve: "I believed that the commitment was correct—freedom of choice, self-determination, save the country from Communism—and that we were doing the right thing because the government *did* the right thing. In those days you didn't question it."[46]

Those days were over by 1968, and probably well before that. Murray Polner, who interviewed more than two hundred veterans in the late sixties for his book *No Victory Parades: The Return of the Vietnam Veteran,* concluded that, "not one of them—hawk, dove, or haunted—was entirely free of doubt about the nature of the war and the American role in it.... Never before have so many questioned as much, as these veterans have, the essential rightness of what they were forced to do."[47]

Furthermore, American soldiers had ample cause to distrust their leaders' strategy for winning the war: the strategy of attrition. "Through most of its wars," writes military analyst, historian, and author James F. Dunnigan, "the United States successfully used the attrition approach. It is easier to be proficient at this type of warfare. You need to master only the simplest military skills and possess enormous quantities of arms and munitions."[48] The United States

Army certainly had that in Vietnam, where attrition amounted to an 11 or 12 to 1 casualty ratio.[49] As General Westmoreland put it, "We'll just go on bleeding them until Hanoi wakes up to the fact that they have bled their country to the point of national disaster for generations."[50] To that end, the army developed an awesome arsenal of high-tech weapons and delivery systems, based on the assumption that the enemy would play by the ready-aim-fire rules of traditional warfare. It was quite obvious to both sides that the Vietnamese resistance forces would lose such an unequal fight badly and quickly.

Instead, the Vietnamese chose what has since become known as asymmetrical warfare, which the National Defense University's *Strategic Assessment* defines as "not fighting fair." This kind of fighting "can include the use of surprise in all its operational and strategic dimensions and the use of weapons in ways unplanned by the U.S."[51] Why it would surprise army planners that the Vietnamese would use sharpened bamboo stakes when they had no access to B-52s is another question altogether. More relevant to this discussion is that the North Vietnamese Army, the NVA (or, as they preferred to call themselves, the People's Army of Vietnam, PAVN) and the National Front for the Liberation of Southern Vietnam, the NLF (or, as they were referred to by U.S. soldiers, the Viet Cong) used whatever means they had at their disposal to level the playing field, to create capabilities and conditions more favorable to themselves. They often didn't wear uniforms. They used women, children, and elders. They used snipers and sappers and disappeared into the jungle whenever possible.

The Americans had not been trained to fight a guerrilla war. Their uniforms were ill-suited to the climate. Stories abound of rot of one kind or another affecting feet or genitals. The ultimate indignity was perhaps what Colonel David Hackworth calls "The plastic, no-account M-16 rabbit shooter."[52] The rifles jammed frequently, and the plastic handgrips were prone to breakage. Shay quotes one veteran whose rifle let him down under fire, who spoke for many: "I started feeling like the government really didn't want us to get back, that there needed to be fewer of us at home."[53] The fact that the handgrips were plastic, were manufactured by the Mattel toy company, and, at least when first introduced, came imprinted with the Mattel logo did little to enhance the gun's reputation. "You can tell it's Mattel" became a common refrain.[54]

UNIT COHESION: THE SOCIAL AND PERSONAL RELATIONSHIPS OF COMBAT

"Try to imagine," Shay asks, "going to war with strangers at your side! Do they know what they're doing? Can you trust them? Will they care what happens to you? Do you talk the same language, figuratively speaking, or even literally? . . . And yet, American military culture, policy, and habit—with a few noteworthy exceptions since WWI—has treated soldiers' connectedness to one another as irrelevant."[55]

Group cohesion among American forces in Vietnam was undermined by a variety of factors. Some of those factors were demographic, not unconnected to the implicit and explicit racism of both the draft and military society. Others were the result of specific military policies that ignored the accumulated lessons of military psychiatry in favor of bureaucratic efficiency.

The racial imbalance among the combat troops in Vietnam would itself have undermined group cohesion. The inequities of the draft, the unequal representation of soldiers of color in the rifle companies and on the casualty lists, and the absence of Black officers were ongoing sources of resentment and tension. According to Lieutenant Commander William S. Norman, an African American who served in Vietnam, "These men belonged to a generation that was far, far more outspoken than any generation of Black men before them. They were there to kill and be killed. About to die. To do first-class dying. Yet in terms of their assignments and promotions and awards, they were getting second-class treatment. It created a special brand of bitterness."[56] At least in the early years of the war, African Americans died in disproportionate numbers: between 1961 and 1966, they constituted about 10 percent of U.S. men at arms, but accounted for almost 20 percent of Vietnam combat fatalities.[57]

On the other side of the color line, there were some white soldiers still clinging to racist traditions and resistance to the Civil Rights movement. In this, the first integrated American army in history, in theory if not in fact, the young Black men drafted and sent to Vietnam were too often confronted with Confederate flags, racial slurs, cross burnings, and a plantation mentality in much of the officer corps.[58] PFC Reginald Edwards, for example, had a platoon commander from Arkansas who called him "chocolate bunny" and "brillo head."[59]

Thus, the inequities of the selection process injected racial tension, anger, resentment, and distrust into every aspect of a soldier's life in Vietnam. In itself, that would have compromised the ability of individuals to bond successfully into effective units. Once they were selected and trained, however, army policy concerning the assignment of soldiers to units virtually ensured their emotional isolation.

Previous wars had identified two reliable measures as proven to protect soldiers from psychiatric wounds. First, it was known that being able to trust those next to you, those on whom your life depends in a dangerous situation, was the most important factor in a soldier's ability to withstand the stress of combat.[60] And second, it had likewise been proven that given adequate exposure to combat, anyone would eventually crack.

In Vietnam, the army chose to limit combat exposure of individual soldiers, but to ignore what was known about the importance of the group. Through a policy known as DEROS (Date of Expected Return from OverSeas), every soldier who served in Vietnam knew before leaving the United States that he was scheduled to return exactly twelve months from his date of departure (thirteen for the marines). Every soldier knew just how long he had to hold out. DEROS ostensibly offered soldiers a way to leave the war as other than a physical or psychiatric casualty, but in practice, the physical, emotional, and moral isolation that was its consequence made Vietnam what Grossman calls "a war of individuals."[61] The endless comings and goings, and the interrupted attempts at bonding and trust undermined effectiveness in the short run and sanity in the long run.[62]

Unlike recruits in previous wars, soldiers who went to Vietnam were arbitrarily separated after boot camp from those with whom they had trained. The bonds they had established were severed, and they had to start from scratch, alone in a new community. They were given individual assignments and inserted like interchangeable parts into the military machine. The process was bureaucratically streamlined and convenient to administer, but certain to increase the number of psychiatric casualties.

When a recruit first arrived in Vietnam, he was the FNG (fucking new guy) in his unit. He was an unknown quantity, distrusted, distrusting, and terribly alone. His lack of experience made him a threat to group survival. He was initially shunned but, once he had settled in, the ticked-off days on his calendar were a constant reminder that he was getting "short," getting close to his departure date. If he wanted to make it home alive, he, in turn, had best stay away from the newest transfer. For the last two or three months of their tours, "short-timer syndrome" often so compromised soldiers' behavior that they had to be moved to noncombat positions, where issues of "survivor guilt" over the buddies they had left behind, both dead and alive, became another source of stress.[63] An indication of the extent to which those feelings of guilt were a common experience is that, in stark contrast to the endless reunions of World War II veterans, Vietnam vets almost never try to contact their former comrades. Though there may be other explanations for that phenomenon, many believe it is because they are too frightened to find out what happened to those they feel guilty for abandoning.[64]

LEADERSHIP: COMPETENCE, ETHICS, TRUST, AND SUPPORT

In addition to the general troop rotations, the army also undermined the leadership potential of its officer corps by rotating officer commands. For a career soldier, combat experience was an essential criterion for advancement, and Vietnam was the only war in town. "We decided everybody would have a chance to command; he would have six months. We have found out that has been wrong," General Bruce

Clarke conceded in his 1971 testimony before Congress. "Not everybody is qualified to command, and certainly not for six months."[65] Given the year-long general rotation for troops, a six-month tour for an officer virtually guaranteed that inexperienced officers would be assigned to more experienced combat troops. Six months was not a great deal of time for an officer to prove himself, either to his subordinates or to his superiors. Trust, respect, and loyalty are established over time and through shared experience. "In Vietnam," write Richard Gabriel and Paul Savage, two sociologists and former army officers, "the result was a kind of 'military anomie'—a situation where troops came to have no sense of belonging and became increasingly hostile to their officers."[66]

That hostility was exacerbated by the racial imbalance throughout the armed forces, especially that between officers and enlisted men. By the late 1960s, and following the assassination of Martin Luther King, draft policies, recruitment efforts, and service assignments that appeared to unfairly target African Americans were increasingly seen, both among Black troops in Vietnam and among civilians, as an extreme form of racism. Colin Powell, who served two tours in Vietnam, wrote in his autobiography that he would "never forgive a leadership that said, in effect: These young men—poorer, less educated, less privileged—are expendable (someone described them as 'economic cannon fodder'), but the rest are too good to risk."[67]

Reflecting a growing disillusionment with the army and the war on the part of more educated African Americans, the mounting racial tension both in the service and at home actually translated into a *decrease* in the number of Black officers in the already shamefully segregated officer corps, from 3.6 percent in 1965 to only 2.6 percent in 1970. The absence of Black officers to serve as role models and to mediate interracial friction lethally undermined the army's ability to cope with the increasingly active resentment that flared among troops in Vietnam in 1970 and 1971.[68]

Finally, the lack of effective leadership in Vietnam was also the result of a singularly grotesque aspect of how success was measured. Competition among officers for coveted commands in Vietnam was fierce. Promotions were dependent on quickly demonstrated performance, and the gauge of success in Vietnam was not territory, but enemy "body counts." Soldiers were asked to sacrifice their lives and the lives of their comrades to gain control of an area one day, only to see the area abandoned the next. Body counts determined the success of their missions. Those officers who did not produce dead bodies were threatened with replacement, so counts were often falsified to create the illusion of progress or to excuse American losses.[69] Body counts were used by commanders to justify their commands, by politicians to prove that the war was being won, and by soldiers to win a few days of R&R.[70] By that perverse reckoning, any dead Vietnamese became "Viet Cong." "More ominously," acknowledges military historian E. B. Riker-Coleman, "the focus on enemy casualties created a casual attitude towards Vietnamese lives that contributed to the My Lai slaughter and countless other less dramatic incidents of civilian casualties."[71] It also led to macabre methods of quantification that have become an insistently haunting piece of Vietnam lore. PFC Charles Stephens of the 101st Airborne Division testified that "they didn't believe our body counts. So we had to cut the right ear off everybody we killed to prove our body count. I guess it was SOP [Standard Operating Procedure], or Battalion SOP, but nothing was ever said to you."[72] There are a lot of similar ear, scalp, or worse stories from Vietnam, and it is a temptation to blame the warped individuals who wore their trophies around their necks, keeping score; but it is facile to dismiss such behavior as atypical and sick when dead Vietnamese bodies were the standard gauge of success used by politicians and generals alike.

The threat of replacement also made it tempting for officers to take unnecessary risks at the expense of the safety of their men. It was a temptation many officers found irresistible. Ninety-five percent of the combat units in Vietnam were so-called "search and destroy" units. Their mission was to flush out NLF troops, to engage them in battle, and then to call in the massive firepower of helicopter gunships to wipe them out. "Humping the boonies" was about *attracting* ambush, luring the guerrilla fighters out into the open. American soldiers were not blind to the fact that they were being used as live bait.[73] Search and destroy missions were at best enormously dangerous for infantry soldiers. Inexperienced commanders who chose to ignore or dismiss that danger, who ordered high-risk missions to attract personal attention, to inflate their reputations or to advance their careers, put the lives of their men in excessive jeopardy. Not only did that threaten morale, it provoked rage.

Ethical behavior among the officer corps was increasingly perceived to be detrimental to one's chances of promotion. Pleasing superiors with statistical results and optimistic reports took priority over meeting the needs or developing the competence of their units. "Careerism" in the officer corps replaced Duty-Honor-Country, the defining principle of West Point since it was founded two hundred years ago. It also effectively diluted the kind of loyalty to ideals that would lead an officer to share the risks of combat with his men. Officers behaved more like corporate bureaucrats and less like inspirational leaders. The higher an officer's rank, the lower was the probability of his death in combat. Enlisted men, Black or white, were ten times more likely to die than their officers.[74] "In Vietnam the record is absolutely clear on this point," Gabriel and Savage write, "the officer corps simply did not die in sufficient numbers or in the presence of their men often enough . . . and [the troops] came to despise them for it."[75]

HOMECOMING

Above and beyond the ways in which "what's right" was betrayed for Americans fighting in Vietnam—the ways in which their training and equipment left them vulnerable, both physically and mentally; the ways in which the selection process contributed to the undermining of unit cohesion; and the ways in which the body counts, the absence of Black officers, and army policies virtually ensured inadequate leadership—above and beyond all that, all of which contributed to a generally chaotic, horrific experience for soldiers in-country, a Vietnam-era soldier's homecoming was also fraught with adversity. Soldiers left Vietnam alone, with a planeload of strangers, often on a commercial airliner, exactly one year after they had arrived. They were sitting in their parents' living room or in the local bar, watching the war on television, days—sometimes hours—after their last firefight. In contrast, World War II soldiers often spent weeks coming home on troopships, in the company of the men with whom they had fought their war. Lost comrades, shared terror, disturbing memories, and invasive guilt that only a fellow traveler would understand, all could be communally processed and grieved. Gabriel compares the long ride home to the purification rituals traditional societies required of their warriors before they were allowed to rejoin their communities. It was assumed that war had rendered them impure. They had lived and acted outside the boundaries set by society. They needed space and time, even ritual and ceremony, to shed personas no longer appropriate, personas that might be a danger to themselves and to others. Space and time afforded them an opportunity to reclaim their former selves and lives. That painful and psychically dangerous exchange, Gabriel writes, can only be successfully accomplished in a supportive communal environment where those who have shared the experience can serve as "a sounding board for their own sanity."[76]

Soldiers returning from Vietnam were denied such cleansing rituals. There were no slow-moving ships, no weeks to fill with reminiscence, shared with empathy and without judgment. There were no debriefings, no decompression, no welcoming crowds, no accorded honor. There was no communalization of their trauma.

Returning vets did not experience homecoming as the sweet end to their ordeal they had imagined; the reality was far more painful. We who were their homes found it difficult to listen. They were alive, but often their friends were not. The streets of their hometowns had changed. As the war ground on overseas, the war at home became an unavoidable fact of life in every community in the United States. The assassinations of Dr. King and Robert Kennedy, the killings at Kent State and Jackson State, Watergate and Nixon's impeachment perhaps stand out as emblematic of a time that was marked by violent social conflict, rebellion, and excessive response. Vietnam vets were called baby-killers by some and losers by others; it was not an easy time to claim veteran status with pride. Unemployment was high. Many had learned to self-medicate with drugs or alcohol. Benefits were less generous than they had been after World War II, and even those were not available to the thousands who had received less than honorable discharges. One veteran with an administrative discharge said bitterly, "I've got friends who've robbed liquor stores who can get jobs easier than me."[77]

Given their war experiences, the returning veterans were disinclined to look to the government for help. If they had had occasion to interact with psychiatry in Vietnam, it was what Robert Lifton appropriately called "the psychiatry of the executioner." Its explicit goal was to return men to the front as quickly as possible.[78] After the war, those whose sanity began to unravel were especially loath to turn to the V.A. According to David Marlowe, writing in a 2001 Rand Corporation study commissioned by the secretary of defense:

> [The Vietnam conflict provided] a conceptual and political undermining of the operations of military medicine, including its ethical behavior, approaches, therapeutic techniques, and overall legitimacy. It would not be untoward to consider that the Vietnam conflict played a major role in persuading patients to believe in a conspiratorial antipatient view of much of institutional medicine (equivalent to the role it played in the widening evolution and development of such views of government in general). It is out of the cauldron of Vietnam that the views were popularized of government and 'establishment institutions' as the 'enemy of the people' and, putatively, their conscienceless users and abusers were popularized.[79]

Veterans' options for treatment were further limited by the inadequacy of existing facilities and professional understanding. During and after the Vietnam War, there were only two V.A. hospital programs in the entire country equipped to deal with psychiatric casualties. Those, according to a National Research Council evaluation, "were found to be dismal in treatment of their psychiatric patients." They were understaffed by underqualified practitioners. Patients were overmedicated and received almost no therapy—"as little as 2.9

average planned treatment hours per patient" in total![80] Until 1980, when PTSD was finally included in the DSM, those who had been discharged from the service with no official record of mental or physical disabilities found themselves ineligible for treatment at V.A. hospitals. If the symptoms appeared more than a year after discharge from active duty, the V.A. did not consider them to be service-related problems. Veterans were routinely misdiagnosed as suffering from depression, paranoid schizophrenia, character disorders, or behavior disorders.[81] Arthur Blank, who became second director of the V.A.'s new Readjustment Counseling Services, acknowledged that "Many Vietnam veterans were both clinically and socially victimized through non-diagnosis and non-treatment of PTSD," and by the fact that "no system-wide services for post-war psychological difficulties were provided by the VA."[82]

Furthermore, the DSM-I, originally published in 1952, had included a diagnosis of "gross stress reaction" that covered victims of stress, including combat-induced stress. In 1968, at the height of the war in Vietnam, the American Psychiatric Association (APA) published the DSM-II, from which that diagnosis was dropped entirely. "Gross stress reaction" was replaced with "(transient) adjustment disorder of adult life." The only mention of combat—as "fear associated with military combat and manifested by trembling, running, and hiding"—was put in the same category as an "unwanted pregnancy."[83]

The reasons for that disappearance have been the source of much speculation among the experts in the field. When Arthur Blank was drafted to serve as a psychiatrist in Vietnam in 1965, he began diagnosing traumatic war neurosis in his Vietnam veteran patients long before most of his colleagues, and he believes the omission was politically motivated. He believes that a highly complex convergence of social and intellectual phenomena had "deeply affected the recognition and appreciation of accurate guidance by organized psychiatry," such that a usable diagnosis that would have afforded veterans appropriate treatment options and support simply vanished.[84] Blank is not suggesting that this denial was either conscious or unconscious. He is suggesting that rather than investigating their own conflicted responses to the war and its veterans—responses that may have ranged from ordinary aversion to painful realities on the part of professionals, to compassion fatigue on the part of caregivers, to anxiety on the part of funding sources anticipating possible financial consequences—the APA allowed any version of combat-induced trauma to be dropped from their diagnostic manual in 1968, the year of the Tet Offensive, the year when it became clear to most Americans that the war was, at best, out of control, or at worst, being lost. Instead, the APA allowed the veterans to become the scapegoats, the most convenient diversion from the magnitude of the problem. But the problem was not just the human and financial debts already incurred. The real problem was that it was becoming increasingly clear that diagnostic and curative models would *always* be prohibitively expensive. The only real solution was preventing the trauma in the first place.[85]

In an effort to fill the gap left by the dearth of facilities and the inadequate diagnostic categories available to even the most sympathetic professionals, two psychiatrists, Robert Lifton and Chaim Shatan, started a "rap group" for veterans at the New York office of Vietnam Veterans against the War (VVAW) in 1971.[86] The informal gathering of veterans and facilitators was organized with the express purpose of creating a safe environment in which the unspeakable could be shared. "[Veterans] associate [the VA] with the war-military-government establishment," said Lifton, "with the forces responsible for a hated ordeal, or with their suspicion . . . that the VA doctors are likely to interpret their rage at everything connected to the war as no more than their own individual problem."[87] These groups helped convince the vets that, though the aftereffects of the war had certainly become a problem for each of them as individuals, there were identifiable aspects of their suffering and its origins that they shared. As Lifton reported, "There was not only a relief of pain but, virtually always, an expanded insight concerning self, war and society."[88] Though Congress was repeatedly petitioned to fund similar programs across the country, it was not until 1979 that the Readjustment Counseling Service, or Operation Outreach, was officially established—almost a decade too late for many returning veterans.

Operation Outreach established eighty-seven community-based "Vet Centers" across the country, modeled after the original VVAW groups. They were run on a self-help, peer-counseling model, staffed almost exclusively by veterans. The counselors were trained to emphasize that posttraumatic stress is a normal and expected response to a traumatic experience and that it can be managed, if not cured, with treatment.[89] Aside from these groups, the Vet Centers offered a broad range of readjustment services (therapeutic, psychosocial, referral, and the like) that took into account the many ways in which PTSD was recognized as life-disabling. Veterans came, and they have continued to come. Today there are 207 storefront Vet Centers in communities across the nation, and they are the most positively evaluated program run by the V.A.[90] The concept has been judged a "success," though to call it that is a bitter and sad reminder of how long this war has lasted and how deeply it has hurt our nation.[91]

In the early '80s, after PTSD had finally been officially recognized, Congress mandated the *National Vietnam Veterans Readjustment Study (NVVRS),* to determine "the prevalence and incidence of PTSD and other psychological problems in readjusting to civilian life.[92] Published in 1990, the *NVVRS* was an epidemiological study of a random sample of Vietnam-era veterans and a random sample of demographically similar civilian controls. (To my knowledge, this is the most comprehensive and the most recent study undertaken, and it is still being used as the basis for many government-funded research projects.) The study found that more than one-third of Vietnam veterans met the full APA diagnostic criteria for PTSD. And it is this study that is said to "prove" that there is in fact such a syndrome. So far, the ability to describe and explain combat trauma has not been accompanied by a commensurate increase in the efficacy of therapies directed against it. Neither have identified and understood prophylactic measures been instituted with any consistency or commitment, either before, during, or since the war in Vietnam. That is a failure Shay simply calls "unethical."

The horrific experiences of combat have reshaped lives—drastically shortening some, blighting the promise of others. Psychiatric casualties are implicated in what the medical anthropologist Arthur Kleinman calls "social suffering": the complex set of connections by which the woes of one person engender woes for many.[93] The "social suffering" that ensued when American soldiers came home from Vietnam has never stopped rippling outward. The veterans of that war who are dead by their own hand are one of the vectors by which such suffering can be marked and measured. By most reliable accounts, there are more of them than there are names on the Vietnam Veterans Memorial Wall.[94]

BARBARA CHISM

I would never remarry. I'm in a relationship now, and I love Eliot, the man I'm with, but I don't want to be that close to anyone again. It's not really the institution of marriage I'm against, it's just the whole idea of being committed to someone and having them hurt you so bad by killing themselves.

Mack and my brother Mike were best friends all through high school. They joined the service together when they graduated. Mike joined the navy. Mack joined the marines and was sent to Vietnam. His company came under fire two months and two days into his second tour. He told all of his people to take cover and disregarded his own safety to remain on the gun. He lost one leg at the hip and the other one at the knee. Mike and my mother flew out to Philadelphia to see him get his medals. He was awarded the Purple Heart, Silver Star, National Service Defense medal, Vietnam Service medal, Vietnam Campaign medal—lots of medals. My Mack was dedicated to his country. He was a Marine. He was tough, but he looked pretty sad when they gave him those medals. I saw the pictures.

Every day we were apart during the engagement Mack called me or wrote me letters. Just the other day, I reread some of them. Even then he was telling me that he didn't feel like he could go on, but I didn't hear it. I was young and so in love. I wanted him to be the father of my children and I couldn't wait to be married. His family wanted me to make him wear the artificial legs. He hated them. They were heavy and cumbersome and they didn't fit right. He walked to our wedding, and that's the only time I ever saw him walk.

I was ambitious and gung-ho. He was reserved. After we were married, I got him into wheelchair basketball. I convinced him to buy an all-terrain vehicle so he could go hunting. And I got him to go to Southern Illinois University for a degree in industrial technology. I was going to save him, and I thought I was doing a damn good job of it. I was going to help him quit drinking and get him all straightened out. He kept promising me, but I realize now that everything he did was for me.

I never asked him to talk about the war. I didn't think he wanted to, so I protected him. He used to sit up alone and watch war movies after I went to bed. I would wake up three, four in the morning and go into the front room. There he'd be with a bottle at the table, smoking cigarette after cigarette, watching those old-fashioned war movies. I would say, "Honey, you should come to bed." But when he did, he was like, sweating in the bed, and tossing and turning all night. I think he was drinking a lot more than I realized, and probably taking a lot of Valium and other various pills that I didn't know about. I was so young. I knew he was taking medicine and I just accepted it. Then one day I came home and he was lying on the floor with an overdose of pills. My mother said, "What did you do to him to get to this point? Why didn't you try to save him?"

This was the first suicide attempt that I knew about. I called 911. They wanted to admit him to the psychiatric ward, but I decided that if he was going to kill himself, nothing was going to stop him. I told him, "We're staying married, we're having another baby, we're going to be happy." So he got out of the hospital, and everything was supposed to be fine. But it wasn't fine.

Mack graduated from college in 1974, and he got a job in Georgia. I stayed at SIU to finish my master's degree. I went to visit him in January. He wanted me to stay, but I wanted to finish school. When I got home to Illinois, he called and said, "I'm going to kill myself. I've got the gun right here and I want you to hear it." We had talked about suicide and crisis intervention in my classes at school, so I knew what to do. I told him to hold on, that our daughter Kim had just fallen down the stairs, and then I used another phone to call the local crisis center. They called the crisis center in Georgia, and the police went to his house while I still had him on the phone. They took his gun and saved his life that night. But the next day, January 18th, my brother Mike showed up at my door. He said he'd just stopped by with supper, but he lived three hours away and he never came to see me, so when the police showed up half an hour later, I already knew. Mack had called my brother and told him to come be with me when I got the news.

He left a suicide note addressed to his mom and family saying he was sorry to hurt them, but that he didn't want to go on living. His family decided that I must have been the one who made him feel that way, that I wasn't being a good wife, so they all blamed me. I couldn't put "your loving wife" on the tombstone. I felt like he walked out on me—and Kim too. I buried him in Mattoon, Illinois, where he was born, where his family lives, and I have never gone back.

When Kim was nine years old, she developed ulcerative colitis. She was very ill, hospitalized at least once a year. The last year of high school, she was in the hospital almost the whole year. The doctors told her she had to have her intestines removed when she was eighteen. She said she would rather die, but I pleaded with her and she finally agreed to have the surgery, and then another after that. She almost died more than once.

I didn't understand anything about benefits, so I was paying all her bills for years when they could have been paid for by the government. When I got really desperate, I started writing letters to anyone I could think of. The Brandy Shive's Children's Fund got me a counselor and paid every bill I couldn't pay. They also taught me about Agent Orange. Mack had been exposed in Vietnam and Kim's symptoms were typical. She was an Agent Orange poster child when she was fifteen.

Kim is now twenty-nine. We're very close. She's in California, teaching third grade. She's fragile, and she gets sick easily. I wanted to be strong for her, and I think, in her eyes, I have been. But I was fifty-three in December, and I still feel like something's blocking me. I got my PhD in 1978, and I've never done anything with it. I had aspirations of doing something wonderful, but when I got job offers I was afraid to go try. I was afraid that I'd be expected to do something that I couldn't do.

Kim says I used to wake up talking in my sleep, and I had flashbacks about my marriage. I never had a dream about Mack that wasn't about fighting. Not physical fighting. Me fighting for myself, fighting for survival. I'm always saying, "Don't do this to me. Don't pull me down." I don't want to say Mack's suicide ruined my life, but maybe if I'd had someone telling me I was good, that I could do it, it would have been different. Instead, everyone was saying, "What did you do to that poor man?" and "Why didn't you save him?" It's like I still hear my mother's voice in the back of my mind: "You've done something to get him to this point of killing himself. Maybe you don't deserve to live." I try not to let that rule me, but it's always in the back of my mind.

KIM CHISM

Sometimes I wonder if the memories I have of my father are really mine or not. They might just be stories that people have told me. I was three when he died. I have memories of riding in his wheelchair with him. I remember that I had long hair and every night after my bath I would come and sit in front of him and he would brush out my hair. He had kind of a big belly and I remember him bouncing me on his belly. And I remember him walking on his hands. When he was home he didn't use his wheelchair. His legs were amputated so far up that there was really nothing to drag. He had huge strong arms, and he used them as if they were legs. I do have memories.

I just got my master's degree in elementary education, and I've been working with children with autistic spectrum disorders for the last two years. I love my work. I love my life, and then I think that when my mother was my age, she was already widowed and she had me to take care of. I can't imagine what that must have been like. I've never heard her talk about posttraumatic stress disorder. I don't think she has really gotten that yet. I think everything that happened is still too personal to think about in clinical terms.

I remember her struggling a lot with depression when I was a child. Every year around the time of my father's death, she would get depressed. She's gotten better as she's gotten older, but I don't think she has ever fully mourned for herself. I know she doesn't feel completely responsible for my father's death, but his side of the family really blamed her. My grandmother wrote her a letter right after my father's death. It said that my mom must not have shown him enough love and made him feel like a man, and that if she had been a better wife, he wouldn't have done what he did. For a long time, I harbored a lot of anger towards my grandmother over that. A few years ago, my aunt told me how she blamed my mom, too, and how horrible she was to her after my father's death. Now, my aunt understands more and she feels really bad, but she's never apologized.

My Uncle Mike was my dad's best friend. He's the one I talk to most about my father. When I was fifteen, I asked him about my dad, and he said, "I've been waiting for you to ask. Your father asked me to help you understand." Uncle Mike told me stories about what happened to my father in Vietnam. I love who I think my dad was, from what people told me about him, and I often wonder what our lives would have been like if he had lived. But I could never imagine the hell he must have been living, and I don't blame him for taking his life. I don't blame him at all. I think it had everything to do with Vietnam.

That's the rational side of me. But there's another side. Whenever I see pictures of my father and me, I always think, "Look at this beautiful little girl. Why wasn't I enough to make him want to live?" My therapist said, "So what you're saying is that you're not good enough?" I said, " 'Good' never comes into it for me. Just, 'I'm not enough. Why aren't I enough?' "

CHAPTER FOUR

THE COLLAPSE OF THE ARMED FORCES

> Captain Rice: We're going to move out on the road, period. Either we're going to move out and they [his men] are going to be left behind, or I'll take point and they can follow me if they want to.
>
> Soldier: I'm not going to walk down there. Nothing doing. My whole squad ain't walking down that trail....
>
> —"The War in Vietnam," *Newsweek*, April 20, 1970

IF I HAD BEEN ASKED, before I began doing research for this book, to identify the reasons that the United States pulled out of Vietnam, I would have said, first, the fierce and passionate commitment of the Vietnamese resistance and, second, the antiwar movement at home. It would not have occurred to me to say that U.S. forces themselves played a major role—that is, that American GIs effectively sabotaged the armed forces from within.

By 1973, the United States military had been rendered virtually unusable. David Cortright, whose *Soldiers in Revolt,* in 1975, was one of the first books to document the extent of the GI revolt, wrote later:

> Although it is not widely known or understood, the GI resistance movement had a major part in the Vietnam experience. Never before in modern history had the American armed forces faced such widespread internal resistance and revolt. Often at great personal risk, hundreds of thousands of soldiers, marines, airmen and sailors dissented and disobeyed military

commanders, in order to speak out for justice and peace. Their struggle hastened American withdrawal from Indochina and played a major role in finally bringing that tragic war to an end.[1]

Some of the dysfunction of U.S. troops in Vietnam is part of collective memory—the drugs, certainly, and perhaps the "fraggings" (a term used to describe attempts by soldiers to kill or injure their own officers by tossing a fragmentation grenade into a tent or a latrine). But what was known at the time as the GI Movement has been effectively erased from official history. The mechanisms responsible for that erasure dart through shadows both public and private. This chapter is about the elusiveness and the treachery of memory. I want to frame Vietnam-era PTSD with a variety of historically visible betrayals of U.S. soldiers, betrayals of thémis, of "what's right," to use Shay's term again. A significant betrayal these soldiers have experienced since their time in combat has been the erasure from official histories of what they did in Vietnam to undermine what they knew to be wrong, their heroic attempts to preserve a precious portion of their humanity in an environment that threatened its destruction.

Since I began to uncover information on the GI Movement, I have been conducting an entirely unscientific survey of friends, colleagues, and acquaintances. That sample is heavily weighted with current or former peace activists who are old enough to remember the war years, but who saw them, as I did, through the lens of the antiwar movement in the U.S. It is stunning to me that I have not found one person who remembers much about what the GIs did to subvert the war effort. No one remembers the mutinies, the sabotage, or the extent of the fragging. No one remembers seeing, much less reading, the front-page articles in the mainstream papers, the *New York Times* and the *New York Post,* the cover stories in *Life* and *Newsweek* that heralded the collapse of the U.S. armed forces in Vietnam.

In 1970 and 1971, the army commissioned two reports that analyzed the dissent in the Vietnam-era army.[2] Those reports divided protest into two separate categories: dissidence and disobedience. Dissidence covered such activities as participation in demonstrations or contributing to GI newspapers protesting the war. In other words, "dissent" included verbal and formal acts of conscious political opposition. Disobedience included insubordination, refusing orders, sabotage, fragging, drug use, and desertion. I will use those distinctions in this chapter for a number of reasons. First, I want to expand the notion of resistance among the armed forces to include both explicit rebellion based on a rejection of government policy and a more personal, emotive, but equally profound rejection of the war. Second, I want to argue that PTSD—and PTSD-related suicide—has to be seen as one among many forms of moral and psychological response to a betrayal of "what's right." And third, I want to pose a question that I cannot answer and that, as far as I know, cannot be answered without further statistical and psychosocial research.

That question has to do with the relationship between forms of resistance and PTSD. It seems likely to me that some forms of largely nonviolent defiance might have been a way of warding off PTSD because they were a way of holding onto a sense of self, a sense both of morality and of agency. It seems to me equally credible that other forms, such as fragging, inevitably drew individuals deeper into the moral chaos of the war and so contributed to what was once called "post-Vietnam syndrome" and is now called PTSD. I recognize this view as perhaps a comfortable one for someone who worked and marched with veterans in the antiwar movement, as I did. I saw them as allies, ached for their pain, and stood in awe of what they knew about evil. I never spat at them, and though I might not have felt the same kinship with Daniel had he *chosen* to go to war, I never held him or other veterans *primarily* responsible for the ways they managed to survive.

Now, having learned what I have about GI resistance to the war, I suspect that we civilians who joined the antiwar movement owe the profoundest of apologies to those whose histories of resistance were erased. If, in commitment to a cause we felt to be just, too many of us were distracted from the efforts of would-be allies, shame on us all. If, in the heady excitement of acting righteously and communally, we forgot that others had risked far more, shame on us again. If we are lacking in compassion for those who were driven by desperation or fear or self-preservation to destructive or self-destructive forms of resistance, it will surely come back to haunt us. The despair that motivated their rebellion has much to teach us about what kinds and degrees of moral behavior can be asked or expected of men (or women) in combat, and under what conditions. The Vietnam era offered an opportunity for communication across the boundaries of class, education, race, and experience in the search for a better solution than war. Forgetting what has been tried in the past, whether or not those attempts were successful, has made us poorer and far less prepared for the present and for the future.

In the early years of the war, before 1969, "combat avoidance" was routinely practiced by enlisted men and even by some officers. "Ghosting" (inventing an excuse to be sent to the rear, or going temporarily AWOL) and "sandbagging" (calling in false coordinates while taking a nap in a safer place) were common enough. Such practices, which very possibly put others in increased danger, were generally frowned upon, but if exposed, the punishment might be a few weeks in the stockade. To many soldiers, a few weeks in the stockade didn't seem such a bad trade.[3] As John Saar noted in *Life* magazine, "Military justice has no answer to the grunt's ironic question, 'What can they do to me; send me to Vietnam?' "[4]

The August 26, 1969, front-page banner headline in the *New York Daily News* proclaimed: "Sir, my men refuse to go."[5] All sixty men of A Company, Third Battalion, 196th Infantry, refused a direct order from their commanding officer to advance down what they perceived to be a dangerous road. According to strict military code, that could have been an offense punishable by death. Instead, the officers and the men "worked it out," and no one received so much as a reprimand.[6] This was the first reported incident of mass mutiny in Vietnam.[7]

From 1969 on, as such incidents multiplied, "search and destroy" increasingly became "search and avoid," and often just plain mutiny. The following is a list of documented incidents:

- November 22, 1969: Twenty-one men of the First Platoon, B Company, of the Second Battalion, Twenty-seventh Infantry, refused to advance. As the *Cleveland Press* reported, they decided the risks were too great.[8]
- April 1970: CBS newsman John Laurence filmed (and aired) a live "performance." Soldiers in the First Air Cavalry Division Charlie Company (Second Battalion, Seventh Cavalry) flatly refused to advance down what they considered to be a dangerous road. The enlisted men informed the captain, in front of the camera, that his order was nonsense and they would not obey.[9]
- May 7, 1970: Sixteen soldiers of the Third Battalion, Eighth Infantry, stationed at Fire Base Washington, refused to advance with their units into Cambodia.[10]
- June 1970: At Camp Evans, nine Black soldiers from A Company, First Battalion, 506th Regiment, refused to report to duty.[11]
- November 1970: At Camp Eagle, six Black soldiers of C Company, Third Battalion, 187th Infantry, refused to join a combat operation, claiming "they would be endangered by racist commanders."[12]
- December 29, 1970: Twenty-three enlisted men *and their officer,* Lieutenant Fred Pitts, C Company, Second Battalion, 501st Infantry, formally refused a direct order to advance. The next morning Pitts was removed from the unit, but his sentence was suspended.[13]
- March 1971: A front-page headline in the *New York Times* read: "General Won't Punish GI's for Refusing Orders." Fifty-three of Brigadier General John Hill's men (Troop B, First Squadron, First Cavalry, Americal Division) had refused a direct order to secure a damaged helicopter. "I suppose if I went by the book," the general said, "I could take them out and shoot them for refusing an order in the face of the enemy, but they're back in the field, doing their duty. I don't think it should be blown out of proportion."[14]
- October 9, 1971: Fifteen men of the Third Platoon, B Company, First Battalion, Twelfth Infantry, refused to advance into enemy

territory. *Newsweek* quoted one GI saying, "I'd rather be court-martialed and be alive." On October 10, when the rebels were actually threatened with court-martial, other platoons rallied to their support. Bravo Company was moved to a base near Saigon, and there were no disciplinary repercussions.[15]

- April 1972: One hundred troops of C Company, Second Battalion, First Infantry of the 196th Brigade, stationed in Phu Bai, refused to advance into enemy territory. They were finally convinced to advance, not because of a court-martial threat, but because A Company would have been endangered by their refusal.[16]

There is no way to know how many other such incidents took place out of sight of reporters and investigators. The *New York Times* quoted a soldier writing from Cu Chi, "They have to set up separate companies for men who refuse to go. If a man is ordered to go to such and such a place he no longer goes through the hassle of refusing: he just packs his shirt and goes to visit some buddies at another base camp."[17] Using figures provided by official testimonies to the U.S. Senate, Richard Gabriel suggests there were as many as 254 "combat refusals" in 1971 alone.[18] The euphemistic "combat refusal" was the military's preferred term. "Mutiny," counters Cortright, "is a potent and evocative term, but it accurately describes what in fact took place frequently in Vietnam."[19] But whether it was combat refusal or mutiny, from 1968 until the troop withdrawal in 1973, American soldiers increasingly simply refused to go.

Desertion was a further indication of collapse. "Nearly one-quarter of all GI's walked away from their units for periods ranging from a couple of weeks to years."[20] In 1971 alone, nearly 100,000 soldiers deserted.[21] The Nixon administration sought to label them all "malingerers, criminals or cowards," citing Pentagon studies that ostensibly showed that only 5 percent of deserters were motivated by antiwar feelings.[22] GIs interviewed by Robert Musil in 1973 said otherwise. Musil quotes attorney Robert Rivkin, who defended many of those charged with desertion: "Experience has taught us that many GIs are away without leave because of something the military did or failed to do." The GIs, Musil concludes, "like so many refugees, voted with their feet."[23]

Others created chaos from within. On April 20, 1971, Senate Majority Leader Mike Mansfield introduced his colleagues to what was perhaps the most macabre development of the war in Vietnam: fragging. Fragmentation grenades were the weapon of choice in most such killings, their advantage being that the evidence was destroyed with the crime. Violent attacks on officers by enlisted men were not unknown in previous twentieth-century wars, but they were relatively rare.[24] After the Tet Offensive in 1968, considered by many to have been the turning point of the war, fragging became endemic among U.S. forces. In response to Mansfield's testimony, Senator Charles Mathias called fragging the most tragic word in all the lexicon of war, "with all that it implies of total failure of discipline and depression of morale, the complete sense of frustration and confusion and the loss of goals and hope itself."[25]

The U.S. Army does not have exact statistics on how many officers were killed in Vietnam in this manner, but in December 1972 the Defense Department acknowledged between eight hundred and one thousand actual or suspected fraggings.[26] It also admitted that it could not account for the deaths of over fourteen hundred other officers and NCOs.[27] It should be noted that this number does *not* include incidents that occurred in other branches of service. Neither does it include attempts to kill by other means. In eloquent militarese, Gabriel and Savage write, "The category of assaults by 'explosive device' excludes attempts to kill 'leadership elements' by other means, such as a rifle, automatic weapons fire, ambush by claymore mines, and misdirection to hostile ambush."[28] These figures suggest that 20 to 25 percent—if not more—of all officers killed during the war were killed by their own men.[29] In 1971, the Americal Division (of My Lai infamy) was experiencing one fragging a week.[30] The army was clearly at war with itself.

Fraggings may have been carried out by individuals, but few were the result of personal vendettas. Far more often, individual soldiers acted with the approval, or at least the acquiescence, of the group.[31] Over eleven days in May of 1969, Colonel Weldon Honeycutt ordered and led an attack on Ap Bia Mountain. His men were so bloodied, so "ground up," in the assault that they renamed the mountain Hamburger Hill. Seventy Americans died on Hamburger Hill, four hundred were wounded, and there were hundreds of NVA casualties in the attack, which resulted in the capture of the mountain. Adding insult to injury, the prize was abandoned less than a month after it was taken.[32] The underground GI newspaper, *GI Says,* subsequently placed a $10,000 bounty on Honeycutt's head—and on that of any officer who ordered such attacks in the future.[33] In spite of the reward, Honeycutt actually made it home, but Hamburger Hill marked the end of major American ground combat operations in Vietnam. "Another Hamburger Hill," a veteran major maintained, "is definitely out."[34] Or as a young captain "happily" told *Life,* "Charging up hills has gone right out of fashion."[35]

Officers eventually awoke to the reality that ordering their men to fight ultimately posed a risk to themselves. Captain Barry Steinberg, an army judge who presided over fragging trials, called it "the troops' way of controlling officers." He added, "it is deadly effective," for whether or not the fragging actually takes place, the threat is enough to intimidate an officer and force him to consider the possible consequences of any order he might give. He thus becomes "useless to the military."[36]

Bounties and rewards were not uncommon in forward units (though the bounty on Honeycutt was larger than most), but they were more frequently initiated in rear units, where the effects of drugs, racial tensions, and the stress of authoritarianism without apparent justification were felt more acutely. REMFs ("rear-echelon motherfuckers"), officers who enforced military discipline with pettiness or rigidity, were most frequently targeted. Typically, they were given warnings, *Time* reported: first a smoke grenade, then tear gas —"then comes the more lethal stuff."[37] "The frustrations that spawn fraggings," Eugene Linden summarized in the *Saturday Review,* "have to do with the collision of a people who don't accept our mission in Vietnam and those who do. We are still killing people in Vietnam; yet there are no convincing arguments to continue doing so. If you can kill Vietnamese without convincing arguments, you can kill officers without them too, because to the battle-weary grunt the gung-ho, nit-picking officer is as inhuman and remote as the gook."[38] And, I would add, every bit as much a threat to his survival.

The army's response to the fragging epidemic was revealing of an institution that had lost the ability to critique and evaluate its own internal culture: they took the soldiers' guns away and restricted their access to explosives. By 1970, in many units, only those soldiers on guard duty or patrol were allowed to carry their weapons. An enlisted man quoted in the *New York Times* claimed that "the American garrisons on the larger bases are virtually disarmed. The lifers have taken our weapons from us and put them under lock and key."[39] The *Saturday Review* called it "symbolic of the Army's plight" that "the men are not even trusted to carry the weapons necessary to fight the war they have been sent to wage."[40] Military Police units were also expanded and used to quell any actual or threatened insurrection.[41] American guns turned on unarmed American boys was no less of a tragic irony in Vietnam than at Kent State in Ohio or Jackson State in Mississippi.

The "Nixon Doctrine," or "Vietnamization," which Nixon unveiled shortly after his first election, purported to shift the burden of the fighting onto the Vietnamese forces so that American troops could be withdrawn "with honor." In fact, the morale and discipline of the U.S. ground troops in Vietnam had so broken down that they were no longer a reliable fighting force. The U.S. government was forced to shift the burden of supporting its South Vietnamese allies from the army to the navy and the air force. "The Nixon administration claimed and received great credit for withdrawing the Army from Vietnam," writes historian David Cortright, "but in fact it was the rebellion of low-ranking GIs that forced the government to abandon a hopeless and suicidal policy."[42]

Shifting the burden of the war effort, however, only served to expand resistance into the other branches of service. Resistance in the air force and the navy grew commensurately with their direct involvement. In early 1970, officers on the aircraft carrier U.S.S. *Hancock* demanded the right to open discussion of the war and signed a letter to Defense Secretary Laird demanding immediate withdrawal from Vietnam.[43] The destroyer U.S.S. *Richard F. Anderson* was sabotaged in May of 1970, and delayed in port for two months.[44] In 1971, a group of both sailors and civilians unsuccessfully tried to stop the attack carriers U.S.S. *Constellation* and U.S.S. *Coral Sea* from sailing. Thousands of sailors signed antiwar petitions and supported the dozens of sailors who jumped ship, refusing duty in Vietnam.[45] On July 10, 1972, a fire on the U.S.S. *Forrestal* caused seven million dollars in damage. It was the worst single act of sabotage in U.S. naval history and caused a two-month delay in the ship's deployment.[46] Three weeks later, a paint scraper and two bolts were inserted into the reduction gears of the U.S.S. *Ranger*, causing one million dollars in damage and a three-and-a-half-month lay-up for repairs.[47] In October of 1972, there were riots aboard the U.S.S. *Kitty Hawk* and the U.S.S. *Hassayampa* in which dozens of sailors were injured.[48] Also in October, open revolt on the U.S.S. *Constellation* forced it to return to San Diego. The *New York Times* called it "the first mass mutiny in the history of the U.S. Navy."[49] A Black sailor described the "Connie" as "a ship as racist as the war it's fighting in."[50] In December, the U.S.S. *Ranger*, having finally been repaired after the previous sabotage, made it to the Gulf of Tonkin, only to be disabled again by a deliberately set fire.[51] The navy admitted that the sabotage of the *Ranger* was the sixth major disaster on a Seventh Fleet carrier since October 1. A 1972 House Armed Services Committee report claimed documentation of "literally hundreds of incidences of damaged Naval property wherein sabotage is suspected."[52]

By November 1972, there were five aircraft carriers out of commission in San Diego. With the army and the navy rendered unreliable, Nixon turned to the air force to continue the war. But the air force, too, was in revolt. By that year, airmen were distributing thirty underground newspapers and protesting "stratolevel technological genocide" outside of major air bases. It was, however, the refusal of combat pilots to fly missions that was most devastating. The so-called Christmas bombings of civilian targets in the North convinced combat pilots Captain Dwight Evans and Captain Michael Heck to refuse to fly. Their story led the TV evening news and made banner headlines everywhere, including the front page of the *New York Times*.[53] Heck, who was serving his fourth combat tour in Vietnam, and who had flown 262 bombing missions prior to his refusal, is quoted as saying "the goals do not justify the mass destruction and killings."[54]

In 1973, when Nixon continued to secretly bomb Cambodia *after* signing the Paris Peace Accords, four other airmen refused to fly B-52 missions and sued the Pentagon, challenging the legality of the bombing.[55] Air force pilot Richard Dawson likewise found he could no longer in conscience participate in the Cambodian bombing, and turned to the courts for redress when he was court-martialed. His claim that the bombing was "illegal" was upheld by every court up to the Supreme Court, at which point the government dropped its charges.[56]

Though it is tempting to blame the mainstream press for not connecting all the dots, it is also unfair to suggest that information about the GI Movement, as it came to be known, was not reported. Stewart Alsop, for example, a veteran journalist with reputed close connections to Pentagon sources, wrote, in a 1970 *Newsweek* editorial, of a "growing feeling among the Administration's policy makers that it might be a good idea to accelerate the rate of withdrawal." The main reason Alsop cited for this view was "that discipline and morale in the American Army in Vietnam are deteriorating very seriously." Though acknowledging risks in such an accelerated withdrawal, Alsop went on to state unequivocally that, "The greatest risk of all is inherent in the constant deterioration of discipline and morale in our Army in Vietnam."[57]

On the other hand, the *New York Times Sunday Magazine* published an article in February 1973, "A Sort of Mutiny: The Constellation Incident," in which the author neglected to make any reference whatsoever to antiwar sentiments as a motivating factor for any of the sailors involved. The article mentioned only racial tension. Just a year earlier, thousands of *Constellation* sailors had signed antiwar petitions, published on-board antiwar newspapers, and supported the dozens of sailors who jumped ship, refusing duty in Vietnam.[58] Eight of the nine sailors charged and court-martialed as the ringleaders in the uprising—who became known as "the Constellation Nine"—were finally given honorable discharges. The ninth chose to remain in the navy. *Up from the Bottom,* one of the many San Diego–based GI publications, reported that, "These men put up a long hard struggle to remind the people that the Air War in Vietnam is still going on and that it starts from the flight deck of carriers which are loaded down with planes which are loaded with bombs to kill the people in Southeast Asia."[59] The *Times* decision to ignore that aspect of the story was certainly an odd one.

Of all the troops in Vietnam, the most rebellious were the African Americans. When Wallace Terry first went to Vietnam in May of 1967, he found that most of the Black soldiers there were professionals, careerists who had joined the army to get ahead.[60] When he returned at the end of the year, the war had chewed up and spat out that older generation of soldier. What Terry found in their place was "a new black soldier" who called himself "Blood." He was "just steps removed from marching in the Civil Rights Movement or rioting in the rebellions that swept the urban ghettos from Harlem to Watts. All were filled with a new sense of pride and purpose."[61] The Bloods knew all about Stokely Carmichael, Malcolm X, and the Black Panthers. They knew that the Black Panther Party Program demanded exemption from military service for Black men who "should not be forced to fight in the military service to defend a racist government that does not protect us."[62] In 1967, Muhammad Ali refused induction into the army with an eloquence that equaled his prowess in the ring: "They want me to go to Vietnam to shoot some black folks that never lynched me, never called me nigger, never assassinated my leaders."[63] Eldridge Cleaver, minister of information for the Black Panther Party and author of *Soul on Ice,* was running for president in 1968 as the candidate of the Peace and Freedom Party. He was on the ballot in some twenty states, running on a platform of immediate withdrawal from Vietnam and support of the Black Liberation movement.[64] "Right inside of the US imperialist beast's army, you are strategically placed to begin the process of destroying him from within," his wife Kathleen exhorted Black soldiers.[65]

Until the spring of 1967, Dr. Martin Luther King Jr. had been largely silent on issues regarding the war. He saw his role as bridging the gap between more radical, militant, and younger African Americans who saw the war as a racist, imperialist venture, and older, more moderate groups that feared antiwar activism would dilute their attempts to press for a civil rights agenda. On April 4, at the Riverside Church in New York City, King took the war on directly in one of his most momentous sermons. In "A Declaration of Independence from the War in Vietnam," King claimed that the war effort was immorally draining resources from antipoverty and civil rights programs. But, he continued:

> [It was] doing far more than devastating the hopes of the poor at home. It was sending their sons and their brothers and their husbands to fight and die in extraordinary high proportions relative to the rest of the population. We were taking the young black men who had been crippled by our society and sending them 8,000 miles away to guarantee liberties in Southeast Asia which they had not found in Southwest Georgia and East Harlem. So we have been repeatedly faced with the cruel irony of watching Negro boys and white boys on TV screens as they kill and die together for a nation that has been unable to seat them together in the same schools."[66]

King's speeches in 1967 and 1968 were increasingly critical of United States policy in Vietnam and increasingly specific about what he thought should be done to redeem our national soul. He came up with a plan that included a bombing halt, a cease-fire, and a timetable for the withdrawal of troops. Perhaps most inflammatory of all, he advocated draft resistance. In April of 1968, he was assassinated in Memphis, Tennessee, and cities across the country erupted in grief and rage.

It was in this political context that African American draftees were given a choice of going to Vietnam or to prison. For the majority of those who "chose" Vietnam, all they wanted to do was their time, to get back to the "world" and to a struggle that had some personal relevance. As PFC John Munn told a *Life* magazine reporter, "I have my life to preserve, but I have nothing against that little man out there. They're fighting for what they believe in, and you can't knock that. I lie on my air mattress at night and I say what am I doing here? I can imagine a war back in the world that I'd fight and wouldn't mind dying in—to keep your people free."[67]

Dr. King's death marked a transitional moment in which a dialogue of nonviolence was drowned out by the militancy of Black Power, both at home and in the military. "Dr King's death changed things," said PFC James Hawkins, a Black soldier. "It made a lot of people angry, angry people with weapons."[68] Black GIs led two of the largest prison rebellions of the war in August of 1968. They were also responsible for several of the combat refusals mentioned earlier.[69] David Addlestone, founder and codirector of the National Veterans Legal Services Program, said that by the time he arrived in Vietnam in 1970, Black soldiers were "very seldom trusted in combat, apparently for fear they might turn their guns around."[70] That was surely an exaggeration, but a recognizable sentiment nonetheless.

The NLF were quick to exploit the racial conflict among U.S. forces. Thousands of propaganda leaflets took advantage of images of U.S. policemen beating Black civil rights workers, of antiwar demonstrations, and of the antiwar statements of politicians, celebrities, and activists in the media. Bulletins proclaiming that "The Vietnam War is being subsidized by the blood, sweat and continued poverty of the poor black man" or "No Vietnamese Ever Called Me a Nigger" were common.[71] Wallace Terry recalled NLF soldiers yelling, "Go home, soul man!" at Black soldiers during combat, and Staff Sergeant Don Browne, who was interviewed in Terry's *Bloods,* described how, "to play on the sympathy of the black soldier, the Vietcong would shoot at a white guy, then let the black guy behind him go through, then shoot at the next white guy."[72] Supporting Browne's perception, Spec. 4 Robert Holcomb remembers that when he arrived in the 101st Airborne, "the white guys would stay close to the black guys in the field because they thought the VC and the NVA didn't shoot at the blacks as much as the whites."[73] The huge numbers of Black soldiers actually killed in combat and the equal maltreatment of Black prisoners of war, however, suggest that the NVA and NLF were simply manipulating the racial discord that already existed within the American ranks.[74]

Viet Cong propaganda was not only aimed at African American GIs. As Colonel Robert D. Heinl Jr. noted in 1971, the increasing tendency of troops to refuse, disrupt, and evade "has not gone unnoticed by the enemy [and] is underscored by the Viet Cong delegation's recent statement at the Paris Peace Talks that communist units in Indochina have been ordered not to engage American units which do not molest them."[75] Joe Urgo, who traveled to Hanoi in 1971 as a representative of the Vietnam Veterans Against the War (VVAW), reported being "given a statement the Front . . . had sent to all its commanders in the field: instructions that any American soldier who wears a button or any physical display of a button of a rifle turned upside down, or carries his rifle in the down position, should not be shot at. . . . People started to wear the VVAW emblem as big as their T-shirt." Urgo recalled, "We saw pictures of the logo as large as the shirt. They were having the mama-sans sew the VVAW emblem on their fatigue shirts."[76]

Whether or not the document Urgo was given was genuine, whether or not the policy was ever implemented by the North Vietnamese Army, is unknown. What is evident, however, is that virtually everyone in uniform in Vietnam in the early '70s was aware of such propaganda. They were also aware that the United States had decided not to try to "win" the war. From June of 1969, when Nixon ordered the first troop withdrawals and the implementation of Vietnamization, there didn't seem to be any good reason to risk dying. "Grunt logic," as Saar wrote in *Life* magazine, "argues that since the U.S. has decided not to go out and win the war, there's no sense in being the last one to die."[77]

Such "grunt logic," it would seem, was eminently sane. Indeed, one of the ironies of Vietnam, given both the moral chaos during the war and the high rates of PTSD that followed, was that in-country "psychiatric" casualties were startlingly low, less than 1 percent, compared to the 43 percent from World War II. There was, at least initially, a great deal of self-congratulation at the Pentagon over those numbers. What they appear to have missed is that, in the midst of a collective breakdown, one that could be recognized in terms of both politics and social psychology, the armed forces could only measure the psychic costs of war through the individual symptomology of past wars. It was all happening again, only this time it was a collective response.

Credit for the low rate of psychiatric casualties was shared by a number of new protocols and initiatives. First, unlike the armed forces in World War II and Korea, the U.S. Army arrived in Vietnam with trained psychiatrists, though their number never exceeded twenty.[78] Most of the work with combat troops was done not by psychiatrists, but by psychiatric technicians, college-educated and fast-tracked in basic military psychiatry.

Second, for the first time in military history, aggressive use was made of powerful tranquilizers and antianxiety drugs.[79] The drug interventions were credited with reducing the incidence of psychiatric casualties *on the battlefield,* casualties that would otherwise have demanded evacuation. The tragic, long-term price paid for short-term gains was, however, soon to become apparent. According to one military psychologist, "if drugs are given while the stressor is still being experienced, then they will arrest or supercede the development of effective coping mechanisms, resulting in an increase in the long-term trauma from the stress. What happened in Vietnam is the moral equivalent of giving a soldier a local anesthetic for a gunshot wound and then sending him back into combat."[80]

The drugs prescribed by doctors, of course, were not the only drugs available. The war in Vietnam coincided with a dramatic increase in drug use among civilian populations, both nationally and internationally. In the spring of 1967, 5 percent of U.S. college students reported having used marijuana. By 1971, that figure had risen to 51 percent.[81] In Vietnam, marijuana's relaxant and euphorgenic qualities made it the drug of choice for many soldiers. One company commander told *Life* magazine he estimated that 70 percent of the men in his company were stoned whenever the breeze wasn't blowing in his direction. His men enthusiastically reported that the number was closer to 85 percent.[82] Perhaps one of the most provocative stories, reported widely in the press, was that of Spec. 4 Peter Lemon, who "fought the enemy single-handed and dragged a wounded comrade to the rear before collapsing from exhaustion and three wounds. [He] refused treatment until more seriously injured men had been cared for." Lemon received for his heroism the Congressional Medal of Honor. He was later quoted in the AP dispatch saying, "You get really alert when you're stoned because you have to be."[83]

When the army clamped down on marijuana use in 1969, one soldier told a *New York Times* reporter, "It's getting so hard to score marijuana around here, guys have to turn to skag."[84] "Skag," as troops called heroin, was cheap: $2 for a vial, 98 percent pure, that would have sold for $150 in the U.S.[85] It was easy to find, more easily concealed, and far more dangerous.[86] In 1970, Congressmen Robert Steele and Morgan Murphy stunned the country with a report that 15–20 percent of American servicemen in Vietnam were addicted to heroin.[87] Others suggest that their figure was low, that 35 percent was probably closer to the truth.[88] The thought of tens of thousands of "soldier-junkies," trained in guerilla warfare, returning to the streets of America was chilling. Nixon responded by declaring a "War on Drugs," but it was not particularly effective. By the following year, more soldiers were being sent home for drug addiction than for war wounds.[89]

The use of marijuana and heroin by U.S. forces in Vietnam, I would argue, should be seen as part of the broader pattern of resistance outlined here. At the same time, it was a form of self-medication, a way of distancing oneself from the horror and the fear. But, like the drugs prescribed by the doctors, the most self-medication could do was postpone the onset of stress-related symptoms.

The best example I have ever heard of General Westmoreland's characteristic unwillingness to entertain criticism or admit fault was his absurd insistence, in a 1968 speech to a group of Florida businesspeople, that Phan Thi Kim Phuc, the little girl in Nick Ut's Pulitzer Prize–winning photograph, running naked and burned from a napalm strike on her village, had merely been the victim of a hibachi accident. The photograph, which landed, front-page, on breakfast tables nationwide, is credited with having helped turn the country against the war. As a result, it was a major embarrassment to the military, and especially to the man responsible for the war's prosecution. "My god," he is quoted as saying, "if she was hit by napalm, she would not have survived."[90]

By 1970, however, blaming the failures of his army on a civilian society run amok was sounding whiny and worn. The irritating and insistent questions about the performance of his army just wouldn't go away, and Westmoreland was finally cornered into an uncharacteristic moment of apparent openness. The Army War College was commissioned to investigate and report. The resulting report, called the *Study on Military Professionalism,* was a devastating document that unabashedly blamed the army's own internal policies, rather than external influences, for its problems.[91] "There was no significant evidence," the report read, "that contemporary sociological pressures—which are everpresent—were primary causes of the differences between the ideal and the actual professional climate in the Army; the problems are for the most part internally generated; they will not vanish automatically as the war in Vietnam winds down and the size of the Army decreases." Under "Solutions," the first and most pressing recommendation was, "Disseminate to the Officer Corps the pertinent findings of this study."[92] Reverting to type, Westmoreland ordered the report classified, and it was not released for thirteen years.

In 1971, however, Colonel Robert D. Heinl Jr., a veteran combat commander with over twenty-seven years' experience in the marines, showed considerably more courage than his boss. Heinl broke the inside story nationally in an article published in the *Armed Forces Journal,* unambiguously titled "The Collapse of the Armed Forces." "By every conceivable indicator," Heinl wrote, "our army that now remains in Vietnam is in a state approaching collapse, with individual units avoiding or having refused combat, murdering their officers and noncommissioned officers, drug-ridden, and dispirited where not near-mutinous."[93] The article went on to document the specifics of his claim, from fraggings to bounties, from mutinies to desertion.

Nixon's armies were collapsing around him. At home, he blamed the failure of the war effort on the protesters, whose anti-American, antisoldier activities were, he insisted, undermining the morale of the troops in Vietnam. It was this homegrown "fifth column" that was causing us to lose the war. "Let us understand," Nixon had said, in his famous "Silent Majority" speech in 1969, "North Vietnam cannot defeat or humiliate the United States. Only Americans can do that."[94] It was his vice president, Spiro Agnew, though, who really inflated the administration's rhetoric, comparing peace activists to Nazi storm troopers, Brown Shirts, Communists, and the KKK.[95]

The nature of the support structure to which a soldier returns—his family, friends, and community—has certainly been recognized as a factor in whether or not he develops a posttraumatic illness. Support and compassion, a time to mourn and a time to heal, can do much to assuage the pain for many. The suggestion that the Vietnam-era veterans came home to an antiwar movement that singled them out for hostility and blame has been injected into the conventional historic narrative of the war. That is certainly not my memory. There were some entitled, college-educated antiwar activists who assumed the right to speak for the veterans. Conversely, there were veterans who believed that only having been there gave one the right to an opinion. But a version of history that privileges friction over solidarity is overwhelmingly contradicted by the written and visual histories of the time.[96]

One major obstacle to the persuasiveness of this account was the large number of Vietnam veterans who joined the civilian antiwar movement. From the late sixties through the end of the war, veterans led teach-ins on college campuses, spoke at rallies and, in impressive numbers, led demonstrations. Thousands of Vietnam veterans, and even active-duty GIs, were at the forefront of the October 15 Moratorium in 1969, and a month later, the November 15 "March of Death," which drew crowds in the hundreds of thousands to New York, Boston, San Francisco, and Washington, D.C.

In 1971, in response to William Calley's conviction for ordering the massacre of some five hundred civilians in the hamlet of My Lai, Vietnam Veterans Against the War convened the "Winter Soldier

Investigation" in Detroit.[97] Over a three-day period, more than a hundred veterans testified to atrocities they had witnessed committed by U.S. troops against Vietnamese civilians.[98] Their expressed intention was to demonstrate that My Lai was not unique, that it was instead the inevitable result of U.S. policy. The Winter Soldiers' testimonies sought to shift the focus of blame from the soldiers to the policy makers, to McNamara, Bundy, Rostow, Johnson, LeMay, Nixon, and the others they felt were truly responsible for the war crimes that had been committed. What, after all, did people expect when, as William Barry Gault said, "terrified and furious teenagers by the tens of thousands have only to twitch their index fingers, and what was a quiet village is suddenly a slaughterhouse"?[99]

Also in 1971, the vanguard of a Washington, D.C., demonstration of half a million people was a contingent of a thousand Vietnam veterans, wearing fatigues, field jackets, their old "Nam" boots, and their boonie hats. They were longhaired and bearded, and many were in wheelchairs or on crutches. The veterans conducted an operation they called "Dewey Canyon III." (Dewey Canyon I and II were the code names given to the covert incursions into Laos in 1969 and 1971.) Dewey Canyon III was both biting street theater and incisive political protest. The vets conducted "a limited incursion into the country of Congress," throwing their medals and ribbons back at the government that had awarded them.

John Kerry, then a VVAW coordinator, was their spokesperson. In an impassioned speech before Congress, he chastised the government for its characterization of the antiwar veterans as "criminal misfits."

> This administration has done us the ultimate dishonor. They have attempted to disown us and the sacrifices we made for this country. . . . We do not need their testimony. Our own scars and stumps of limbs are witness enough for others and for ourselves. . . . All that they have done and all that they can do by this denial is to make more clear than ever our own determination to undertake one last mission—to search out and destroy the last vestige of this barbaric war, to pacify our own hearts,

> to conquer the hate and the fear that have driven this country these last ten years and more, so when thirty years from now our brothers go down the street without a leg, without an arm, or a face, and small boys ask why, we will be able to say "Vietnam" and not mean a desert, not a filthy obscene memory, but mean instead the place where America finally turned and where soldiers like us helped it in the turning.[100]

For Nixon to credibly blame the veterans, whose credibility was patently enormous, required extraordinary finesse. Much of his political support came from the far more conservative veterans of previous wars. He could hardly afford to paint all veterans with the same broad brush. His solution was first to create images of "good" and "bad" veterans, and then to drive a wedge between the two groups. His "good" veterans won their wars, were proud of their uniforms, joined the VFW or American Legion chapters, kept their hair short, and trusted authority and government. "Bad" veterans smoked marijuana, grew their hair long, disrespected their uniforms, and marched in protests that mocked and challenged government authority. "Bad" veterans had ended up in this sorry state because of insidious radicals who spat on them, victimized them, and further traumatized them in their fragile post-combat states. They had been made ill through ill-treatment, and it was their illness speaking when they took to the streets to protest the war.[101]

Nixon's obsessive attempts to discredit the "bad" veterans, to label them mentally impaired, radical, dope fiends, and the victims of psychic assault from antiwar activists, led to his use of the "plumbers" to infiltrate their organizations, and thus ultimately led to his impeachment. The legacy of his fabrication, however, haunts our political dialogue still. Jerry Lembcke's book *The Spitting Image* is a thoroughly researched and chilling reminder of how insidiously Nixon's spin has infiltrated and reconfigured our collective memory in the intervening years. His premise is that the spat-upon veteran is a myth, that it never happened, but that it was an abuse alleged so often and proclaimed so loudly that over time it infiltrated the public consciousness.[102] In his search through press archives, media images, and written testimonials from the time, he uncovered no evidence whatsoever of such occurrences.

The overwhelming historical evidence indicated rather that antiwar civilians and antiwar veterans recognized their common cause and worked together, if not always seamlessly, to end a war they all believed was immoral. "Remembered as a war that was lost because of betrayal at home," wrote Lembcke, "Vietnam becomes a modern-day Alamo that must be avenged.... Remembered as a war in which soldiers and pacifists joined hands to fight for peace, Vietnam symbolizes popular resistance to political authority and the dominant images of what it means to be a good American."[103]

The myth of the spat-upon Vietnam veteran is just another insidious example of how a widespread and multifaceted rebellion against the war, its authors, and its justifying ideologies has been rewritten as pathology and not as political efficacy. This revision itself represents a betrayal of both the veterans' experiences and their pain. In the current political climate, with U.S. forces again facing down a local citizenry opposed to their presence, it must give us pause.

In the early '70s, press reports began to refer to a "Post-Vietnam Syndrome." An article that appeared in the August 21, 1972, *New York Times* called Post-Vietnam Syndrome a mental illness that was the result, not of wartime experience, but of homecoming. Citing the low psychiatric casualty rate during the war, the author went on to suggest that guilt aroused by antiwar, antiveteran sentiments was the source of the veterans' distress.[104] The insinuation served to further marginalize and stigmatize veterans, while at the same time delegitimizing both their illness and their protest. Perhaps not coincidentally, August 21, 1972, was the opening day of the Republican National Convention in Miami. Whatever the intention of the author or the *Times,* the article played into the Republican agenda. Who, it suggested, need take seriously the rantings of mentally unbalanced extremists who were already gathering in the streets?

It has been recognized for over a century that exposure to combat inevitably causes symptoms associated with trauma. The fact that veterans of the war in Vietnam exhibited relatively few of those symptoms until after their return home was a surprise to many, but the suggestion that interactions with civilian antiwar protesters were responsible for veterans' subsequent psychiatric illnesses has never, that I am aware of, been taken seriously enough to have been the subject of scientific inquiry. There is certainly no evidence to support that claim. There is, however, overwhelming evidence that every soldier stationed in Vietnam "experienced, witnessed, or was confronted with an event or events that involved actual or threatened death or serious injury, or a threat to the physical integrity of self or others" and that their responses "involved intense fear, helplessness, or horror."[105] They were all traumatized by their war experience. Why so few manifested the traditionally recognized array of symptoms during their war years is still a largely unanswered question. So, too, is the question why some became symptomatic and others did not. But it seems fatuous to suggest that simply because old criteria didn't fit, the illness wasn't there.

In any event, we have now lived for decades with an awareness, if not an understanding, of the ways in which PTSD inexorably diminishes lives. The Vietnam vets who suffer from PTSD have known the loss of stability and focus necessary to hold down a job. They have known how medications (legal and illegal) create intolerable dependence and undermine competence and credibility. And they have had to find ways to avoid stimuli that trigger unacceptable, uncivilized, even illegal responses, ways that often involve removing themselves from the sights, sounds, and intimacies that the rest of us take for granted. I would like to think that those soldiers who protested most cleanly and explicitly have suffered less than others because, in insisting on what Shay called thémis, "what's right," they retained some viable moral integrity. But I do not know that, and I have my own suspect reasons for wishing it to be so. What I do know is that far too many of the veterans of the war in Vietnam have never managed to recover a workable modicum of their humanity. Some will be forever tormented by their demons. Far too many, like Daniel, gave in to despair and suicide.

EMILIA PARRISH

We had decided to have a natural childbirth. After Noel's death my mother became my Lamaze coach. It was so hard to go to the class and see all the other happy couples, and there I was—with my mother. I didn't want to hate them, but I did. They were so happy and I was so miserable.

My son was born on December 24, 1970. When it was time to go to the hospital to deliver, everyone asked me where my husband was. At first I would tell the truth and say, "He's dead, he committed suicide three months ago." But I would get these horrified looks. So I just started saying that he died in Vietnam. It was easier.

I named him Noel, after his father. I had such mixed emotions when he was born. It was just amazing how many gestures and expressions he had that were so very much like his father's. I loved him to death, but I resented him, too. And I kept thinking, "I don't want you to take his place. I want him."

I never screamed and hollered the way that I should have. I had to go back to work immediately after he was born. A few weeks later, I had two baby showers. Life went on as though nothing had happened.

My husband was my high-school sweetheart, a gorgeous man with Paul Newman blue eyes and beautiful curly hair. When he got a low lottery number, he enlisted rather than waiting to be drafted. He chose the Marine Corps because he thought he was a tough, macho guy. They sent him to Vietnam right after boot camp. He was stationed with the 3rd Tanks Battalion in Quang Tri, near the DMZ, and I know that he saw a lot of combat. I could never get him to talk about it. I do remember one story. He said they had access to all the liquor they wanted. One evening there was incoming artillery and some of his friends died because they were too drunk to move.

I didn't know exactly when he was coming home. On Thanksgiving Day, his family and mine were celebrating together, and I got a call, "Emilia, I'm home. I'm at the airport. Come get me." When we got back, everyone was there having Thanksgiving dinner. He was more quiet than usual, like he was in another world. The service never debriefed him. They brought him home from Vietnam—boom!—straight back to civilization with nothing in between.

We got married soon after he got home, but it was a real anxious time. He was stationed at the Marine Corps base in Vallejo and having a lot of problems with alcohol. He knew it, but he just didn't know where to turn. I called the base many times asking for somebody to help him, somebody to do something. I even talked to the chaplain, but he just kept saying that he would be okay. When it got worse, first they demoted him to PFC, and then they discharged him five months early. It was an honorable discharge, but just barely. It was easier to just get rid of him than to try to help.

When he finally came home, we stayed with my parents for a while. I was working, and I was pregnant, and he was trying to find a job. He wanted to be a policeman, but he didn't get hired because they saw that he'd been demoted. That was a big disappointment. He got more and more depressed, his drinking was out of control, and who knows what else he was doing to keep himself sedated. My parents thought he had malaria because he would start shaking and break out in cold sweats. He was real fidgety, couldn't sleep. I had to be careful when I walked into a room to let him know I was there. You could never walk up behind him without saying something because he would turn around and attack. When he began to feel really out of control, he went to live with his brother, Neil. We had been married less than a year.

The last time I saw him was a week before he died, and he scared me to death. He was completely out of it. I thought he was drunk, but it could have been something else. He was dirty. He was always an impeccable man, and there he was with dirty clothes on. He tried to be loving, but I was repulsed. This was not the man I had fallen in love with. This was not the man I married. My last vision of him was—not him.

He called me at 3:00 in the morning the night before he died, to say that he was sorry, but I had heard it so many times before. I didn't think he was serious, but he had bought a gun and he shot himself in the heart.

About ten years ago, I found a suicide support group near my home. It was the first time I had thought to look for help. Everyone else in the group was mourning a recent loss, and I was talking about something that had happened over twenty years ago, but when I started to tell my story, it felt like it had just happened. It was still fresh in my body, mind, and soul because I had never been through a grieving process. It seems that every time I tell my story, it gets a little easier. I can talk about it all now, but it's taken thirty years.

I'll be fifty-two in May. I have never remarried. Sometimes I wonder about being so alone. I guess it's the trust factor. I have a hard time trusting anyone with my heart. It is only recently that I have come to understand how angry I was at Noel for leaving us. He should have been there when his son was born, and now his son has become a father, and he will miss his grandson. He loved babies. He was a gentle man. I think Vietnam ripped his heart apart. The bullet just finished what the war had started.

RUTH MURTAUGH

My son, Don, was a nice boy, a hardworking boy, but then he hit that teenage stage and he thought he knew everything. He wanted to be on his own and he thought the best way was to join the army. He volunteered for Vietnam. We didn't want him to go, and we could've stopped him, but I just don't believe in doing things like that. If he wanted to go, that was his prerogative. He acted like he couldn't wait to get away, but the first month we had huge telephone bills. He was so young.

After the first year, he came home on leave, and I don't remember thinking he had changed much. But then he reenlisted, went back for another year, and when he came home the second time, it was horrible. He had been busted in Vietnam. He was a Spec 4 when he went and he got busted back to a private. I have no idea what the reason for it was, but he was very bitter about the whole thing, about the war. Our boy was very patriotic, but he was carrying on about this rotten country and how they don't give a damn about anything.

We live in McAllen, Texas. McAllen is a conservative town and, when the war started, I think most people felt, like I did, that it was a bad situation, but there was nothing you could do about it; you had to more or less accept it. But by the time it had finished, by the time I had seen what it had done to these boys, how they came back and were so bitter, I felt disgusted. I tried to put on a brave front, but I was angry about all the young men who had gone off to a useless war. And I think that's exactly what it was.

When Don was sober, he was wonderful, but when he was drunk, he was disgusting. He'd show up at my house and I'd feed him and he'd sit there for a while and sort of slobber, and then he'd say he was going home. I don't know how many DUIs he got. Oh, he made me mad! I probably should have gotten angrier with him, but I don't think it would have saved him. I tried to do everything I could to help him. We all tried to guide him along the right ways. I know I never said, "Don't come back."

For a while, he went to San Antonio to the V.A. They diagnosed him as a manic-depressive, but that was in the mid-'70s, before they knew about PTSD. It wasn't helping, so he stopped going, and decided to build himself a house outside of town, where it was quiet. The house was really nothing but a shack out of used lumber, but he was so proud of it. In Vietnam they taught them how to survive by themselves, plumbing, electrical work, anything. He had a toilet in there, and a shower, a telephone, and a parrot. I never could understand what that bird was saying, but it was the meanest damn thing I ever saw.

About a week before he died, Don called each one of us. He was in terrible shape, and we were all so disgusted with him. Neither of my daughters would answer their phones. When he called me, I think I knew he was getting ready to do it. He told me he was going to someplace in Mexico for scuba diving lessons. When I told him he couldn't afford it, he laughed and said that he had an American Express card and was going whether he could afford it or not. I think I knew he was going to have a last fling and to hell with the consequences. I didn't really try to stop him. When he came back, he overdosed in a rental car just outside of town by the 7-11.

I'm a very forgiving person, but I am still bitter about this: right after he died I got in touch with the Vietnam Veterans office here. I believe that posttraumatic stress was the cause of my son's death. All I wanted was an acknowledgment of that. I wasn't looking for a pension. I already have a pension. I just wanted them to say that this was the reason why this boy did what he did. I believe that it was to blame for what other boys went through, and I don't think the girls or wives or mothers or whoever is left behind should blame themselves for the way it turned out. It wasn't their fault. I didn't get any response from them. I'm sorry to say that, but it's true.

My daughters both felt so guilty because they thought he was reaching out to them for help and they didn't give it to him. I told them, "I don't want you blaming yourselves. It's not your fault. It was Don's time to go." It will probably sound wicked to you, but I prayed to God to end it. I'm afraid that's a wicked thing for a mother to do, but he had really had enough. I think that that's the reason God took him.

CHAPTER FIVE

SUICIDE IN THE AFTERMATH OF VIETNAM

> We were survivors of a shipwreck, consumed by guilt for having failed to save the dearest people in our lives and ashamed at being alive and abandoned. We were dazed by our helplessness, confused by the anger that laced through our mourning.
>
> —CARLA FINE, *No Time to Say Goodbye*

IN THE 1980S, REPORTS BEGAN to circulate in the mainstream media claiming that more Vietnam veterans had killed themselves since coming home than there were names on the Wall. First, in 1980, this claim was made in a Disabled American Veterans manual on the treatment of posttraumatic stress disorder.[1] Then, in 1981, the *Seattle Times* published a front-page story, "Vietnam Legacy: veterans' suicide toll may top war casualties," that put the number at 50,000.[2] In 1985, *Discover* magazine claimed the number was 58,000, and it was up to 60,000 or more in books published in 1986.[3] In 1987, a guest on CBS's *60 Minutes* put the number at more than 100,000,[4] and in 1988, a CBS report, "The Wall Within," asserted that between 26,000 and 100,000 suicides had occurred among Vietnam veterans, "depending on which reputable source you believe."[5]

It was a breathtaking, heartbreaking story—if it was true. In 1990, an article in the *American Journal of Psychiatry* attempted to trace the sources of those reports. They found that the story had apparently taken on a life of its own, one source quoting another, and though those sources included some of the most respected newspapers, magazines, and television news programs in the country, none of the reports was apparently based on documented evidence.[6]

By the late 1980s, however, similar reports had also begun to appear in professional and scientific journals and reports. Unlike reports in the popular press, articles published in academic and professional journals were based on clear evidence, specifically small-scale qualitative studies and in-depth work with veterans suffering from PTSD. For example, in 1986, Norman Hearst et al. published an article in the *New England Journal of Medicine* that found that "veterans were 65 percent and 49 percent more likely [than nonveterans] to die from suicide and motor-vehicle accidents, respectively."[7] The authors specifically blame "military service during the Vietnam War" for those deaths. In 1988, psychiatrist and trauma specialist Jacob Lindy stated that "Fifty-eight thousand [young Americans] were killed [in Vietnam]. Tens of thousands more committed suicide after returning home."[8]

What was still missing, however, was a large-scale study that would identify the scope of the problem. Because of the expense and necessary access to information, such a study could only be done by the government. Between 1986 and 1988, the federal government did indeed undertake what it called "the most far-reaching and comprehensive national mental health study ever attempted with any population." The *National Vietnam Veterans Readjustment Study (NVVRS)* was published in 1990. As I mentioned in Chapter Three, its findings are still being used as the basis for many government-funded research projects. It claimed to represent "virtually every segment of the veteran population"—every segment, that is, with the astonishing exception of those veterans who had died by their own hand, those who had attempted to die by their own hand, or those whose lives had been turned upside down by constant and intrusive thoughts about ending their lives. The *NVVRS never mentions* suicide or even suicidal ideation.[9]

Lindy's report, *Vietnam: A Casebook,* served as the preliminary study for the *NVVRS*. In 1988, he had written, "In our own samples, we have been repeatedly impressed with the frequency and severity of the problem of suicide. One hundred percent of our treatment sample and 72 percent of the clinical sample from the NIMH [National Institute for Mental Health] study reported suicidal thinking in the past week. In addition, 37 percent of the NIMH clinical sample had attempted suicide and 8 percent of the non-clinical sample had as well."[10] It is hard to imagine what might have happened between 1988 and 1990 when the government study was published, to explain such an omission.

The truth is that nobody knows how many Vietnam veterans have taken their own lives since the war ended. Jonathan Shay, certainly one of the foremost authorities on PTSD in Vietnam veterans, says that "the most commonly heard guess, 'as many (suicides) as there are (KIAs) on the Wall,' is one I readily believe."[11] Shay is an extremely credible witness, but however educated the guess, it is still a guess.

Claims concerning suicide among Vietnam vets are still the subject of contentious debate. Government agencies have consistently denied the numbers as just another fabrication of the irresponsible, sensationalist media playing loose with the facts. Even some veterans' groups have passionately rejected claims that they felt were slandering the strength, courage, and manhood of American soldiers. Thus it is that, three decades after the American withdrawal from Vietnam, as veterans of that war continue to take their own lives, and as ominous stories appear in the news of suicides among American troops in, or recently returned from, Afghanistan and Iraq, the relationship between military service and suicide is treated as a novel and perplexing phenomenon. It becomes the stuff of sound bites and brief stories that have no staying power, stories that are subject to denial, denunciation, and disingenuous surprise.

There are many reasons that, whatever the actual number, an epidemic of veteran suicides has been allowed to pass unacknowledged, erased from our memories and the official histories of post-Vietnam. In this chapter, I want to focus on a number of closely related reasons that have to do with cultural beliefs concerning suicide. I want to ask how our cultural beliefs have contributed to the invisibility of suicide in general, and more specifically of military suicides. I want to show how those beliefs have been exploited by a government unwilling to gather credible information, who has paid the price for that lack of information, and whose agendas have thus been served.

Under the best of circumstances, suicide statistics are imprecise. Only one in five or six suicides actually leaves a note.[12] In her profoundly moving and insightful book *No Time to Say Goodbye,* Carla Fine devotes an entire chapter to statements from people who have tried to keep the suicide of a loved one secret. Survivors, those who are left behind, feel guilt at their failure to intervene, or shame that they weren't enough to make a difference. They feel, and often are, judged by families and communities that would hold them responsible, or by religious communities that would withhold the comforting rituals of death. They cover up evidence, hide notes, and even pressure professionals to falsify death certificates. In some cases, officials are sincerely unable to establish whether a death was accidental or intentional. If a death is officially determined to be suicide, many life insurance companies will refuse to honor a claim.[13] Some coroners or medical examiners will only classify a death a suicide when a note is found.

Among other factors that complicate suicide statistics are the many different understandings of what constitutes a suicide. Even sociologist Emile Durkheim's rather broad definition of suicide—"all cases of death resulting directly or indirectly from a positive or negative act of the victim himself, which he knows will produce this result"—may not go far enough.[14] It is not much of a stretch to call the Russian roulette player's death a suicide, though it cannot be said for certain that he *knows* what will happen when he pulls the trigger. The same is true of street drugs, which every user knows can vary unpredictably, often lethally, in purity. And "suicide by cop," in which an individual deliberately creates a situation designed to provoke a deadly response from police, can circumvent the stigma or the fear of self-destructive behavior.[15] Likewise, it is impossible to know how consciously suicidal reckless driving is.[16] The individual may be less than fully conscious of the self-destructive impulse behind behaviors or "accidents." That is why researchers such as the Hearst team cited above include statistics about motor vehicle accidents in their accumulated data.

It appears certain, however, that for any or all of the reasons above, suicides are underreported. The Centers for Disease Control and Prevention (CDC) admits that, "Because suicide is particularly subject to inaccurate determination, the incidence of suicide may be underestimated by 10–50 percent."[17] Even so, it ranks eleventh in the most common way Americans die. In 2000, according to the World Health Organization, suicide was the greatest single cause of violent death around the world, almost equaling deaths from homicide and war *combined*.[18] David Satcher, the U.S. Surgeon General, wrote in 1999:

> Compounding the tragedy of loss of life, suicide evokes complicated and uncomfortable reactions in most of us. Too often, we blame the victim and stigmatize the surviving family members and friends. These reactions add to the survivors' burden of hurt, intensify their isolation, and shroud suicide in secrecy. Unfortunately, secrecy and silence diminish the accuracy and amount of information available about persons who have completed suicide—information that might help prevent other suicides.[19]

Statistics can be an affront to those of us who cannot help but attach an individual beloved face and a life-shattering experience to them. But without them, how are we to understand the magnitude of a problem that few acknowledge unless, and sometimes even when, it has touched them personally? The murder rate in this country is the highest in the world, yet the suicide rate is 50 percent higher still.[20] During the worst years of the AIDS epidemic in this country (1987–1996), almost 1,500 more young men took their own lives than died from HIV/AIDS.[21] Earlier, during the Vietnam years, almost twice as many young American men died from suicide as there were combat deaths. Yet suicide is less visible in our national awareness than murder, AIDS, or war. Religious prohibitions, social taboos, shame, guilt, disgrace, and fear have all contributed to the gap between public perception and the reality of suicide. Suicide remains a most hidden death.

Different times and cultures have understood the act of suicide very differently, and whether or not suicide is in itself "permissible" has a long history of debate. The right to choose death has provoked religious, legal, moral, and philosophical debates that remain unresolved. Suicide has been seen as a crime, a sin, a sickness, or a combination of those three. Statesmen, philosophers, priests, poets, and, more recently, sociologists and psychologists have argued about whether suicide was a heinous crime or the most basic human right, the ultimate sin or the ultimate romantic gesture. They argued about whether or not law, culture, or religion should acknowledge an exception for insanity, and then whether or not the taking of one's own life was, in and of itself, a sign of insanity. The arguments always began with the responsibility of the individual to law, the community, or a god. Those historical categories still inform the attitudes and beliefs that exist in our culture today.

For the ancient Greeks, suicide was primarily a philosophical issue.[22] Socrates believed that the impure body imprisons the perfect soul, and thus stands between it and wisdom, but still a "man should wait, and not take his own life until God summons him." But then he is said to have added, before drinking the hemlock, "as he is now summoning me."[23] Plato and his student Aristotle agreed that suicide is "contrary to the right rule of life," but where Plato posited an obligation to the gods, Aristotle substituted an obligation to the state. Both agreed, however, that the suicide thereby forfeits the right to be buried as a citizen.[24] The Roman Stoic Seneca, writing in the first century CE, essentially agreed that fate is of divine origin and must be accepted and endured, but only up to a point. "The wise man will live as long as he ought, not as long as he can."[25]

The early Christians took issue with any idea that the individual's first loyalty might be to the self, or even to the state. A Christian's first loyalty was emphatically to God. Still, at least in the early years, there was an exception that contemporary scholars estimate up to 100,000 souls took advantage of.[26] Specifically, one had the option of delivering oneself to God, confessed and clean, and going directly to heaven. There was always the little problem of the gap between confession and death into which some little sin, some little sinful thought, might creep. So better yet, if a little persecution could be arranged, martyrdom was an automatic heavenly pass. By the fourth century CE, the Christian Church was facing a virtual plague of suicides that threatened its extinction. Augustine took it upon himself to staunch the flow. In *The City of God*, he closed the suicide loophole by decreeing that to die by one's own hand was "the most monstrous" sin.[27] It was worse even than murder because it was a willful rejection of God's gift of life and hence a rejection of God. Augustine's position is essentially that of the Catholic Church today.

Medieval Christian laws concerning a suicide were neither gentle nor generous. They combined stern Christian prohibitions with age-old superstitions concerning the troubled and restless soul of a suicide and a typically medieval sense of the grotesque. Often the corpse was dramatically and publicly abused, with stakes driven through the heart, and the body buried at busy crossroads to confuse an errant spirit that might otherwise come back to haunt the living. The family estates of suicides were confiscated, and those whose attempts at self-destruction failed were subject to punishment—in some cases, ironically, death. Thomas Aquinas's thirteenth-century *Summa Theologica* is essentially a restatement of Aristotle and Augustine: Suicide is contrary to "the inclinations of nature," it "injures the community," and it is stealing from God.[28] The punishment would be certain and eternal damnation. Dante, writing at about the same time as Aquinas, dispatched suicides to the seventh circle of hell to hang for eternity, fed on by Harpies whose sharp bite gives agony.[29]

The harshness of European law was transplanted briefly to the original American colonies. Colonial Virginia, for example, required an ignominious burial as well as estate forfeiture to the crown,[30] but by 1647 exceptions were being made for a "mad or distracted man."[31] The "insanity exception" had crept in, but it took another century and the rational, empirical, and, above all, secular attitudes characteristic of the Age of Reason, for the definition of suicide as a disease rather than a sin to achieve status in the American legal system.

The organized religions in the United States, however, have stubbornly resisted, as they continue to resist, redefining suicide in terms of disease. Like the Christians, Jews and Muslims have historically condemned suicide, and for essentially the same reason: deliberate destruction of one's own life is seen as a denial of God and an attempt to thwart divine will.[32] Jewish funeral rites were denied: there was no rending of clothing, no eulogizing, and no burial in a Jewish cemetery.[33] The Qur'an is also explicit in its prohibitions against suicide: "My slave has caused death on himself hurriedly," the Prophet (SAW)[34] is quoted as saying, "so I forbid Paradise for him."[35]

In recent years, there has been a trend toward relaxation of traditional prohibitions and sanctions among some religious teachers and some congregations, but religious doctrines still largely cleave to the belief that suicide is a sin. It has been the law and science, including the social sciences, that have taken the lead in advocating for more compassionate paradigms. But lest that shift be interpreted as progressive or unproblematic, it is perhaps valuable to point out that sin and mental illness have a number of common attributes. Like sin, mental illness is associated with the mysterious, the unholy, the secretive, and the undisciplined. It is the stuff of possession and superstition, of shame and fear. For, above all, the mind, as the location of mental illness, is as elusive and invisible as the soul.

I will argue later that the invisible quality of diseases of the mind and their association with shame, fear, and superstition are still factors in issues of public health policy, access, delivery, and reimbursement. What can be examined and quantified continues to be respected and privileged above what can only be described or felt. But for the moment, I want to address another association that the social scientific paradigm concerning suicide shared with the previous religious paradigm: that of a breakdown in morality.

In the earliest socio-scientific discussion of suicide, Emile Durkheim related it to a condition of social deregulation in which the bonds or norms of society disintegrate. Without such bonds and norms, individuals are left without a moral compass and are vulnerable to despair. Since Durkheim's *Suicide* was published in 1897, the despair that so often leads to suicide has been seen not just as the result of a genetic propensity to mental illness, but as the result of the social circumstances that ease or aggravate such a propensity. In other words, affirmative support structures such as family, community, and meaningful work might serve to counter a genetic inclination, while the psychic devastation of combat experience might amplify the same inclination.[36] Contemporary trauma theory takes Durkheim's premise a bit farther, arguing that experience can actually change an individual's brain chemistry, turning what was a relatively fluid propensity into a hard-wired reality.[37] The PTSD suffered by combat veterans is now thought to involve just such brain chemistry alterations, and it is not yet known whether or not they are reversible.[38]

When Daniel first began talking about suicide in 1971, and even when he made his first attempt in 1975, much less was known about the connections among war, PTSD, and suicide. The same was true for the husbands of other women whose stories are included in this book. News reports and the early scientific studies claiming a more direct correlation between combat and suicide began appearing in the 1980s—*after* PTSD had been officially included in the DSM-III —and the implications were enormous. If the survivors and dependents of suicides were added to the already vast numbers of veterans filing disability claims for other health-related issues, they would add millions to the government's liability for the cost of the war in Vietnam, and, for that matter, any future war. Disability compensation is expensive, and it is far easier to deny a claim for a wounded mind, a wound that does not show, than for an obviously wounded body. Over the years, as more and more veterans gave up hope and the desire to live, as the frequency of their final choices became increasingly obvious to medical and mental health practitioners, the government had a choice: investigate further, in the hope of preventing present and future pain and loss, or camouflage, downplay, and cover up information.

Granted, the relationship between war trauma and suicide is

complex. The origins of individual despair are many and are often related to events and circumstances that precede military service. The invisibility of psychic wounds has made diagnosis more difficult and benefit claims harder to substantiate. And the effects of brain chemistry disruption as a result of combat often manifest themselves only months, years, or even decades later.

That said, what is *not* known about PTSD and its relationship to suicide, combined with all the historically associated stigma and fear, has been exploited by our government and our military institutions. Answers have not been honorably sought, and the absence of answers has been used to deny responsibility and avoid disability claims. Answers would, in all likelihood, be expensive. They would, in all likelihood, tarnish the romanticized warrior image. And information about veterans who take their own lives is not good for recruitment. In the meantime, the grief of the women whose stories I have gathered has not been honored, access to the rituals of mourning has not been accorded them, and communal and financial support that should have been theirs has not been granted.

How has this been allowed to continue? Those veterans who were exposed to Agent Orange have never stopped lobbying to force the government to acknowledge the relationship between their war experiences and their illnesses. Those who were exposed to depleted uranium and other toxic substances in the first Gulf War are still a vocal and visible advocacy group. In the case of suicide, the most appropriate advocates, the veterans themselves, are dead.

Most of us who were left behind were too overwhelmed by grief, guilt, and shame, or too depressed after the chaotic stress of living with a PTSD veteran for six months or twenty-five years, to aggressively pursue redress. A few family members of the deceased tried to access the V.A. healthcare system, only to be met with institutional recalcitrance. When the psychiatrists and the culture told us it was our fault, we folded our hands. A budget item had been sidestepped.

Conspiracy theories to the contrary, the fact that the government has denied a relationship between Vietnam service and suicide does not, of course, prove that such a relationship exists. It is difficult to argue a case based on what has not been done, on nonexistent information. Given the complexity of individual cases, studies involving large numbers of veterans would perhaps have been the best, the most just, way to determine the incidence of war-related suicide. Those studies were not and have not yet been done.

There are, however, two groups of studies, the results of which offer compelling circumstantial evidence: the parallel response of government to other veteran health issues and the response of other governments and institutions to the issue of combat-related suicide. First, the pattern of obfuscation that characterized our government's response to Agent Orange directly parallels its response to the issue of suicide; the same agencies of government responsible for stonewalling on the health effects of Agent Orange were also entrusted with oversight of the government's investigation into the connection between PTSD and suicide. Second, the prevailing American response to that connection differs markedly from that of other countries, such as Australia, our ally in Vietnam.

In the decades following the war in Vietnam, the impetus for advocacy came largely from two groups of veterans. Those living with PTSD gained traction in their efforts with the inclusion of their illness in the DSM-III, but at the same time a whole new category of complaints began to emerge. Veterans and their children were suffering a wide variety of physical illnesses that they believed were linked to service in Vietnam, specifically to exposure to Agent Orange and other dioxin-based herbicides. When veterans sought compensation for these illnesses, they were stonewalled. By 1983, more than 106,000 veterans had requested and received Agent Orange examinations at V.A. facilities.[39] The V.A. had awarded compensation to 1,461 veterans, claiming that the only disease proven to have a direct causal link to dioxin exposure was a skin rash.[40]

In response to the activism of veterans concerned about the long-term health effects of Agent Orange exposure—and a growing body of scientific evidence that encouraged their fears and supported their claims—Congress passed the Veterans' Dioxin and Radiation Exposure Compensation Standards Act of 1984. That act required the V.A. to decide the merit of claims by giving veterans "the benefit of the doubt" when there was an "increased risk" or a "significant correlation" between dioxin and their illnesses.[41] Responsibility for conducting investigations into dioxin-related illnesses was taken away from the V.A. and given to the CDC.

The next twenty years are a litany of shame. The V.A., in direct opposition to the congressional directive and subsequently that of the courts, continued to use a cause-and-effect standard, denying the vast majority of veterans' claims.[42] The CDC, for its part, produced a series of studies ostensibly designed to track the ways the war in Vietnam had affected the lives of veterans. The *Vietnam Experience Study* was actually four studies: "The Health Status of Vietnam Veterans,"[43] "The Selected Cancer Study,"[44] "The Agent Orange Exposure Study,"[45] and "Postservice Mortality Among Vietnam Veterans."[46] All four were deeply, cravenly unsound. Admiral Elmo Zumwalt, testifying before the Department of Veterans Affairs in 1990, called them "so flawed as to be useless,"[47] showing "a discernible pattern, if not outright governmental collaboration, to deny compensation to Vietnam Veterans."[48]

Zumwalt had very personal reasons for attacking the CDC's studies. As commander of U.S. naval forces in Vietnam from 1968 to 1974, he supervised the spraying of Agent Orange. His son, who had served under his command, died in 1988 of an Agent Orange cancer. The father subsequently became an eloquent and tireless advocate for veterans' health benefits. He held the Reagan White House responsible for orchestrating the cover-up, calling the coordinators "a cabal . . . which had as its assignment the manipulation of government studies" because "it would be costly for the government . . . and corporations would be exposed to tort liabilities."[49]

Zumwalt's conclusion that the study results "suggested not merely disagreements in data evaluation, but the perpetration of fraudulent conclusions" led him to gather for Congress refutations of the contaminated conclusions by outside evaluators.[50] His testimony points to the available information the CDC scientists chose to ignore and documents the ways in which the Veterans Administration made use of the CDC conclusions to circumvent the express wishes of Congress.

"The Health Status of Vietnam Veterans," for example, contradicted the evidence of numerous independent studies (including those of Dow Chemical, the primary manufacturer of Agent Orange)[51] in claiming that the only difference between the health of Vietnam veterans and Vietnam-era veterans (veterans who were in the service during the war years, but were not stationed in Vietnam) was that those who had served in Vietnam had "more hearing loss." The "Health Status" study also claimed there was no difference in the rate of birth defects among the children of Vietnam veterans, in defiance of even military acknowledgment to the contrary. Similarly, "The Selected Cancer Study" found only a slightly elevated risk from dioxin for non-Hodgkin's lymphoma, and none for five others categories of cancer, all of which had, at the time, been shown to have statistically significant correlations with dioxin exposure, and all of which have since been included on the list of service-connected cancers warranting compensation.[52]

The "Agent Orange Exposure Study" was canceled in 1986, after four years and $63 million in federal funds, because the military claimed it was impossible to determine individual "exposure status."[53] That claim was challenged at the time by Richard Christian, a retired army lieutenant colonel and the head of the Pentagon's Environmental Study Group. Christian testified before Congress[54] that not only was this conclusion false, but that he had personally informed the CDC that adequate military records existed to identify company-specific movements as well as spray locations.[55] In 2003, Christian was part of Dr. Jeanne Stellman's team of scientists who finally managed to untangle the knot of information and disinformation. Their study finally provided the incontrovertible proof veterans could use to establish their wartime herbicide exposure in Vietnam.[56]

The Agent Orange Act of 1991 pointedly assigned further study to the National Academy of Sciences, "an independent nonprofit scientific organization with appropriate expertise which is not part of the Federal Government," to oversee, review, and evaluate available scientific evidence.[57] Since then, thirty-eight diseases have been added to the list recognized by the V.A. as service-related to dioxin exposure, and that does not include birth defects in veterans' children. The V.A. still does not make it easy to receive compensation for the illnesses on the list. In March 2002, David Brunnstrom reported that, to date, "More than 100,000 veterans have asked the U.S. Veterans Administration for help for illnesses they believe are linked to Vietnam service. Only 7,500 are receiving any assistance."[58]

The fourth segment of the CDC's *Vietnam Experience Study,* "Post-Service Mortality Among Vietnam Veterans," was published in 1987 in the *Journal of the American Medical Association.*[59] In keeping with the other segments of the study, the CDC challenged the conclusions of nongovernmental researchers such as Hearst et al., finding only a slight rise in suicide rates for veterans—and only for the first five postservice years. After that, "regardless of the place of service," the authors claimed, "the suicide rate among these veterans was not unusual."

In a letter published in the *New England Journal of Medicine,* Hearst et al. explained why the CDC came to such different conclusions from their own.[60] The CDC scientists had used the general male population for their comparison group, ignoring what is known as the "healthy worker effect." Comparing veterans to the general male population "would be fine," Hearst et al. wrote, "if entrants into military service were randomly selected from the general population. In fact, veterans represent a highly selected group of healthy men from which those with serious medical or psychological problems are presumably excluded. This selection process is so effective that veterans have substantially lower mortality rates than the general population for more than 20 years after discharge."[61] Hearst et al. used the lottery to define their comparison group, "men who were alike in every way except for their luck of the draw in the draft lottery."[62] Against that more appropriate control group, the greater number of suicides was marked.

Nonetheless, the CDC's finding that suicide was not a serious postservice health risk might explain why the issue was completely ignored in its next major governmental study, the *National Vietnam*

Veterans Readjustment Study (NVVRS), which, as I discussed in Chapter Three, never mentions suicide or even suicidal ideation. The omission seems irresponsible at best.[63] At worst, it was a cynical strategy to avoid taking responsibility for a population that was emotionally incapable of protecting itself. The increased likelihood of suicide for PTSD vets and the torment of living with thoughts of self-annihilation were central to the literature that preceded and provoked the study,[64] just as they are central to contemporary literature.[65] The *NVVRS* chose to ignore it altogether.

When similar rumors about elevated rates of suicide among their Vietnam veteran population began to circulate in Australia, the initial response of the government was not unlike the American response. Like the early American studies, several Australian studies in 1984 and 1985 found little or no statistical increase in the suicide rate.[66] The problem was "solved."

The rumors continued to circulate, however, and over the next decade, the Vietnam Veterans Association of Australia (VVAA) kept constant pressure on the government to reexamine both the methodologies and the findings of those studies.[67] Their efforts resulted in a series of studies, commissioned by the Australian government,[68] that have made available increasingly nuanced information about the health of Vietnam veterans and their families. Consequently, more illnesses are now recognized by the Australian Bureau of Veterans Affairs as service-connected than by the V.A.

The Retrospective Cohort Study published in 1997, for example, compiled a nominal roll of *all* Australian veterans who had served in Vietnam[69] and compared their vital statistics with those of veterans of the same era who had not served in Vietnam. The study spanned the years from 1982 to 1994 and found, among other things, a 21 percent increase in suicide among the Vietnam veterans.[70] A further study, instigated by information gathered in the original *Cohort Study,* found that "the number of deaths of Vietnam veterans' children from the combined causes of accident and suicide is 250 percent higher than for other young Australians."[71]

To create the Nominal Roll, the Australian government had to get in touch with each of the almost sixty thousand veterans who had served in Vietnam. The willingness to commit this level of time and resources suggests a willingness to invest in the future of their veterans' health. To quote Keith Horsley, one of the authors of the Australian *Cohort* studies, "The Nominal Roll process is slow, but once you have built it you have it forever."[72] To be sure, tracking the three million American veterans of Vietnam would be even costlier in terms of time and resources, but the record of the United States government concerning comparable issues does not suggest a comparable willingness to uncover information that might be useful to veterans.

In the (alleged) absence of documentation, for example, it took the Stellman team at Columbia University until 2003 to recreate patterns of Agent Orange usage in Vietnam so that veterans could prove exposure and claim compensation.[73] Veterans who believe they were given the malaria drug Lariam, which is now being blamed for a myriad of dangerous side effects, including suicide, are similarly faced with an absence of documentation and are advised by the National Gulf War Resource Center (NGWRC) to find a *civilian* neurologist and to get their diagnoses in writing before approaching the V.A.[74] And though the United Nations Sub-Commission on the Promotion and Protection of Human Rights has declared depleted uranium, a component of U.S. armaments since the first Gulf War, to be a "weapon of mass destruction" and its use a "breach of international law," the United States continues to insist it is safe and is stonewalling in the face of multiple studies suggesting otherwise.[75] Given that litany of denial, the government's refusal to keep track of veteran suicides or investigate their origins is hardly uncharacteristic.

In the past decade, two American studies have been done exploring the relationship between PTSD and suicide. The first, in 1994, found the overall mortality rate for Vietnam veterans with PTSD to be 71 percent higher than that of a similar group of non-PTSD vets, based on a sample of 16,257 veterans. A 2003 study also found rates of suicide to be significantly elevated in PTSD vets, based on a sample of 110 veterans. That study concluded that "Prospective studies using larger, national samples of veterans receiving PTSD treatment are needed to better clarify the mortality risk and patterns associated with chronic combat-related PTSD."[76]

In the decades since the war in Vietnam, U.S. veterans who got sick, eventually if not immediately, heard that there were thousands of others suffering similar complaints. They banded together, unionized as it were, and began to advocate for themselves. They were sick, many sick unto death, and they were furious that the V.A. was treating them like adversaries rather than heroes and martyrs.

But what of those who could not advocate for themselves? What of those who had no visible wounds to show, who self-medicated to placate their demons, but whose demons destroyed not only their own inner sanctuaries, but the homes and families they so needed to survive and heal? The role of advocate was left to their wives and their parents and their children, those whose own lives had been traumatized by living with the nightmares and the numbness and the violent outbursts, those who had feared for their own lives and those of their children, those who were grieving, those who were blamed, those who had failed to save, those who had walked away, and those who were secretly ashamed of their relief. They were the ones who looked on while the agencies that should have helped told their loved ones to go home and take pills, get another job, and, like Robert Paterakis (see below), live on eighty-seven dollars a month.

Instead of acknowledging the psychic dangers of military service, instead of investigating ways to protect those who serve and those who care for them, the American military and the government left us in the dark. We were what Joyce Garcia calls "communities of one," not only alone with our grief, but suffering the additional burden of blame. The families whose lives were turned upside down forever were told by community, church, and government that we, as individuals, had fallen down on the job. Or that our tragedies were isolated incidents, and those we loved and lost were simply victims of their own unique despair. Every one of us has, on top of our loss, suffered the anguish of trying to explain to a child or a mother, a friend, and especially to ourselves, why we didn't see it coming, what we wish we had or hadn't done that might have made a difference.

Instead of compassion in our time of grief, we got the bottom line. A simple public acknowledgment when the patterns began to be observed, when the numbers started coming in, that suicide is often a direct result of combat PTSD, would have profoundly changed our expectations, our inclination to seek help, and the load of guilt and failure we have lugged around ever since. Perhaps we *should* have taken up their fight, and perhaps we would have, had we known there were others out there. We thought we were alone. We were exhausted. We had no proof.

In recent years, suicide among veterans has been widely discussed in the international community. In addition to the Australian studies previously mentioned, British papers in 2002 claimed that "More veterans of the Falklands War have killed themselves in the years since the 1982 conflict ended than died during hostilities."[77] In 2003, *The Guardian* (UK) reported, "According to MoD [Ministry of Defense] figures, there have been 107 suicides among veterans of the first Gulf war—compared with 24 who died in combat." The British Gulf Veterans Association argues that hundreds more killed in "accidents" should be reclassified.[78] The Coalition for Work with Psychotrauma and Peace, a nongovernmental agency working in East Croatia, has documented ninety-four suicides among veterans of the Balkan wars in one county in 2001 alone.[79] Writing about Norwegian studies that found a 43 percent increased mortality from suicide and a 28 percent increase in other forms of violent death among their United Nations Interim Forces in Lebanon,[80] Weisaeth et al. identified suicide and suicidal behavior as "the most severe short-and-long-term consequence of serving in the UN peacekeeping forces."[81]

Given our participation in international conflicts and the number of our soldiers whose health—if not their lives—is at stake, the United States certainly has a commensurate stake in gathering such information. This book is being written at a time in which U.S. forces are again at war. While the moral and budgetary implications of the invasion of Iraq are many, the response of the government to combat-related illness should surely be one of them. Suicide has already become an issue for the U.S. troops currently serving in Iraq. In January 2004, the Associated Press reported that the suicide rate for troops in Iraq was 24 percent higher than in the military as a whole and 26 percent higher than the overall U.S. rate.[82]

Today, there are Web sites dedicated to gathering information about Vietnam veteran suicides.[83] Those Web sites are a "virtual Wall," designed to honor those whose deaths have not been officially acknowledged. They are a well-meant effort, but hardly take the place of studies that might finally prove or disprove the relationship among war, PTSD, and suicide. Those studies still have not been done. Those in a position to fund them are apparently not interested in hearing what they might reveal. Armed with information about the frequency of service-related suicide, survivors might find it easier to lay the blame and the responsibility where they rightly belong, and citizens, better understanding the real cost of war, might make more informed decisions. The evidence has been there for decades. But so has deniability.

DEBBIE PATERAKIS

He was back from Vietnam in November of 1973, and it wasn't long after that I ran into him. We knew each other when we were kids. He was fun; he was a dancer; he was outgoing, good-looking. I was drinking at the time myself, and it was party, party, party. We both woke up one day, hung over as hell, and he said, "Let's get married today." I said okay. We partied for two days.

Bob never talked about Vietnam. Only in our arguments, when he was drunk, he would say, "I've killed better men than you." I thought it was just drunk talk, but when it was brought up in his PTSD group years later, he showed me pictures from his file. He said, "See those two guys on the ground. I shot them." Then I realized he wasn't joking.

For twenty years, he was walking around with that stuff in his head. I don't know if he was trying to be strong, but he never showed weakness to me. Maybe he wanted to protect me. Maybe he thought I wouldn't understand.

Gradually his drinking became worse. In 1984, his work told him to go to a treatment center for thirty days or be fired. I committed myself to a treatment center too because he said we couldn't stay together if I didn't. Bob stayed clean, except for once—and except for the medication the V.A. put him on. I never had another drink until after he died.

Then on June 5, 1987, his son, Adam, died. He was seventeen years old and he drowned in a swimming accident. I look back on it today and thank God Bob and I had each other to hold. He went into an emotional tailspin. He knew he was messed up. That's when he said he was going to get some help from the V.A.

He had been hospitalized twice before, but after Adam died, he was in and out of the V.A. so often I lost count. Even though the psychiatrists detected that this was posttraumatic stress disorder, they denied him benefits. The army said they had lost his service records.

"Not confirmed by evidence of record," they said. I even had to bring his snapshots from Vietnam to his PTSD group because he said they didn't believe he had even been there. Everything Bob said in those groups, I think they thought he was blowing smoke out his butt.

In 1993, Bob finally asked the governor of Wyoming to help him get his records from the army, and he got them, no trouble. They showed that Bob's story was true. After six years of appointments and papers, applications, denials, and filling him full of drugs, he finally had the evidence of record, and the V.A. sent him to Cheyenne for a PTSD evaluation. I never saw his evaluation until after his death. Why they never warned me is beyond me. This is what the report said:

> The patient has been in three different PTSD groups. Copies of his most recent psychological testing show significant elevation of PTSD scales, as well as depression scales.
>
> This patient . . . has suicidal ideas that occur for two months at a time, especially worsened by what he calls panic attacks. . . . He jumps and startles when people surprise him from behind, and . . . also has remembrances. He has three nightmares which are repetitive and says he awakens soaking wet. . . . This patient has had 37 jobs since coming back from Vietnam. He says that he is unable to work. . . .
>
> This is a cooperative sad faced man who has tears in his eyes when he describes Vietnam. He has brought papers from Dr. Hackman, a Ph.D. psychologist from Sheridan and these notes written in October of 1993 say "too disturbed for the PTSD program." He is described as having been tested and having severe PTSD.

That's the part I never saw, but this part I did see:

"We carefully considered your disability claim. The evidence establishes the following service-connected condition(s): Post Traumatic Stress Syndrome—10 percent." They gave him $87 a month!

After he heard the news, Bob went on a hell of a drunk. The Highway Patrol arrested him driving on the wrong side of the highway. I truly believe he was trying to kill himself. I told him to appeal the V.A.'s decision, but he said, "Fuck 'em. I'm tired of it."

The last five years of our marriage we slept in twin beds pushed together. He was shaking his legs at night like he was riding a bicycle. He'd wake up in a cold sweat, get up, get a drink of water, smoke a cigarette, and come back to bed—just up and down, up and down, fifty times during the night. And he thought I was out to get him. He called me at work twenty times one day and cussed me out for taking his slippers. He thought I'd taken them because I didn't want him going anywhere. I didn't have his slippers. It must have been some medicine he was on. I thought I was going crazy just being around him. It was to the point where it was my fault if he couldn't sleep or if he couldn't eat, my fault if the phone rang, my fault if he forgot to take a pill, my fault if it was raining.

Every time he went to the V.A., they just gave him more medicine and sent him home. The police counted fifty-four bottles of medicine the day of his death. He would carry it in a paper bag all day long, from room to room. The thorazine made him sit in a chair and drool. Another pill he'd be on sometimes would make him rock in that chair a hundred miles an hour and talk so I could hear him across the street. I believe the V.A. deliberately tries to discourage people, drugs them, and hopes they will give up. Well, it worked. He gave up. On October 29, 1994, he put a gun in his mouth and pulled the trigger. October 29 was Adam's birthday.

The phone calls were day and night, people just wanting to know what happened and why. I didn't know myself! People I never heard from in twenty years would call. Not, "How are you? Are the kids OK?", but, "What happened?" They were just curious. That's a horrible feeling. I felt like people were staring at me, pointing out the girl whose husband did himself in, and I just wanted to crawl under a rug.

My friend Cheryl asked me if I'd received the $1500 from the V.A. for Bob's burial expenses. I called them and asked why they hadn't told me I was entitled to the benefit, and they said because I didn't ask. That really made me mad. They were playing head games with me and I thought, "I'm going to get educated, mister. I'm going to find out what else you keep secret." I decided to take up where Bob left off. I knew he should have been 100 percent PTSD disabled.

I was at it for six years. I had to go to Washington, D.C., to testify, but it was worth it. On October 3, 2000, I received a letter from the Department of Veterans Affairs. It said that Bob's condition had increased in severity. This is six years after his death, but never mind! They raised his PTSD rating from 10 to 100 percent, retroactive to 1993. I won. I won because I was right, and because I just wouldn't quit. But I'm not a veteran on medications. He is the one who truly deserved it.

It's been seven years now, and it's a whole different world for me. I still don't quite know how to act. My whole life was around Bob, and every day I see or hear something that reminds me of him—the way someone walks, or smells, or whistles. If you asked me now if I would marry him again, the answer would be yes. The kids think he's better off where he is. They knew he was suffering. In his suicide note, he told them it was like putting Puppy to sleep. They accepted that.

GLORIA FLUCK

We were part of a generation brought up to believe in family, God, and country. You had your family and your ability to worship God because of the country you lived in. You defended it. You stood up when the flag went by. You honored the president and the office—which I can't say I do now. But then I did.

His name was James Cassel Fluck. He was funny, adventurous, and daring. I was into studying. He was into running around. Then he got his draft notice and enlisted. He wanted to be in the army, Special Forces. I think he looked at it as an adventure. So he went to Vietnam, and I went to nursing school.

When Jim came back from Vietnam, he went into the First Armored Cavalry at Fort Meade, which meant he could come home on weekends. I didn't notice the changes at first. But things started to show. He couldn't be out in a crowd. He didn't sleep a lot, had nightmares. Then he hit a commissioned officer. I think it came from his frustrations and his fears. He had spent twelve months sleeping in the jungle, and suddenly he can't make his own decisions. He was given the choice of a general discharge or court-martial, and he chose the general discharge.

You know, it makes so much sense. You take a nineteen-year-old out of this area (Lancaster County, Pennsylvania), and this area twenty years ago was a lot more country, a lot more laid back than it is now. You knew your neighbor; you didn't lock your house. You take him out of here, you send him thousands of miles away to the jungle. He's never seen a jungle. You put a gun in his hands and say go fight. He's fighting someone he doesn't know or know anything about. He's spending every second of every day wondering if he's going to see tomorrow. It's got to affect you. Especially if you're young.

He didn't want to talk about it. Nothing. Well, once in a while he'd talk about the snakes and the jungle. And once he told me he had shot someone and they later found out it was a kid, around sixteen. In my mind, he just tried to block it out as a chapter of his life he wasn't going to revisit. I respected his silence. I knew that eventually if people want to talk about something, they will. The only comment he'd ever say is, "If I ever have any sons, and there's another war, I will personally drive them to Canada."

He came home and started college, but he just couldn't do it. He got into plumbing, and from plumbing he got into business with a friend of his selling cars. Nothing seemed to work. We went through a phase where, if I lost weight, he said I had a boyfriend, and if I gained weight, I was fat.

The last year was bad. We were in a bankruptcy. He lost his business, the house, everything. I was working full-time, trying to keep the family together. I always took very high-stress, high-level positions because they gave me some time flexibility and a better salary. I was working nights and I really didn't want to leave him alone with the kids, so his mother came. We got up one morning and he had no idea where he was, didn't even know his mom. He was totally and completely out of touch with reality.

When he signed himself into the hospital, they called it acute depression, and blamed it all on the business and family. Nobody connected it to the war. I should have, but when you're so close to a situation, you don't always see. And this was 1976. Posttraumatic stress wasn't even recognized until 1982. I looked at his medical records later. They don't even say he was in the military.

When he was discharged, it was one of those—see you in six weeks. A mental health disaster. He was still on heavy sedation. He'd get up, take pills, go back to bed. He slept twenty-four hours a day. I knew it was serious, but he refused to sign himself back in. He should have been taken involuntarily because he had made threats, but the laws are very difficult to deal with. People used to put people away just to get rid of them. I was an RN who dealt with commitments through the emergency room all the time, and they still wouldn't listen to me. But, he followed through with his threats. When they found him, the mental health person who had refused to sign him into the hospital showed up with the state police. One of my coworkers just looked at her and said, "She told you, and you didn't listen."

Those were hard years, after Jim died. Mike was the oldest and he was only seven. I was working long hours, tired all the time. My parents helped, but money was always an issue. I pulled away from my friendships. Nobody wants to hear about a suicide. I don't go to high-school reunions. I don't go to nursing reunions. I don't want to have to rehash my life. You pull in and you become very private. You don't share at all. So that's the worst part.

The second worst part is you get to this age, and it's like—god, where'd my life go? I don't regret anything I did or didn't do, but it's like, well, this is the part of my life where things should be different. And they're not. I'm still working sixty hours a week and I'm still tired. I turn fifty-five this year. My feet hurt, my knees are gone, my back's gone, I'd like to ease off. It's not the life I would've chosen, but I don't think in life we're given a whole lot of choices. Jim had a choice. I think he would have been in a psychiatric ward for the rest of his life, and that would have been devastating to him. He didn't feel he was worthy of living, and I think that that's why he chose the path he chose. I think his choice probably was the best. Whatever life brings you, you deal with it.

And I was one of the fortunate ones. I had a profession that paid better than a lot of people's. If I had had to raise three kids at minimum wage, where would I have been? It's an election year, and I'm waiting for it to come out again that the problem with the world is single-parent families. That's a slap in the face to every single parent who has sacrificed to raise children to be productive members of society. I'm a single parent and I'm proud of my kids. Two of them have gone through college and come out owing nothing because I have sacrificed to get them through. I haven't asked the government to give them loans, grants, or anything, and yet they tell me I'm the reason society's in such bad shape. It really irritates me. If this had been dealt with right, if I had the benefits of a widow of a battle-related death, my life and my children's lives would have been very different. I would not have had to work full-time. I would have had more time to spend with my kids. And now, I would have enough to retire. To me, if people serve their country and something like this happens, the country owes them. The democracy and the government that you so support and believe in, you shouldn't have to fight. I'm not an activist or anything like that, but I shouldn't have to do this. But they want paperwork going back twenty-five years, and I'm on the third appeal.

Am I angry at him? Yes, some days. Do I feel sorry for him? Some days. Do I wish my life had been different? Well, yeah I do, but if it was, what kind of different person would I be? Someone told me God only gives you what you can handle. I've decided God maybe has a little bit of Alzheimer's and forgets, and he keeps giving me a little more.

CONCLUSION

Daniel was the first person who made me feel really loved. He was achingly sensitive, desperate to be nurtured, and he seemed to want nothing except for me. We got married in 1972, rented an ugly little house in Santa Barbara, and furnished it with orange crates and bulrushes. I grew sweet potato vines on the kitchen walls. My mother sent out wedding announcements and gave us monogrammed towels. I don't think our bathroom had a door, much less a towel rack.

Daniel's sister, Kerry, was fourteen when the local fire department realized that their mother, her bourbon, and her cigarettes were a community hazard. She was committed to Camarillo State Hospital, and Kerry came to live with us. Daniel and I finished photography school, and Kerry finished high school. We were three emotional orphans, living on our own for the first time, taking care of each other as best we could.

My last real memory of Kerry was her sitting with me in the emergency room while Daniel was waking up after his first suicide attempt. He had tubes coming out of every orifice, draining fluids of ominously primary colors into a variety of plastic containers. His face was bloated with poisons and rage as he fought the restraints that prevented him from pulling his plugs. "As soon as I get out, I'll do it again," he screamed at me. "Bitch!"

Feeling extorted by Daniel's threat to try again, and at the same time frightened and helpless, I loaded up my dog and cameras and headed cross-country for home. Back in New York, I found an apartment in the Village and worked as a stringer for the *New York Times*. Daniel's old army buddy Bobby agreed to take him in until he got back on his feet. I am ashamed that, after a year, I went to visit. I wanted to touch once more that feeling of being loved best. I knew I wouldn't stay, and I knew my visit would make things harder for him.

It was a lonely time. Daniel and I wrote letters trying to sort the ways we had failed each other. I kept my favorite picture of him taped to the inside of a kitchen cabinet. He looked like a barely warm-blooded soul fading into a cold blue haze. His beauty still makes me wince. I don't remember Kerry calling to tell me he was dead. I don't remember why I didn't go to the funeral. I can't imagine what I was thinking.

Gone, too, are any good memories of the years we lived together. Almost without exception, what I can remember are the times when I behaved badly. Like combat flashbacks, they are the lurid, guilty remains of those years. There is no balance, no perspective, to my memories. People have fights; they hurt each other; they do ugly things to each other in anger or frustration or immaturity. Doors get slammed. Coffee cups get thrown. Uncivilized, ill-considered, cruel things get said. Sometimes the anger passes and the meanness can be forgiven. Sometimes the relationship ends. Sometimes there is relief, sometimes pain.

But Daniel didn't simply slam a door. He got the last word because he was dead, and the person I was angriest with was the one I needed to mourn. I learned to numb, to distance, and to protect. I rehearsed a version of events that emphasized my own faults and wore it like a secret amulet to protect me from intimacy, from being so hurt again.

When my children were twelve and ten, their father and I separated. I had stayed in this second marriage for too long, ostensibly for the sake of the children, but really because I was afraid that if I left, he too would kill himself. That fear had nothing to do with him. It was a mutation, a rotten seed grown in contaminated soil. In the aftermath of the divorce, my daughter began to complain of ringing in her ears, and I discovered that she had been taking aspirin in large doses to kill the pain in her heart. My son, a gymnast, wrote an essay for school describing his fantasies about tumbling from windows. I got them both into therapy and began to wonder seriously if I was contagious. Suicide seemed to follow me like a devoted dog.

When I finally called Kerry, almost thirty years had gone by. I expected her to blame me for Daniel's death, and I expected her to blame me for having abandoned her. Instead, she insisted on driving the two hours to meet my plane, reserved a room in an airport hotel so we could talk all night, and then took me home to meet her family. She introduced me to her children as Aunt Penny, to friends as her sister-in-law.

It was Kerry who has helped me reconstruct the past, who has offered me a balancing image of who I was. She says I helped her negotiate the bureaucracy of high school. She says I helped nurse her through the melanoma that was discovered on her chest when she was eighteen. She says I played the part of mother, sister, and friend. But perhaps most importantly to me, she remembers that I loved her brother—not always as well as I might have wished, but she remembers how hard I tried.

Daniel's old friend Bobby offered to cook us dinner. Daniel and Bobby had been caught by the draft at the same time, met at induction, and gone through boot camp together. Bobby worked as a counselor during the war and is now a social worker in Los Angeles. I imagined he would have heard terrible stories about me in the year he harbored Daniel, and I imagined too that he would have feelings of resentment at being left so absolutely holding the bag. The dinner we shared was instead filled with hilarity and loving memories. Bobby hated boot camp, hated the war, but he had gathered some great stories from the seditious, stoned moments he and Daniel shared.

It became clear in the course of the evening that Daniel had not told Bobby any more than he had told Kerry or me about his experiences in the war zone. We three were his closest friends, and our pooled memories amounted to virtually nothing. Daniel and Bobby had, however, gone through induction together, and when I pushed Bobby for insight into what it might have been that Daniel had found so intolerable, what might have pushed him over the edge, Bobby came up with a theory that made perfect sense to me:

> It was either Canada, prison, or the army. You can go to Canada, freeze your ass off, leave everything. You can never go home and see your family. When your friends die, you can't go home to bury them. Or you can go to prison and be some-

> body's butt buddy. Or you can join the army and see if you can survive there. That's it. That's all there is. Here you are in a line. Are you going to step forward and swear?
>
> Danny stood on that same line, and when he stepped over it, he would never be the same again. Couldn't be. At that moment, we learned something about ourselves we never wanted to know. When I stepped forward all I thought was, "Can I do this? I will do it! I'll kill somebody if I have to. I'll kill somebody I don't even know. I'm going over and I'm coming home." If you swear that oath, what you are saying to yourself is, "I'll go and do whatever I have to do to survive. I'll be the worst person in the world, because if I'm the second worst, I will die. So I gotta be the worst person there is. I'll kill them. I'll fucking kill them. No question man, I'll chew their faces off. That guy back there, he doesn't exist any more. He's dead. But the new guy, he's coming home no matter what."

According to Bobby, it mattered less to Daniel what he had actually *done* when he was in Vietnam than what he had been forced to acknowledge he was capable of doing. That was a fearsome and abhorrent acknowledgment of an identity I can readily believe Daniel rejected, a face he couldn't bear to look at in the mirror, and finally, someone he chose not to let live.

"THIS MAY NOT BE VIETNAM, BUT, BOY, IT SURE SMELLS LIKE IT."

SENATOR TOM HARKIN

There is a version of history that holds that, after the fall of Saigon, the citizens and policy makers of the United States suffered flashbacks and panic attacks every time someone suggested using American soldiers to resolve an international conflict. The "revulsion at the use of military power that afflicted our national psyche for decades after our defeat," to quote columnist William Safire, became known in the '80s as the Vietnam syndrome.[1] The Vietnam syndrome, in other words, was a national mental illness, a form of collective

PTSD, characterized by the reluctance to go to war, and not by the experience of war itself. According to this same version of history, Grenada, Panama, Bosnia, and Kosovo (to name only those conflicts in which the U.S. military was *directly* involved) afforded tentative little doses of immunizing military action to fortify our depleted national psyche. Desert Storm was the final restorative injection. In his March 1991 victory speech, an exuberant G. H. W. Bush declared us cured: "By God, we've kicked the Vietnam syndrome once and for all! The specter of Vietnam has been buried forever in the desert sands of the Arabian peninsula."

This version of history is tragic. If there ever was such a thing as a Vietnam syndrome (and the numerous American military ventures since the mid-'70s suggest that a reluctance to use military force has been relative at best) it might have been seen as an opportunity, rather than an illness—an opportunity to reexamine closely held beliefs about who we are as a people and as nation. Instead, "kicking" the Vietnam syndrome has not been a feat of healing, but one of forgetting. It suggests that what must be forgotten is what the war in Vietnam truly cost us, in terms of blood and honor and national unity. The calculation of that price, this book argues, must always include the price paid by traumatized veterans and their families. If we forget that, then all the death and sadness and horror will have taught us nothing.

There is, however, another version of history. "The 'post-Vietnam syndrome,'" wrote psychiatrist Chaim Shatan, "confronts us with the unconsummated grief of soldiers, an 'impacted grief' in which an unending, encapsulated past robs the present of meaning. Their sorrow is unspent, the grief of their wounds is untold, their guilt is unexpiated."[2] The post-Vietnam syndrome that Shatan describes, the cluster of symptoms that a decade later would be officially included in the DSM-III as PTSD, has as a central precept that war is an evil that causes irreparable wounds and unending sorrow for those who come too close. Only by remembering them, and they are legion, and by carrying with us the burden of their sorrow, can we honorably weigh decisions about what is worth forgetting, what wars, if any, should be fought, and what should be buried in the sand.

The same notion of impacted grief can be used to describe those of us they left behind. I, and I suspect all of the women in this book, lived the war and its aftermath so intimately and personally that we have suffered a form of secondary PTSD in our own right. We have all felt trapped in cycles of remembering our shattered lives and alternately looking for solace in oblivion, the oblivion that is so often falsely proffered as help: put it behind you and move on. We all would wish some of the pain to go away, but not if the price is emptiness. On the other side of the grief, and the guilt, and the alternating cycles of numbness and pain, all the memories that were sweet and loving beckon.

There were so many moments in which, listening to another widow speak, I felt a profound compassion for her, only to realize it was a compassion I had denied myself. It was so often clear that the telling and retelling was a compulsive search for a version of self who, with practice, would come to find the memories tolerable. We were searching for ways to hold on to what we so loved without losing ourselves. We were looking for forgiveness, certainly, but more to the point, we were/are looking, not for a way to leave something behind, but for the strength that will allow us to carry it along. We choose to feel its weight because it is precious. It has become us, and it is what makes us better lovers, better parents, better citizens.

I am both angered at and frightened by the ways in which amnesia, numbness, and denial—our collective PTSD, as it were—are getting in the way of confronting the costs of this, our newest, war. Had we consciously set out to recreate the situation that led both to the ignominious American defeat in Vietnam and to an aftermath that has continued to claim lives for over thirty years, we could hardly have done a better job than the current situation in Iraq. We have again invaded another country in the name of freedom. We are again treating a civilian population as collateral damage.[3] We have again heard our government characterize those Americans who do not support administration policy as unpatriotic. And, perhaps most crucially for the subject matter of this book, we have again betrayed the soldiers who are fighting in our name, soldiers who were told they would be greeted as liberators and who were given inappropriate training and shamefully inadequate equipment, who were kept beyond their allotted time and asked to risk their lives for reasons that have repeatedly changed as they have been exposed as lies.

I understand that there are many Americans who see this war as necessary and legitimate, and who would disagree with me on many points. I even accept that, however passionate my own feelings, history's final judgment concerning the war in Iraq is beyond the scope of this book. What I am concerned with here, however, is something about which I believe all Americans can, or should, agree: namely that there were lessons made available to us in previous wars, specifically during and after the war in Vietnam, that we have an obligation to keep in mind—an obligation to those we ask to risk their lives in our name. Specifically, this new war will inevitably, predictably, result in psychiatric as well as physical casualties. It is simply no longer reasonable, however politically expedient, to deny them equal respect, compassion, and support.

As I write, there is a growing concern that Iraq may prove to be an even more devastating experience than Vietnam. In October 2004, the army released a new study, published in the *New England Journal of Medicine,* reporting that one in six of all Iraq veterans suffers from PTSD or depression. Given that well over one million U.S. troops have fought in the wars since September 11, 2001 (as of January 1, 2005, the exact figure, according to the Pentagon, was 1,048,884, or approximately one-third the number of troops ever stationed in or around Vietnam during the fifteen years of that conflict), that would mean that at least 166,000 men and women already are living with serious mental illness as a result of their war experiences.[4] But the *Journal* article went on to say that of those soldiers included in the army estimates, fewer than 40 percent have sought professional help, and that those who have *not* sought help are generally the most vulnerable, the most fragile, the most likely to develop serious and lasting symptoms. More ominous still, the data thus far available concern only the acute cases. The delayed and the chronic cases have yet to manifest themselves.

In the face of this evidence, the military's failure to institute changes based on well-documented experience and history is remarkable. There were, in the immediate aftermath of the war in Vietnam, some perfunctory paroxysms of self-criticism and reform. The *Study on Military Professionalism*,[5] which General William Westmoreland commissioned in 1970, addressed some of the most glaring examples of military dysfunction. Specifically, as I discussed in Chapter Three, it criticized the ways in which traditional American military culture and organization in the Vietnam era undermined unit cohesion, ignored the most basic tenets of military psychology, and thereby failed to support and protect its soldiers, both physically and emotionally. Westmoreland shelved that report, and its findings were dismissed. Other studies followed, but as Major Donald E. Vandergriff, a vocal and credible contemporary critic of the army's intransigence, points out, "The Army has considerable experience with a variety of surveys beginning with the *Study of Professionalism*. It is the use of data, not the gathering of it, that has been the primary flaw in the Army's survey efforts."[6]

Into the void left by all this unused and inconveniently embarrassing data, both the armed forces and the U.S. administration have fallen back on clichéd notions of masculinity, heroism, and cowardice. Soldiers may mourn or fear or feel conflicted about the agony they have seen or caused, but they are duty-bound to do so in silence. The entrenched code of military conduct does not admit to loss of heart or mind, and the stigma that attaches is the direct descendant of that which in the past attached to the weak-minded, the malingerer, the hysteric, the sissy.

American soldiers still in Iraq can, in theory, ask to see a psychiatrist if they are upset, but half of those who have screened positive for mental health problems say they are not given time for therapy sessions. More than half say they fear the stigma.[7] They have learned to hide their problems, to seek help outside the V.A. system, to self-medicate. In too many cases, they have turned to domestic or self-destructive violence.

Fort Carson, Colorado, is a reentry point for soldiers returning from Iraq. According to Richard Bridges, the army's Fort Carson spokesman, returning soldiers *must* receive seven hours of counseling. None of the soldiers interviewed by United Press International (UPI) in May 2004 said the army had followed through on that obligation. Kaye Baron, a clinical psychologist in Colorado Springs, who treats soldiers in her private practice and helps the V.A. evaluate the mental health of soldiers leaving the army, told UPI's Mark Benjamin that she thinks the army isn't doing nearly enough to protect the veterans. "Why are they disposing of people? Do they not have the resources? Are they in denial? Is it corruption? I'd like to know," Baron said. "My belief is that we should honor these soldiers and acknowledge that these people are going to be affected."[8]

The soldiers interviewed by Benjamin did, however, refer to the case of another Fort Carson soldier, Staff Sergeant Georg-Andreas Pogany, who was accused of cowardice after he apparently asked his chain of command for help with what he said was a panic attack in Iraq.

On November 23, 2003, a front-page story in the *Denver Post* reported that Pogany, after just two days on active duty in Iraq, caught sight of the mangled body of a dead Iraqi soldier. The body was ripped almost in two, with a large hole and strips of ripped flesh where the man's chest should have been. Pogany said he experienced a "panic attack," found it difficult to breathe and, for hours, couldn't stop throwing up. He sought the help of a chaplain and an army psychologist, both of whom assured him he was suffering a very common stress response and filed reports to that effect.

His commanding officer, however, thought otherwise. In front of Pogany's fellow Green Berets, the commander berated him as "a shit bag" and "a fucking coward" with his "head up his ass." Pogany was stripped of his weapons and sent home to face court-martial for cowardice, a crime still officially punishable by death.

Staff Sergeant Pogany was vilified in the media as a disgrace to his country. CNN ran footage of Jessica Lynch and Pogany subtitled "Heroes and Cowards." Paula Zahn led her evening broadcast with "Heroism and cowardice, both are in the headlines tonight."[9] "How do you fix that?" asked Pogany's lawyer, Richard Travis.[10] Veterans' advocates agree that if soldiers were running scared before Pogany got sent home, there is no way in hell they will report problems now.[11]

The kind of vendetta directed at Pogany has also been directed at members of the media who challenge this administration's world-view. The administration and its neoconservative allies have poured a steady stream of money into think tanks that produce reports that look like science, that have all the compelling charts and numbers, but are in reality not based on research at all. From Darwin to global warming, in spite of overwhelming scientific consensus, these so-called "scholars" have managed to create the illusion of scientific controversy. They are engaged in what the *Department of Defense Dictionary of Military and Associated Terms* refers to as *perception management,* defined as "actions to convey and/or deny selected information and indicators," specifically to influence "emotions, motives, and objective reasoning."[12] "Perception management" is, in other words, double-speak for sleight of hand with truth, or disinformation. The decision by the Pentagon (and many media outlets as well) to exclude the wounded from their published casualty statistics is an example of perception management, and it is important to note that the exclusion applies not only to those soldiers wounded in body, but also to those wounded in mind.[13] Neglecting to keep records of state-side suicides or homicides among veterans is another form of perception management. Neither the Pentagon nor the V.A. has ever kept such records, so statistics tend to be anecdotal, but a small weekly newspaper in western Washington state reported in August 2005 that in their local area alone, ten young people, all soldiers or recent veterans of Iraq or their partners, had been killed or had killed themselves since the 2003 invasion of Iraq.[14]

Steve Robinson, head of the National Gulf War Resource Center in Maryland, says data on such violent incidents are almost impossible to trace, but he believes that the spate of deaths in Washington is not an isolated phenomenon. Last year he tracked "as many as 35 suicides [nationwide], but [he's] sure it's higher now." The National Gulf War Service Center estimates that as many as ninety soldiers and vets have taken their own lives while serving in Iraq or Afghanistan or after returning home.[15] The combination of all these hidden casualties, the suicides and the homicides, the physically wounded and the anticipated 30 percent of *all* veterans who will suffer from PTSD in some form, looms ever more ominously.

Clearly anticipating that PTSD will be difficult if not impossible to keep out of the public debate, the Bush administration and its domestic allies are attempting to preempt the issue; they are trying to claim the moral high ground and the mainstream discourse through perception management. To that end, they are creating what *New York Times* editorial writer Paul Krugman has described as "a sort of parallel intellectual universe, a world of 'scholars' whose careers are based on toeing an ideological line, rather than on doing research that stands up to scrutiny by their peers."[16] American Enterprise scholar Sally Satel, for example, blames psychiatrists for over-diagnosing PTSD and veterans for allowing themselves to be seduced into believing they are really sick. According to her faux science, which has been published in newspapers all over the U.S., there's nothing wrong with the vets that the distraction of a good job wouldn't cure. Unfortunately, she would have us believe, the lazy bums have instead been handed the perfect excuse to just lie back and collect benefits.[17] It's the diagnosis that is ruining lives, and not the horror of warfare.

Compounding the image Satel has drawn of an opportunistic cabal of psychiatrists and veterans using PTSD diagnoses to defraud the public, the V.A. decided in August 2005 to review the cases of over 72,000 veterans who have already been awarded the maximum disability compensation for PTSD. That means that those veterans with the most serious mental problems will have to prove their case all over again. The V.A.'s justification for the move is that their own agents have been inconsistent in awarding benefits and that some veterans have inflated their claims. Aside from the injustice of choosing to reevaluate only those cases where veterans received 100 percent disability and not cases where they were either awarded inappropriately low ratings or unfairly denied disability altogether, the V.A.'s pursuit of the most vulnerable vets with PTSD and the high-decibel accusations of potential fraud promote the stigma attached to mental trauma. "There is flat-out discrimination against PTSD on the part of many people, both in the military and [in] the V.A.," says Rick Weidman, director of government relations at Vietnam Veterans of America. He calls the V.A. review "a biased and bigoted view of neuropsychiatric wounds."[18] Once again, it is the vets who have been made ill by their combat experiences who are being denounced and disavowed, and the timing sends a menacing message to those soldiers who are now returning from Iraq and Afghanistan.

In the same way as combat stress was inexplicably dropped as a diagnostic category from the DSM-II at the height of the war in Vietnam, as suicide was erased from the *NVVRS* study in 1980, and as the effects of Agent Orange poisoning were stonewalled for a decade, bogus ideas about PTSD are now being peddled in the hopes that they will defuse what is already an explosive topic, one that promises to be politically destabilizing, monumentally expensive, and very bad for recruiting. Arthur Blank now predicts that when the DSM-V is formulated, PTSD will have similarly, conveniently, disappeared.[19]

Given that we now seem to have embarked on a vaguely defined war-without-end, it is hardly surprising that the architects of current U.S. military adventurism are attempting to spin the issue of PTSD. Retired colonel Harry Holloway, an army psychiatrist for thirty years, recently told *New Yorker* reporter Dan Baum that "as soon as we ask the question of how killing affects soldiers, we acknowledge we're causing harm, and that raises the question of whether the good we're accomplishing is worth the harm we're causing." Holloway goes on to say that the army is reluctant to admit its psychological casualties because "if we get into this business of talking about killing people, we're going to pathologize an absolutely necessary experience."[20]

I would suggest that it is more than appropriate for soldiers and citizens alike to question, and question deeply, the absolute necessity of every war and whether or not the good we're accomplishing is worth the harm we're causing. Without acknowledging the social context within which the traumatic stress occurs, we condemn ourselves to unending cycles of both individual and national illness. It is the veterans, however, who most immediately pay for our lack of courage and imagination and compassion.

Acknowledging the psychic costs of combat in the service of one's country implies an ethical responsibility to those affected. The connection between combat and PTSD has been firmly established over time. The connection between PTSD and suicide has been established, if not by our own government then by experts in other countries, as "the most severe short-and-long-term consequence" of military service.[21] Some would say that veterans have always complained that government was not doing enough, but, as Baum points out, "providing the same level of therapy that, say, the New York Police Department gives a cop involved in a shooting incident would be an unimaginable burden." At the same time, Baum continues, "Given what combat does to soldiers, it's hard to imagine any amount of services being 'enough.' "[22]

Finally, the military is having difficulty convincing young people to sign up. In spite of intense efforts, the army has failed to meet its recruitment quotas for 2005.[23] Even when territories like American Samoa, where the annual per capita income is $8,000, are aggressively targeted, and in spite of enlistment incentives as high as $100,000 for more skilled personnel, nothing seems to help—not accepting recruits without high-school diplomas, not increasing the age limit for Reserve and National Guard recruits to thirty-nine, not even hiring 20 percent more recruiters. Caught between tough and hungry superior officers and a public increasingly skeptical about this particular war—whatever the inducements—recruiters are having a hard time. In March, the *New York Times* ran an exposé about how they have been managing to feed both beasts. Army records for 2004, the *Times* reported, show over a thousand allegations of recruitment "improprieties," including falsifying documents, making false promises to recruits or telling them outright lies, and suggesting that recruits lie about medical problems or police records. Their own investigations substantiated half of those allegations; the rest they called errors. "Gen. Richard A. Cody, Army vice chief of staff, told Congress on March 16 that he is concerned about whether the Army can continue to provide the troops the nation needs."[24]

Millions of words have been written about our longest war, the war we lost. Threaded through the justifications, the explanations, the criticisms, the excuses, and the apologies, there is often to be found a genuine attempt to disentangle some strands of meaning, some worthwhile lessons from what went so terribly wrong. But there is also a kind of communal numbing or amnesia, a tragic temptation to swathe all the unpleasantness in a cocoon and hope against hope that whatever monstrousness gestates will never find its way out. It is a collective response that mirrors the individual response to trauma: the memory is overwhelming, too painful to integrate, and it begs to be hidden from awareness.

The process of writing this book, for me, has been an attempt to push back against amnesia and numbness, both my own and that of my country. The collateral damage from a thirty-year-old conflict is still being tallied, and the true costs have yet to be acknowledged, much less paid. I am deeply disturbed by the ways in which the temptation to forget, to avoid the pain of the memories, has been encouraged and exploited to serve a political agenda, making it possible to repeat the mistakes of the past. I have tried to tease out the machineries that have distorted and colonized our collective memory. I am interested in sabotaging them in any way possible. The wrong questions only produce solutions that avoid the central issue. Don't we owe it to ourselves to pick apart those aspects of our culture that allow us to cleave to the illegitimate and unjust belief that PTSD is a reflection on the character of the sufferer? Instead of asking why one is afflicted, should we not ask why not another, or why not everyone? Should we not as citizens insist on communalizing the responsibility of caring for the wounded among us? Is it time to check our indulgence in fear and our reliance on military power? Is it time to stop being what Chaim Shatan calls "stretcher-bearers of the social order" and instead "try to eliminate the sources of PTSD in the social order"? If not, Shatan warns, "PTSD—an outgrowth of war and persecution—will remain with us unchanged—under whatever name from shellshock to K.Z. syndrome, from DSM-III to DSM-X."

Horace said that it is a sweet and fitting thing to die for one's country. However hollow and inadequate a comfort that might seem to those who are left with memories and a folded flag, the sentiment is still central to the allure and romance of military culture. I have never heard it suggested that there is anything sweet or fitting about being a psychiatric casualty for one's country, though surely veterans who were injured in their minds pledged the same and risked as much as their fallen comrades. Nothing that has been learned about PTSD has done anything to challenge that inequity. The psychically wounded are not even counted as official casualties. Yet when those veterans can no longer tolerate their injuries, when what they have learned about themselves or the world they have inherited becomes unbearable, their injuries are as fatal as any bullet or bomb.

Those injuries to mind, and the deaths they so often provoke, do not deserve to be erased. They deserve to be included in an honest and honorable reckoning of war's cost. They deserve to have a public as well as a private meaning. Perhaps the naked magnitude of the cost will convince us that finding peaceful solutions to our problems, though a tall order, offers a compelling, motivating ideal. Perhaps we can come a little closer if we accept the truth that war itself is an illness that sickens our society as surely and in much the same way as it sickens our citizens and our soldiers. When we, both as a nation and as part of an international community, decide that we must find a cure, memory will be a good place to start.

ACKNOWLEDGMENTS

This has been a hard book to write because the material is so close, so intimate, and still so raw. It would have been harder still without the support of a number of people who eased my process in ways for which I will be eternally grateful. First, Kerry has been the loyal caretaker of our shared memories for decades. She has lovingly helped me shape a gentler version of my history and taught me that pain can be sacred. To my brave friends, Joyce Garcia, Judy James, Maryallyn and Jean Marie Fisher, Emilia Parrish, Linda Robideau, Debbie Paterakis, Barbara and Kim Chism, Gloria Fluck, Ruth Murtaugh, and Paula Elvick, I cannot extend a deep enough gratitude. I like to think that in some ways this process has been healing for you, as it certainly has been for me, and I know we all share the hope that our cautionary tales might *at least* spare someone else our experience of isolation. My children, Charlie and Sophie, gave me the reason and the courage. And Elana, who shares my despair and my joy, and my wonder at a universe that can be so generous with both, has been endlessly patient as first reader and editor. She used her own glittering brilliance to find order in the chaos of my thoughts, words, and feelings, and loved this book with a fierceness I often had to borrow. I never forget what a lonely walk this would be without you.

Bobby Lanz loved Daniel, took him in when he was truly bereft, and offered me another way to think about what happened. Sheila Okin is always the wise woman in my life. And Brian Halley, my editor at Beacon, managed a truly impressive balance of supportive, ruthless, and right, making this a much better book.

Others who were kind and generous with their time, their expertise, their organizations, or their resources include Charlotte Sheedy, Jim Lomax, Alan Jones, Donna Holland Barnes, Keith Horsley, Steve Pennington, Arthur Egendorf, Sam Bloom, Pat O'Toole, Jennifer Selin, Bev Donovan, Ruth Coder Fitzgerald, Alvin F. Poussaint, Amy Alexander, Louvon B. Brown, Gaspar Falzone, Cynthia Falzone, Joy Ilam, Altha Stewart, Genevieve Douglass, Pauline Laurent, Patty Lee, Tracee Bryant, Mike Gillen, Kent Drescher, Rumi Kato Price, Dan and Lynda King, Marilyn Koenig, Moekie Porter, Edmee J. Hills, Ron Leonard, Robert Gebbia, Megan Abbott Francisco Muñiz, Ben Chitty, Rachael Prinsloo, Henry Louis Gates, David Davis, Cheryl Glidden, Mike Fluck, Toni Schoonover, and Maury Stern.

I am also grateful to the Ella Lyman Cabot Trust. They generously funded the beginnings of this project in the belief that it held "a promise of good to others."

NOTES

FOREWORD

1. Leon Golden, *Aristotle on Tragic and Comic Mimesis* (American Philological Association, American Classical Studies 29, 1992).

2. For more about this veteran, see *Odysseus in America*, 93–95.

3. Stephen E. Ambrose, *Citizen Soldiers: The U.S. Army from the Normandy Beaches to the Bulge to the Surrender of Germany, June 7, 1944–May 7, 1945* (New York: Simon & Schuster, 1997), 285–286. The people I am referring to as "heaped with honors" are the top leaders who set the training and replacement policies.

4. See Part Three of *Odysseus in America* for an outline of what these preventive measures are.

5. You will notice that I chose my words carefully—enslavement as a social process (e.g., trafficking and prostitution, the literal enslavement of weaker prisoners by more brutal ones in our prisons, various covert forced labor, living on $1 a day and 4 liters a day of water)—is not only very much still with us, but growing.

6. I also believe that, as a practical matter, such a collective security regime would have to intervene to stop wars made by states against segments of their own populations (genocide), in addition to the compelling ethical and humanitarian reasons to stop these. Often a genocide in one country provokes war with at least one other country, usually a neighbor.

7. For a rigorous education about the military-industrial-congressional complex, read the studies by Franklin C. (Chuck) Spinney, archived in Defense and the National Interest, www.d-n-i.net. See especially the "Military in Society" section.

INTRODUCTION

1. U.S. Army Surgeon General, *Operation Iraqi Freedom (OIF) Mental Health Advisory Team (MHAT) Report* (December 16, 2003), Annex A, "WRAIR Report of Soldier Health and Well-Being Assessment," and Annex D, "Review of Soldier Suicides," D-7 and D-62. Available online at www.globalsecurity.org/military/library/report/2004/mhat.htm.

2. *Operation Iraqi Freedom (OIF) Mental Health Advisory Team (MHAT)*

Report, Annex A, "WRAIR Report of Soldier Health and Well-Being Assessment," A-3.

3. Richard Allen Greene, "US Veterans' Invisible Wounds," *BBC News,* UK Edition (August 16, 2005), available online at http://news.bbc.co.uk/1/hi/world/americas/4122602.stm; Mark Benjamin, "Military Injustice," Salon.com, June 7, 2005, http://archive.salon.com/news/feature/2005/06/07/whistleblower/.

4. Richard A. Gabriel, *No More Heroes: Madness and Psychiatry in War* (New York: Hill and Wang, 1987). Cited in Lieutenant Colonel Dave Grossman, *On Killing* (New York: Little, Brown and Co., 1996), 43.

5. Judith Herman, *Trauma and Recovery: The Aftermath of Violence—from Domestic Abuse to Political Terror* (New York: Basic Books, 1997), 47.

6. R. Anderson, "Vietnam Legacy: Veterans' Suicide Toll May Top War Casualties," *Seattle Times,* March 18, 1981, 1; "The War That Has No End," *Discover Magazine,* June 1985, 44; "Vietnam 101," *60 Minutes,* CBS, October 4, 1987 (transcript); "CBS Reports: The Wall Within," *CBS News,* June 2, 1988 (transcript).

7. Air Force Pamphlet 14-210 Intelligence, February 1, 1998: *USAF Intelligence Targeting Guide,* Attachment 7: "Collateral Damage," A7.1, available online at www.fas.org/irp/doddir/usaf/afpam14-210/part20.htm.

8. NVA casualty data were provided by North Vietnam in a press release to Agence France Presse (AFP) on April 3, 1995, on the twentieth anniversary of the end of the Vietnam War. See the Web site *Vietnam War,* "Vietnam War Casualties," at www.vietnam-war.info/casualties/.

9. First and most obviously, the subject matter of any such conversation would be fraught with many feelings, but anger and pain would most certainly be among them. There is still a great deal of bitterness in Black communities about who was asked to fight in Vietnam and at what risk. Too many African Americans were drafted and too many died. Promotions were rarer for Black soldiers, punishments more severe, and service assignments more dangerous. Why would a widow take the risk that a lack of sensitivity to those special circumstances might add another layer of pain to an already devastating experience?

I suspect that another factor might be attitudes within the Black community toward suicide. According to Dr. Alvin Poussaint and Amy Alexander, whose *Lay My Burden Down* (Boston: Beacon Press, 2000) is a rich combination of personal testimony and cultural analysis, Black Americans "have become accustomed to downplaying outward signs of depression or suicidal thinking" (Poussaint and Alexander, 16). Among the reasons for this is "the unmistakable resistance that many blacks have to seeking help from the medical community ... [which] can be traced to a long and sullied track record where blacks and the

American medical psychiatric/psychological establishments are concerned" (14). Poussaint and Alexander also point to the church, which has traditionally taught "that while drinking, drug abuse, spouse abuse, or criminal activity should be forgiven, suicide is a sin that will keep one's soul from entering the kingdom of heaven" (105–6). Also implicit in the church's teaching is the suggestion that having survived three hundred years in the United States, Black people have learned to "bear up" at any cost, to "take (their problems) to the Lord" (105). "In a racist society, there are many ways for black men in severe emotional distress to invite death, and in such an environment, a man might view dying by self-provoked violence as a more 'honorable' way to go" (119). This last conclusion stretches the traditional definitions of suicide, and, given the associated stigma, might well have discouraged women from agreeing to speak with me because they couldn't acknowledge themselves, either publicly or privately, to be the widows of suicides.

Furthermore, the conventional definition of "widow" might have discouraged some economically disadvantaged women from speaking with me. In the '60s and '70s, means-tested social service programs, such as housing subsidies, TANF (Temporary Assistance for Needy Families), food stamps, and Medicare, as well as the tax code, discriminated against married couples and encouraged couples not to legally formalize their relationships. As public policy has influenced the cultural understanding and normative meaning of marriage, it has concurrently influenced the meaning of the word "widow."

CHAPTER ONE: FROM IRRITABLE HEART TO SHELL SHOCK

1. Jonathan Shay, *Odysseus in America: Combat Trauma and the Tensions of Homecoming* (New York: Scribner, 2002), 4.

2. *Diagnostic and Statistical Manual of Mental Disorders (DSM-IV),* 4th ed. (Washington, D.C.: American Psychiatric Press, 1994). See http://omi.unm.edu/PTSD-DSM-IV.html.

3. Judith Herman, *Trauma and Recovery: The Aftermath of Violence—from Domestic Abuse to Political Terror* (New York: Basic Books, 1997), 33.

4. According to myth, the hero Achilles was dipped at birth into a magic potion that would render his flesh as invincible as an immortal's. The spot on the back of his heel, however, where he was gripped by his mother's hand, failed to touch the magic potion and remained dry. It was a spot of vulnerability, an Achilles' heel.

5. Agamemnon enraged Achilles by appropriating his battle prize, a beautiful woman.

6. Jonathan Shay, "Cohesion, Confidence, Command Climate: Keys to Preventing Psychological and Moral Injury in Military Service," in *Leadership: Theory and Practice,* Gene R. Andersen, ed. (Needham Heights, Massachusetts: Simon and Schuster Custom Publishing, for the United States Naval Academy, 1999). Excerpted from a panel of the same title at the Joint Services Conference on Professional Ethics, National Defense University, January 1998. Available online at www.belisarius.com/modern_business_strategy/shay/shay_prevent_psy_injury.htm.

7. Jonathan Shay, *Achilles in Vietnam* (New York: Touchstone, 1995), 20.

8. Nicholas L. Rock, et al., "U.S. Army Combat Psychiatry," Chapter 7 in *Textbook of Military Medicine: War Psychiatry* (Washington, D.C.: Office of the Surgeon General, Department of the Army, 1995), 153. Available online at *Virtual Naval Hospital: A Digital Library of Naval Medicine and Military Medicine,* www.vnh.org/WarPsychiatry.

9. Eric T. Dean, *Shook over Hell* (Cambridge, Massachusetts: Harvard University Press, 1997), 68–9.

10. Dean, *Shook over Hell,* 126–7.

11. John Whiteclay Chambers II, *The Oxford Companion to American Military History* (New York: Oxford University Press, 1999), 212.

12. John Ellard, "Principles of Military Psychiatry," *ADF (Australian Defense Force) Mental Health* 1 (2000): 81, available online at www.defence.gov.au/dpe/dhs/infocentre/publications/journals/NoIDs/ADFHealthAproo/ADFHealthAproo_1_2_81-84.pdf.

13. Dean, *Shook over Hell,* 85.

14. Ibid., 100.

15. *Records of the Colony of New Plymouth in New England,* hypertext version of the Plymouth Colony Laws, based on *The Records of the Colony of New Plymouth in New England,* "Printed by Order of the Legislature of the Commonwealth of Massachusetts," David Pulsifer, ed. (Boston: William White, 1861), 17. Available online at http://etext.lib.virginia.edu/users/deetz/Plymouth/laws1.html.

16. See Chambers, *The Oxford Companion to American Military History,* 750.

17. Chambers, *The Oxford Companion to American Military History,* 750; Dean, *Shook over Hell,* 143.

18. Dean, *Shook over Hell,* 148.

19. Herman, *Trauma and Recovery,* 11.

20. Sigmund Freud, *The Aetiology of Hysteria,* J. Strachey, trans., std. ed., vol. 3 (London: Hogarth Press, 1896, 1962), 203.

21. Herman, *Trauma and Recovery,* 14.

22. Ibid., 13–14.

23. Pierre Janet, "The Mental State of Hystericals: A Study of Mental Stigmata and Mental Accidents" (first published in French in 1893 as *L'État mentale hysterique*), Caroline Rollin Corson, trans., in Robert H. Wozniak, ed., *Classics in Psychology, 1855–1914: Historical Essays* (Chicago: University of Chicago Press, 1999). Cited in Jean Côté, "The à-propos of Pierre Janet in the false-memory controversy," available online at www.provirtuel.com/doc/falsememory.html.

24. Denis Winter, *Death's Men: Soldiers of the Great War* (New York: Penguin, 1978), 129.

25. Paul Fussell, *The Great War and Modern Memory* (New York: Oxford University Press, 2000), 13.

26. Ibid., 13.

27. Ben Shephard, *A War of Nerves: Soldiers and Psychiatrists in the Twentieth Century* (Cambridge, Massachusetts: Harvard University Press, 2000), 40.

28. Ibid., 46–47.

29. Winter, *Death's Men*, 140. In 1993, in light of what had subsequently been learned about PTSD, a campaign was initiated in the British parliament to grant retroactive pardons to those soldiers who had been executed for crimes of desertion or cowardice during the war years. The British prime minister, John Major, refused, justifying his decision with the claim that the practice was necessary to maintain morale and discipline. See Shephard, *A War of Nerves*, 67.

30. Winter, *Death's Men*, 129.

31. Ellard, "Principles of Military Psychiatry," 81.

32. Herman, *Trauma and Recovery*, 21.

33. Gregory Mathew Thomas, "Posttraumatic Nation: Medical Manifestations of Psychological Trauma in Inter-War France" (doctoral dissertation, University of California at Berkeley, 2002), 66–67. Abstract available online at www.gregthomas.net/academics/abstract.html.

34. Shephard, *A War of Nerves*, 47.

35. Albert J. Glass, "Psychotherapy in the Combat Zone," *American Journal of Psychiatry* 110, no. 7 (1954): 729.

36. Glass, "Psychotherapy in the Combat Zone," 729.

37. Chambers, *The Oxford Companion to American Military History*, 165.

38. Rock et al., "U.S. Army Combat Psychiatry," 154.

39. Shephard, *A War of Nerves*, 124. Salmon also acquired the xenophobic biases that would later characterize the draft he designed for the next war.

40. *Neuropsychiatry*, vol. 10 of *The Medical Department of the United States Army in World War I*, T. Salmon, ed. (Washington, D.C.: U.S. Army, 1929), 314. Cited in Shephard, *A War of Nerves*, 129.

41. Rock, "U.S. Army Combat Psychiatry," 155.

42. It also earned him the central voice in Pat Barker's brilliant historical fiction, the *Regeneration* trilogy.

43. William H. R. Rivers, "Freud's Psychology of the Unconscious" (paper read at a meeting of the Edinburgh Pathological Club, March 7, 1917, and published in *Lancet,* June 16, 1917), Appendix I in *Instinct and the Unconscious: A Contribution to a Biological Theory of the Psycho-Neuroses*, 168, available online at Classics in the History of Psychology, http://psychclassics.yorku.ca/Rivers.

44. Ibid., 164.

45. Ibid., 167.

46. Ibid., 164.

47. Ibid., 166.

48. Ibid.

49. Stephen Badsey, "World War I: Mass Politics and the Western Front," bbc.co.uk/history, March 1, 2002, available online at www.bbc.co.uk/history/war/wwone/war_media_01.shtml.

50. Siegfried Sassoon, "Statement against the continuation of the War—1917," available online at www.sassoonery.demon.co.uk/sassdefy.htm.

51. *Neuropsychiatry in World War II,* vol. 2, A. J. Glass et al., eds. (Washington D.C.: Office of the Surgeon General, Department of the Army, 1973), 115. Cited in Shephard, *A War of Nerves,* 244.

52. Sons and Daughters in Touch (SDIT) is an organization dedicated to locating, uniting, and providing support to children and other family members of those who died or are missing as a result of the war in Vietnam. See http://sdit.org/.

CHAPTER TWO: PTSD AND MODERN WARFARE

1. *A Historical Guide to the United States Government,* George Thomas Kurian, ed. (New York: Oxford University Press, 1998), 489.

2. "About DAV: The DAV's Long Tradition of Service," available online at Disabled American Veterans, www.dav.org/about/history.html.

3. Albert J. Glass, "Psychotherapy in the Combat Zone," *American Journal of Psychiatry* 110, no. 7 (1954): 726.

4. Major General Smedley Butler, letter written in 1936 and excerpted in *The VVA Veteran,* April 1995, 30. Cited in Jo Knox and David H. Price, "Healing America's Warriors: Vet Centers and the Social Contract" (paper presented to the 1996 Vietnam Symposium, "After the Cold War: Reassessing Vietnam," University of Texas at Arlington, April 18–20, 1996), available online at www

.vietnam.ttu.edu/vietnamcenter/events/1996_Symposium/96papers/healing.htm.

5. Ben Shephard, *A War of Nerves: Soldiers and Psychiatrists in the Twentieth Century* (Cambridge, Massachusetts: Harvard University Press, 2000), 197.

6. Harry Stack Sullivan, "Psychiatry and the National Defense," in Harry S. Sullivan, *The Fusion of Psychiatry and Social Science* (New York: Norton, 1964). Cited in Davis H. Marlowe, *Psychological and Psychosocial Consequences of Combat and Deployment: With Special Emphasis on the Gulf War* (Santa Monica, California: Rand, 2001), 48.

7. John Whiteclay Chambers II, *The Oxford Companion to American Military History* (New York: Oxford University Press, 1999), 165.

8. G.H. Benton, "'War' Neuroses and Allied Conditions in Ex-Service Men," *Journal of the American Medical Association* 77 (1921): 360–364. Cited in Marlowe, *Psychological and Psychosocial Consequences of Combat and Deployment,* 40.

9. Gordon A. Craig, "The X-Files," *The New York Review of Books* 48, no. 6 (April 12, 2001): 57.

10. Joseph W. Bendersky, *The "Jewish Threat": Anti-Semitic Politics of the U.S. Army* (New York: Basic Books, 2002), 309.

11. Nicholas Lemann, "The Great Sorting," *The Atlantic Monthly* 276, no. 3 (September 1995): 84–100.

12. Shephard, *A War of Nerves,* 199.

13. Ibid., 200.

14. Eric T. Dean, *Shook over Hell* (Cambridge, Massachusetts: Harvard University Press, 1997), 35.

15. Jim Goodwin, "The Etiology of Combat-related Posttraumatic Stress Disorders," in *Posttraumatic Stress Disorders of the Vietnam Veterans,* Tom Williams, ed. (Cincinnati: Disabled American Veterans, 1980), 11.

16. John Ellard, "Principles of Military Psychiatry," *ADF (Australian Defense Force) Mental Health* 1 (2000): 83, available online at www.defence.gov.au/dpe/dhs/infocentre/publications/journals/NoIDs/ADFHealthAproo/ADFHealthAproo_1_2_81-84.pdf.

17. Roy Grinker and John Spiegel published *War Neuroses in North Africa: The Tunisian Campaign* in 1943. Forty-five thousand copies were distributed within the medical community, and for some years it was the seminal text for new military psychiatrists. The authors advocated use of Pentothal to encourage patients to talk about their traumatic experiences, calling the technique "narcosynthesis." It was probably the least effective method for getting soldiers back into combat,

as the availability of suppressed memories was more likely to destroy whatever personality defenses had previously served to mask a soldier's horror. Their rate of return to combat was somewhere around 2 percent. The military did not approve. See Shephard, *A War of Nerves,* 212–215.

18. "In September 1943 the discharge rate for neuropsychiatric disorder was 35.6 per 1000 man strength; by May 1944 it was reduced to 11 per 1000 men strength." Ellard, "Principles of Military Psychiatry," 82.

19. Roy R. Grinker and John P. Spiegel, *Men Under Stress* (New York: Irvington, 1979), 53.

20. Robert H. Ahrenfeldt, *Psychiatry in the British Army in the Second World War* (London: Routledge and Kegan Paul, 1958), 271–273.

21. Ibid., 26.

22. Shephard, *A War of Nerves,* 217.

23. Charles M. Province, *The Unknown Patton* (New York: Hippocrene Books, 1983), available online at http://pattonhq.com/unknown/chap08.html.

24. John W. Appel and Gilbert W. Beebe, "Preventive Psychiatry: An Epidemiological Approach," *Journal of the American Medical Association* 131 (1946): 1470. Cited in Judith Herman, *Trauma and Recovery: The Aftermath of Violence—from Domestic Abuse to Political Terror* (New York: Basic Books, 1997), 25.

25. *Neuropsychiatry in World War II,* vol. 2, A. J. Glass et al., eds. (Washington D.C.: Office of the Surgeon General, Department of the Army, 1973), 115. Cited in Shephard, *A War of Nerves,* 244.

26. Grinker and Speigel, *Men Under Stress.* Cited in Herman, 1997, 26.

27. Herman, 1997, 26.

28. Department of Veterans Affairs, Office of Facilities Management, "70 Years of VA History" (Washington, D.C.: Department of Veterans Affairs, April 2001), available online at www.va.gov/facmgt/historic/va_history_highlights.asp.

29. Shephard, *A War of Nerves,* 330.

30. Robert Youngson and Ian Schott, "Brief History of the Lobotomy," 4, available online at www.u.arizona.edu/ffirmertens/Psych381/lobotomy/lobotomy.htm. Material adapted from Robert Youngson and Ian Schott, *Medical Blunders* (New York: New York University Press, 1998).

31. Benedict Carey, "New Surgery to Control Behavior," *Los Angeles Times,* August 4, 2003, F1.

32. Joel Braslow, *Mental Ills and Bodily Cures: Psychiatric Treatment in the First Half of the Twentieth Century* (Berkeley: University of California Press, 1997).

Perhaps the most notorious lobotomy was performed on actress, radical political activist, and rebel Frances Farmer. Farmer was a communist sympathizer whose run-ins with authority and her parents landed her in the Western State Hospital in Washington, where she was involuntarily lobotomized at the age of thirty-four. See Youngson and Schott, "Brief History of the Lobotomy," at www.u.arizona.edu/ffirmertens/Psych381/lobotomy/lobotomy.htm.

33. Shephard, *A War of Nerves*, 342.

34. P. G. Bourne, *Men, Stress and Vietnam* (Boston: Little, Brown, 1970), 74.

35. Albert J. Glass, "Lessons Learned," in *Neuropsychiatry in World War II*, vol. 2, A. J. Glass et al., eds., 995. Cited in Marlowe, *Psychological and Psychosocial Consequences of Combat and Deployment*, 52–53.

36. Albert J. Glass, "Psychotherapy in the Combat Zone," *American Journal of Psychiatry* 110 (1954): 725–31. Cited in Shephard, *A War of Nerves*, 342.

37. Frank Pace, Truman's secretary of the army, implemented the point system in 1951, just as Glass arrived.

38. Goodwin, "The Etiology of Combat-related Posttraumatic Stress Disorders," 6.

39. Bourne, *Men, Stress and Vietnam*, 74.

CHAPTER THREE: (WHY) WAS VIETNAM DIFFERENT?

1. Now Ho Chi Minh City.

2. Richard A. Kulka et al., *Trauma and the Vietnam War Generation: Report of the Findings from the National Vietnam Veterans Readjustment Study* (New York: Brunner/Mazel, 1990), xxvii.

3. "This is a fairly standard procedure used to snare enlistees. In fact, the military regulations state that only the enlistee, not the military, is bound by the specifics of the recruiting contract." See Matthew Rinaldi, "The Olive Drab Rebels: Military Organizing During the Vietnam Era," *Radical America* 8, no. 3 (1974), available online at www.geocities.com/cordobakaf/gis.html.

4. John Whiteclay Chambers II, *The Oxford Companion to American Military History* (New York: Oxford University Press, 1999), 181.

5. "Channeling" was an official publication of the Selective Service System issued in July of 1965 and sent to all local draft boards. It was withdrawn because of the outrage it engendered, but its policies remained unchanged. See Larry G. Waterhouse and Mariann G. Wizard, *Turning the Guns Around: Notes on the GI Movement* (New York: Praeger, 1971), 203.

6. Jim Loughrey, "Basic Overview of Post Traumatic Stress Disorder," Veterans of the Vietnam War, Inc., 1986, www.11thcavnam.com/ptsd.html or www.haditveteransforum.com/135827.htm.

7. Marilyn Young, *The Vietnam Wars: 1945–1990* (New York: Harper Perennial, 1991), 334.

8. Myra MacPherson, "McNamara's 'Moron Corps,'" Salon.com, May 29, 2002, www.salon.com/news/feature/2002/05/29/mcnamara/index_np.html.

9. MacPherson, "McNamara's 'Moron Corps,'" and Young, *The Vietnam Wars*, 320.

10. In December of 1969 a lottery system replaced the system of draft deferments. It was a more equitable method of selection, but the Armed Forces Qualifications Tests (AFQT) administered to all enlistees effectively preserved the channeling philosophy. Those who had had the advantage of quality educations scored higher on the tests and ended up in skilled technical and administrative units. Those who came from dysfunctional, underserved schools scored lower and were channeled into combat units, where most of the casualties were sustained.

11. Christian G. Appy, *Working-Class War: American Combat Soldiers and Vietnam* (Chapel Hill: University of North Carolina Press, 1993), 27.

12. Ibid., 26.

13. Ward Just, *To What End* (New York: Public Affairs, 2000), 71.

14. Kim Moody, "The American Working Class in Transition," *International Socialism*, no. 40, old series (October/November 1969): 19. Cited in Joel Geier, "Vietnam: The Soldier's Revolt," *International Socialist Review* 9, online edition (August-September 2000): 2. Available at www.isreview.org/issues/09/soldiers_revolt.shtml.

15. Lawrence M. Baskir and William A. Strauss, *Chance and Circumstance: The Draft, the War and the Vietnam Generation* (New York: Vintage Books, 1978), 8–10. Cited in Young, *The Vietnam Wars*, 320.

16. Ibid., 319.

17. Jonathan Shay, *Achilles in Vietnam* (New York: Touchstone, 1995), 20.

18. Jonathan Shay, "Preventing Psychological and Moral Injury in Military Service," Commandant of the Marine Corps Study, 2000, available online at www.belisarius.com/modern_business_strategy/shay/shay_prevent_psy_injury.htm.

19. David Grossman, *On Killing* (New York: Little, Brown and Co., 1996), 318.

20. Ibid., 318.

21. Gwynne Dyer, *War* (New York: Crown, 1985), 103.

22. Peter G. Bourne, "From Boot Camp to My Lai," in *Crimes of War*, Richard A. Falk, Gabriel Kolko, and Robert Jay Lifton, eds. (New York: Random House, 1971), 464.

23. See Erik H. Erikson, *Identity: Youth and Crisis* (New York: W. W. Norton

& Co., 1968), 128–130, or Erik H. Erikson, *Childhood and Society* (New York: W. W. Norton, 1993), 261–264.

24. Dyer, *War,* 108.

25. Ibid., 111.

26. Robert Jay Lifton, *Home from the War: Learning from Vietnam Veterans* (New York: Simon and Schuster, 1973), 41.

27. Bourne, "From Boot Camp to My Lai," 466.

28. Richard Falk, "The Vietnam Syndrome," *The Nation,* July 9, 2001, available online at www.thirdworldtraveler.com/Society/Vietnam_Syndrome.html.

29. John Langone, "The War That Has No Ending," *Discover,* June 1985, 44.

30. S. L. A. Marshall, *Men against Fire: The Problem of Battle Command in Future War* (Gloucester, Massachusetts: Peter Smith, 1978), 54.

31. Dan Baum, "The Price of Valor," *The New Yorker,* October 13, 2004, 46.

32. Ibid., 46.

33. Ibid., 50.

34. Wallace Terry, *Bloods: An Oral History of the Vietnam War by Black Veterans* (New York: Ballantine Books, 1985), 5–6.

35. Grossman, *On Killing,* 251.

36. Peter Kilner, "Military Leaders' Obligation to Justify Killing in War," *Military Review,* March–April 2002, available online at www.leavenworth.army.mil/milrev/english/MarApr02/kilner.htm.

37. Ibid.

38. Tim Weiner, "New Model Army Soldier Rolls Closer to Battle," *New York Times,* February 16, 2005, A1.

39. George C. Herring, "'Cold Blood': LBJ's Conduct of Limited War in Vietnam," in *An American Dilemma: Vietnam 1964–1973,* Dennis E. Showalter and John G. Albert, eds. (Chicago: Imprint Publications, 1993), 64.

40. Chambers, *The Oxford Companion to American Military History,* 769.

41. Jeanne Mager Stellman et al., "The extent and patterns of usage of Agent Orange and other herbicides in Vietnam," *Nature* 422 (April 17, 2003): 681–687.

42. Agence France Presse (AFP), April 3, 1995, "Vietnam War Casualties," available online at www.rjsmith.com/kia_tbl.html.

43. Reed Irvine, ed., "Ben Tre: Did Being Destroyed Save It?" *Accuracy in Media Report* 16 (August 8, 1977), available online at www.aim.org/publications/aim_report/1977/08b.html#3.

44. Stanley Karnow, "Ho Chi Minh: He married nationalism to communism and perfected the deadly art of guerrilla warfare," in *The Time 100: The Most Important People of the Century.* See *Time,* online edition, April 13, 1998, available at www.time.com/time/time100/leaders/profile/hochiminh.html.

45. Appy, *Working-Class War,* 233.

46. Young, *The Vietnam Wars,* 314.

47. Murray Polner, *No Victory Parades: The Return of the Vietnam Veteran* (New York: Holt, Rinehart and Winston, 1971), 154, 249. Cited in Appy, *Working-Class War,* 249.

48. James F. Dunnigan, *How to Make War* (New York: William Morrow and Company, 1993), 584–585.

49. Harold G. Moore and Joseph L. Galloway, *We Were Soldiers Once... and Young: Ia Drang—The Battle That Changed the War in Vietnam* (New York: Random House, 1992), 339. Cited in Marlowe, 2001, 112.

50. Guenter Lewy, *America in Vietnam* (Oxford University Press, 1983), 73. Cited in Young, *The Vietnam Wars,* 179.

51. "Asymmetric Threats," chapter 11 of *Strategic Assessment: Engaging Power for Peace* (Washington, D.C.: Institute for National Security Studies, 1998), available online at www.ndu.edu/inss/Strategic%20Assessments/sa98/sa98ch11.html.

52. Colonel David Hackworth, "Maybe this time we'll get it right," WorldNetDaily, *Defending America,* March 30, 2004, available at www.worldnetdaily.com/news/article.asp?ARTICLE_ID=37803.

53. Shay, 1995, 158.

54. Barbara Mikkelson and David P. Mikkelson, "M-16," *Urban Legends Reference Pages,* Snopes.com, July 7, 2002, available at www.snopes.com/military/m16.htm.

55. Jonathan Shay, *Odysseus in America: Combat Trauma and the Trials of Homecoming* (New York: Scribner, 2002).

56. Terry, *Bloods,* 199.

57. *Encyclopedia of the Vietnam War,* Spencer C. Tucker, ed. (Oxford: Oxford University Press, 2001), 4.

58. Terry, *Bloods,* xiv.

59. Ibid., 5.

60. Albert J. Glass et al., eds., *Neuropsychiatry in World War II,* vol. 2, (Washington D.C.: Office of the Surgeon General, Department of the Army, 1973), 995.

61. Grossman, *On Killing,* 268.

62. Davis H. Marlowe, *Psychological and Psychosocial Consequences of Combat and Deployment: With Special Emphasis on the Gulf War* (Santa Monica, California: Rand, 2001), 89–90.

63. Ibid., 90.

64. "How the Vietnam Experience Differed from Previous Wars and Sub-

sequently Predisposed the Combatant to the Posttraumatic Stress Disorder: Delayed and/or Chronic Type," *The DEROS Page!* (Woodland Park, Colorado: PTSD Support Services, accessed September 21, 2005), available at www.ptsdsupport.net/deros.html.

65. House Committee on Internal Security, *Investigation of Attempts to Subvert the United States Armed Services, Part Two: Hearings before the Committee on Internal Security,* 92nd Cong., 2nd sess. (Washington, D.C.: U.S. Government Printing Office, 1971), 6994, testimony of General Bruce Clarke. Cited in Erik Blaine Riker-Coleman, "Reflection and Reform: Professionalism and Ethics in the U.S. Army Officer Corps, 1968–1975" (doctoral dissertation, University of North Carolina, 1997), 28. Available online at www.unc.edu/ffichaos1/reform.pdf.

66. Richard A. Gabriel and Paul L. Savage, *Crisis in Command: Mismanagement in the Army* (New York: Hill and Wang, 1978), 72.

67. Colin Powell with Joseph E. Persico, *My American Journey* (New York: Ballantine, 1995), 148.

68. In a brief presented to the Supreme Court in 2003, three former chairmen of the Joint Chiefs of Staff, former superintendents of the U.S. Military and Air Force Academies, and eleven retired four-star generals opposed the Bush administration's challenge to affirmative action programs, writing "Compelling considerations of national security and military mission justify consideration of race in selecting military officers. . . . In the 1960s and 1970s, the stark disparity between the racial composition of the rank and file and that of the officer corps fueled a breakdown of order that endangered the military's ability to fulfill its missions." See Jerome Karabel, "Race and National Security," *The Christian Science Monitor,* March 29, 2003. Available online at http://search.csmonitor.com/2003/0328/p11s01-coop.htm.

69. James William Gibson, *The Perfect War: Technowar in Vietnam* (Boston: Atlantic Monthly Press, 1986), 116.

70. Appy, *Working-Class War,* 156.

71. Riker-Coleman, "Reflection and Reform: Professionalism and Ethics in the U.S. Army Officer Corps, 1968–1975," 31.

72. Elliott L. Meyrowitz and Kenneth J. Campbell, "Vietnam Veterans and War Crimes Hearings," in *Give Peace A Chance,* Melvin Small and William D. Hoover, eds. (Syracuse, New York: Syracuse University Press, 1992), 133.

73. Appy, *Working-Class War,* 8, 185.

74. Meyrowitz and Campbell, "Vietnam Veterans and War Crimes Hearings," Table 7.

75. Ibid., 16.

76. Grossman, *On Killing,* 272.

77. James Maycock, "War within War," *Guardian Unlimited*, September 15, 2001, available at www.guardian.co.uk/Archive/Article/0,4273,4256062,00.html.

78. Lifton, *Home from the War*, 414.

79. Marlowe, *Psychological and Psychosocial Consequences of Combat and Deployment*, 74.

80. Jo Knox and David H. Price, "Healing America's Warriors: Vet Centers and the Social Contract" (paper presented to the 1996 Vietnam Symposium, After the Cold War: Reassessing Vietnam, University of Texas at Arlington, April 18–20, 1996), available online at www.vietnam.ttu.edu/vietnamcenter/events/1996_Symposium/96papers/healing.htm.

81. Arthur Blank, "Irrational Reactions to Posttraumatic Stress Disorder and Viet Nam Veterans," in S. M. Sonnenberg, A. S. Blank, and J. A. Talbott, eds., *The Trauma of War: Stress and Recovery in Viet Nam Veterans* (Washington, D.C.: American Psychiatric Press, 1985), 74–5.

82. Arthur S. Blank, "Readjustment Counseling Service" *NCP Clinical Newsletter* 2, no. 2 (Spring 1992): 1, 3–4. Available online at www.ncptsd.va.gov/publications/cq/v2/n2/blank.html.

83. Chaim Shatan, "Johnny, we don't want to know you: From DEROS and death camps to the diagnostic battlefield" (paper presented at the founding meeting of the Society for Traumatic Stress Studies, Atlanta, Georgia, September 23, 1985). Cited in Sandra L. Bloom, "Our Hearts and Our Hopes Are Turned to Peace: Origins of The International Society for Traumatic Stress Studies," in *International Handbook of Human Response to Trauma*, Arieh Y. Shalev, Rachel Yehuda, and Alexander C. McFarlane, eds. (New York: Kluwer Academic/Plenum Publishers, 2000), 1. Available online at www.istss.org/what/history.htm.

84. Arthur Blank, "Irrational Reactions to Posttraumatic Stress Disorder and Viet Nam Veterans," 74.

85. Bloom, "Our Hearts and Our Hopes Are Turned to Peace," 4.

86. Lifton, *Home from the War*, 75.

87. Ibid., 35.

88. Ibid., 382.

89. Charles R. Figley, "Weathering the War at Home: War-Related Family Stress and Coping," in *The Military Family in Peace and War*, Florence W. Kaslow, ed. (New York: Springer, 1993), 173–190.

90. House Committee on Veterans' Affairs, *Full Committee Hearing on the Department of Defense and Department of Veterans Affairs: The Continuum of Care for Post Traumatic Stress Disorder (PTSD)*, 109th Cong., 1st sess., testimony of

Alfonso R. Batres, July 27, 2005. Available online at http://veterans.house.gov/hearings/schedule109/jul05/7-27-05f/abatres.html.

91. Alan Fontana et al, *The Long Journey Home IV: The Fourth Progress Report on the Department of Veterans Affairs Specialized PTSD Programs* (West Haven, Connecticut: Northeast Program Evaluation Center, Evaluation Division, National Center for PTSD, 1995).

92. Kulka et al., *Trauma and the Vietnam War Generation,* xxiii.

93. Chambers, *The Oxford Companion to American Military History,* 165.

94. Among the many who quote this statistic, Shay claims to be persuaded and extrapolates convincingly in a note in *Odysseus in America. The Oxford Companion to American Military History* (Chambers, 766) also states unequivocally, "More Vietnam veterans committed suicide after the war than had died in it."

CHAPTER FOUR: THE COLLAPSE OF THE ARMED FORCES

1. David Cortright, "GI Resistance During the Vietnam War," in *Give Peace a Chance: Essays from the Charles DeBenedetti Memorial Conference on the Vietnam Antiwar Movement,* William D. Hoover and Melvin Small, eds. (Syracuse, New York: Syracuse University Press, 1992), 128.

2. Howard C. Olson and R. William Rae, Technical Paper RAC-TP-410, "Determination of the Potential for Dissidence in the U.S. Army," 2 vols. (McLean, Virginia: Research Analysis Corporation, 1971); R. William Rae, Stephen B. Forman, and Howard C. Olson, Technical Paper RAC-TP-441, "Future Impact of Dissident Elements Within the Army on the Enforcement of Discipline, Law, and Order" (McLean, Virginia: Research Analysis Corporation, 1972).

3. Christian G. Appy, *Working-Class War: American Combat Soldiers and Vietnam* (Chapel Hill: University of North Carolina Press, 1993), 244.

4. John Saar, "You Can't Just Hand Out Orders," *Life,* October 23, 1970, 39.

5. Horst Faas and Peter Arnett, *The Daily News,* August 26, 1969, 1.

6. Ibid.; David Cortright, *Soldiers in Revolt: The American Military Today* (Garden City, New York: Doubleday, 1975), 35–6.

7. Cortright, *Soldiers in Revolt,* 35.

8. T. Tiede, "Cu Chi," *The Cleveland Press,* November 22, 1969; Cortright, *Soldiers in Revolt,* 36.

9. "The War in Vietnam," *Newsweek,* April 20, 1970, 51; "Cambodia: We're Cache Counters," *Newsweek,* May 25, 1970, 45; Cortright, *Soldiers in Revolt,* 36; Terry Anderson, "The GI Movement and the Response of the Brass," in *Give*

Peace a Chance, Melvin Small and William Hoover, eds. (Syracuse, New York: Syracuse University Press, 1992), 103.

10. Cortright, *Soldiers in Revolt,* 36-7.

11. *Newsweek,* June 9, 1970, 50; Cortright, *Soldiers in Revolt,* 41.

12. File of Lawyers' Military Defense Committee, in Cortright, *Soldiers in Revolt,* 41.

13. Cortright, *Soldiers in Revolt,* 37.

14. "General Won't Punish G.I.'s for Refusing Orders," *New York Times,* March 23, 1971, A1.

15. Nicholas C. Proffitt, "Soldiers Who Refuse to Die," *Newsweek,* October 25, 1971, 67–8; Cortright, *Soldiers in Revolt,* 38.

16. *New York Times,* April 15, 1972 (no page); Cortright, *Soldiers in Revolt,* 39.

17. Tom Wells and Tod Gitlin, *The War Within: America's Battle over Vietnam* (New York: Henry Holt, 1994), 474; Colonel Robert. D. Heinl Jr., "The Collapse of the Armed Forces," *Armed Forces Journal* 7 (June 1971), reprinted in Marvin Gettleman et al., *Vietnam and America: A Documented History* (New York: Grove Press, 1995), 329.

18. Richard Holmes, *Acts of War: The Behavior of Men in Battle* (New York: Free Press, 1985), 317.

19. Cortright, *Soldiers in Revolt,* 35.

20. Robert K. Musil, "The Truth About Deserters," *The Nation,* April 16, 1973, 496; John Whiteclay Chambers II, *The Oxford Companion to American Military History* (New York: Oxford University Press, 1999), 212.

21. Robert K. Musil, "The Truth About Deserters," *The Nation* 216, no. 16 (April 16, 1973): 495–499.

22. Ibid., 495.

23. Ibid., 498.

24. According to Eugene Linden ("Fragging and Other Withdrawal Symptoms," *Saturday Review,* January 8, 1972, 12): "In World War I, which involved over 4,700,000 American military, fewer than 370 cases of violence directed at superiors were brought to courts-martial. This low ratio was fairly constant through World War II and the Korean police action. It did not change significantly until Vietnam. Since January 1970 alone, a period during which roughly 700,000 Americans were in Vietnam, there have been 363 cases involving assault with explosive devices . . . and another 118 cases termed "possible assault with explosive devices. . . . Officers of the Judge Advocate General Corps have estimated that only about 10 percent of fraggings end up in court."

25. Cortright, *Soldiers in Revolt,* 43.

26. Anderson, "The GI Movement and the Response of the Brass," 105. See also Richard A. Gabriel and Paul L. Savage, *Crisis in Command: Mismanagement in the Army* (New York: Hill and Wang, 1978), Table 3.

27. Anderson, "The GI Movement and the Response of the Brass," 105.

28. Gabriel and Savage, *Crisis in Command,* 41.

29. Ibid., Table 3; Holmes, *Acts of War,* 329.

30. Appy, *Working-Class War,* 246; Wells and Gitlin, *The War Within,* 474.

31. Appy, *Working-Class War,* 246.

32. Lieutenant Colonel D. P Scalard, "The Battle of Hamburger Hill: Battle Command in Difficult Terrain Against a Determined Enemy," Chapter XXIX in Faculty of Combat Studies Institute, *Studies in Battle Command* (Ohio State University Department of History, 2005), available online at eHistory, www.ehistory.com/vietnam/essays/battlecommand/index.cfm.

33. There were several attempts made on Colonel Honeycutt's life, but he managed to make it back to the States alive. See Heinl, "The Collapse of the Armed Forces," 328–9, and Anderson, "The GI Movement and the Response of the Brass," 102–3.

34. Heinl, "The Collapse of the Armed Forces," 329.

35. Saar, "You Can't Just Hand Out Orders," 32.

36. Linden, "Fragging and Other Withdrawal Symptoms," 12; Appy, *Working-Class War,* 246; Saar, "You Can't Just Hand Out Orders," 32.

37. "The War within a War," *Time,* January 25, 1971, 34.

38. Linden, "Fragging and Other Withdrawal Symptoms," 17.

39. Wells and Gitlin, *The War Within,* 474; Heinl, "The Collapse of the Armed Forces," 329.

40. Linden, "Fragging and Other Withdrawal Symptoms," 15; Cortright, *Soldiers in Revolt,* 47; Anderson, "The GI Movement and the Response of the Brass," 105.

41. In September 1971, at Whiskey Mountain, military police served as assault troops against fellow GIs, and in October 1971, MPs were called in to Praline Mountain to protect the company commander, who had been unsuccessfully fragged two nights in a row. See Anderson, "The GI Movement and the Response of the Brass," 105, and Cortright, *Soldiers in Revolt,* 124.

42. Cortright, *Soldiers in Revolt,* 49.

43. Anderson, "The GI Movement and the Response of the Brass," 106.

44. Cited in Anderson, "The GI Movement and the Response of the Brass," 107.

45. Anderson, "The GI Movement and the Response of the Brass," 107;

Cortright, *Soldiers in Revolt,* 126; "'Vietnam Syndrome' Still Haunts the U.S. Bosses," Special *CHALLENGE* Military Supplement, January 2001, available online at www.plp.org/vietnam/vietsuppl1200.html.

46. Cortright, *Soldiers in Revolt,* 127; Anderson, "The GI Movement and the Response of the Brass," 107.

47. Cortright, *Soldiers in Revolt,* 127; "The GI Movement and the Response of the Brass," 107.

48. Cortright, *Soldiers in Revolt,* 127; Matthew Rinaldi, "The Olive Drab Rebels: Military Organizing During the Vietnam Era," *Radical America* 8, no. 3 (1974), available online at www.geocities.com/cordobakaf/gis.html.

49. Henry P. Leifermann, "A Sort of Mutiny: The Constellation Incident," *New York Times,* February 18, 1973, 17.

50. Richard Boyle, "GI Revolts: The Breakdown of the U.S. Army in Vietnam," May 1973, www-rohan.sdsu.edu/ffirgibson/girevolts.htm.

51. "'Vietnam Syndrome' Still Haunts the U.S. Bosses," www.plp.org/vietnam/vietsuppl1200.html.

52. House Armed Services Committee, *Report by the Special Subcommittee on Disciplinary Problems in the U.S. Navy of the Committee on Armed Services,* 92nd Cong., 2nd sess., 1972, serial 17670. Cited in Cortright, *Soldiers in Revolt,* 126.

53. "B-52 Pilot Faces Military Inquiry," *New York Times,* January 11, 1973, A1, and "2nd Pilot Accused of Refusing to Raid North," *New York Times,* January 20, 1973.

54. Anderson, "The GI Movement and the Response of the Brass," 107.

55. "Air Force Takes 3 Officers off Cambodia Runs," *New York Times,* June 6, 1973, 10, and "Rogers Said 'Our Hands Are Clean' on Cambodia," *New York Times,* July 26, 1973, A1; Anderson, "The GI Movement and the Response of the Brass," 107.

56. Marilyn Young, *The Vietnam Wars: 1945–1990* (New York: Harper Perennial, 1991), 284.

57. Stewart Alsop, editorial, *Newsweek,* December 7, 1970, 104.

58. "'Vietnam Syndrome' Still Haunts the U.S. Bosses," Special *CHALLENGE* Military Supplement, January 2001, available online at www.plp.org/vietnam/vietsuppl1200.html.

One petition, signed by 1,500 *Constellation* sailors, demanded that "Jane Fonda be allowed to perform her *Fuck the Army* show on the ship, and when the captain rejected that, some 4,000 appeared at her rally in the city." See Terry W. Anderson, *The Movement and the Sixties: Protest in America from Greensboro to Wounded Knee* (New York: Oxford University Press, 1995), 372.

59. "Connie Eight Skate," *Up from the Bottom* 2, no. 1 (January 17, 1972), G.I.

Publications, San Diego, CA, available online at www.aavw.org/served/gipubs_up_bottom_abstract02.html.

60. Wallace Terry, *Bloods: An Oral History of the Vietnam War by Black Veterans* (New York: Ballantine Books, 1985), xiv.

61. Ibid., xiv.

62. "Black Panther Party Platform and Program," October 1966 (Viet Nam Generation, Inc., 1993), available online at The Sixties Project, http://lists.village.virginia.edu/sixties/HTML_docs/Resources/Primary/Manifestos/Panther_platform.html.

63. James Maycock, "War within War," *Guardian Unlimited*, September 15, 2001, available at www.guardian.co.uk/Archive/Article/0,4273,4256062,00.html.

64. "Letters," *New York Review of Books* 11, no. 8 (November 7, 1968).

65. Maycock, "War within War."

66. Dr. Martin Luther King Jr., "Declaration of Independence from the War in Vietnam" (speech delivered at Riverside Church, New York City, April 4, 1967), excerpt available online at www.ablongman.com/html/jonestour/page18.pdf.

67. Saar, "You Can't Just Hand Out Orders," 33.

68. Maycock, "War within War."

69. The 1970 combat refusals mentioned before, at Camp Evans and Camp Eagle, both involved Black soldiers.

70. Cortright, *Soldiers in Revolt*, 40.

71. Rod Oakland, "Fighting Words and Images: The Use of Leaflets in the Propaganda War in Vietnam, 1945 to 1975," available online at The Vietnam Wars, www.btinternet.com/ffirod.oakland/vietnam.htm.

72. Terry, *Bloods*, 167; Maycock, "War within War."

73. Terry, *Bloods*, 212.

74. Maycock, "War within War."

75. Heinl, "The Collapse of the Armed Forces," 329.

76. Richard Stacewicz, *Winter Soldiers: An Oral History of the Vietnam Veterans against the War* (New York: Twayne Publications, 1997), 286.

77. Saar, "You Can't Just Hand Out Orders," 31.

78. Ben Shephard, *A War of Nerves: Soldiers and Psychiatrists in the Twentieth Century* (Cambridge, Mass.: Harvard University Press, 2000), 343.

79. Ibid.; David Grossman, *On Killing* (New York: Little, Brown and Co., 1996), 270.

80. Grossman, *On Killing*, 271.

81. U.S. Department of Justice, Criminal Justice Research Center, *Sourcebook of Criminal Justice Statistics 1977*, 393.

82. Saar, "You Can't Just Hand Out Orders," 40.

83. *New York Times*, June 22, 1971, cited in E. M. Brecher and the Editors of *Consumer Reports* Magazine, *The Consumers Union Report on Licit and Illicit Drugs*, Chapter 57 (New York: Little, Brown and Co., 1972), available online at www.drugtext.org/library/reports/cu/cumenu.htm.

84. Donald Kirk, "Who Wants to Be the Last American Killed in Vietnam?" *New York Times Sunday Magazine*, September 19, 1971, 66.

85. Linden, "Fragging and Other Withdrawal Symptoms," 14.

86. Kirk, "Who Wants to Be the Last American Killed in Vietnam?" 66.

87. Morgan F. Murphy and Robert H. Steele, *The World Heroin Problem*, 92nd Cong., 1st sess. (Washington, D.C.: U.S. Government Printing Office, May 1971).

88. Alfred W. McCoy, "Drug Fallout," *Progressive*, August 1997. McCoy is a history professor at the University of Wisconsin and the author of *The Politics of Heroin: The CIA Complicity in the Global Drug Trade*. "By 1971," he claims, in "Drug Fallout," "34 percent of all U.S. soldiers in South Vietnam were heroin addicts, according to a White House survey. There were more American heroin addicts in South Vietnam than in the entire United States—largely supplied from heroin laboratories operated by CIA allies." See http://www.thirdworld traveler.com/CIA/CIAdrug_fallout.html.

89. Shephard, *A War of Nerves*, 351.

90. "Vietnam Photo Is Challenged," *Washington Post*, January 1986, cited in Vicki Goldberg, *The Power of Photography* (New York: Abbeville Press, 1991), 245.

91. U.S. Army War College, *Study on Military Professionalism* (Carlisle Barracks, Pennsylvania: U.S. Army War College, June 30, 1970), 30.

92. *Study on Military Professionalism*, 38.

93. Heinl, "The Collapse of the Armed Forces," 327.

94. Richard M. Nixon, "Address to the Nation on the War in Vietnam" (televised speech, November 3, 1969), available online at watergate.info, www.watergate.info/nixon/silent-majority-speech-1969.shtml.

95. Young, *The Vietnam Wars*, 248.

96. For a thorough discussion of this, see Jerry Lembcke's *The Spitting Image* (New York: New York University Press, 1998).

97. The name "winter soldier" was taken from Thomas Paine, who, in the winter of 1776, called all those who failed to rally in support of country "summer soldiers" and "sunshine patriots."

98. Milliarium Zero is rereleasing the film *Winter Soldier* in theaters across the country beginning with its opening in New York in August 2005. There will

be a DVD commemorating the thirty-fifth anniversary of the original Winter Soldier Investigation, to be released in early 2006.

99. William Barry Gault, "Some Remarks on Slaughter," *American Journal of Psychiatry* 128 (October 1971): 450–53, cited in Robert Jay Lifton, *Home from the War: Learning from Vietnam Veterans* (New York: Simon and Schuster, 1973), 418.

100. John Kerry, "Vietnam Veterans Against the War Statement by John Kerry to the Senate Committee of Foreign Relations," April 23, 1971 (Viet Nam Generation, Inc., 1993), available online at The Sixties Project, http://lists.village.virginia.edu/sixties/HTML_docs/Resources/Primary/Manifestos/VVAW_Kerry_Senate.html.

101. Lembcke, *The Spitting Image,* 53–56.

102. Lembcke argues persuasively that the myth had its origins in films of the late eighties and early nineties, that the image served to forward the political agendas of Nixon and the first President Bush, smearing the antiwar movements of two generations by successfully reducing public opinion to emotion and symbolism. "In the United States, the idea that the Vietnam veterans had met with malevolence gained prominence during the fall of 1990, when the Bush administration used it to rally support for the Persian Gulf War. After sending troops to the Gulf in August, the administration argued that opposition to the war was tantamount to disregard for their well-being and that such disregard was reminiscent of the treatment given to Vietnam veterans upon their return home." See Lembcke, *The Spitting Image,* 2.

103. Ibid., 188.

104. J. Nordheimer, "Postwar Shock Besets Ex-G.I.'s," *New York Times,* August 21, 1972, A1.

105. *Diagnostic and Statistical Manual of Mental Disorders*, 4th ed. (DSM-IV) (Washington, D.C.: American Psychiatric Association, 1994), available online at www.psychologynet.org/dsm.html.

CHAPTER FIVE: SUICIDE IN THE AFTERMATH OF VIETNAM

1. Jim Goodwin, "The Etiology of Combat-related Posttraumatic Stress Disorders," in *Posttraumatic Stress Disorders of the Vietnam Veterans,* Tom Williams, ed. (Cincinnati: Disabled American Veterans, 1980), 11.

2. R. Anderson, "Vietnam Legacy: Veterans' Suicide Toll May Top War Casualties," *Seattle Times,* March 18, 1981, 1.

3. Duncan Spencer, *Facing the Wall* (New York: Macmillan, 1986); R. Williams, "Introduction," in *Unwinding the Vietnam War: From War into Peace,* R. Williams, ed. (Seattle: Real Comet Press, 1987).

4. "Vietnam 101," 60 *Minutes*, CBS, October 4, 1987 (transcript).

5. "CBS Reports: The Wall Within," *CBS News*, June 2, 1988 (transcript).

6. D. A. Pollock et al., "Estimating the Number of Suicides among Vietnam Veterans," *American Journal of Psychiatry* 147 (1990): 772–776.

7. Norman Hearst, Thomas B. Neuman, and Stephen P. Hulley, "Delayed Effects of the Military Draft on Mortality," *New England Journal of Medicine* 314, no. 10 (March 6, 1986): 620–624.

8. Jacob D. Lindy, *Vietnam: A Casebook*, vol. 10 (New York: Brunner/Mazel, 1988), xvi.

9. Richard A Kulka et al., *Trauma and the Vietnam War Generation: Report of the Findings from the National Vietnam Veterans Readjustment Study*, vol. 18 (New York: Brunner/Mazel, 1990).

10. Lindy, *Vietnam: A Casebook*, 33.

11. Jonathan Shay, *Odysseus in America: Combat Trauma and the Trials of Homecoming* (New York: Scribner, 2002), 290.

12. George Howe Colt, *The Enigma of Suicide* (New York: Touchstone, 1991), 239.

13. Most life insurance policies include a "suicide clause," which *Merriam-Webster's Dictionary of Law* (1996) defines as "a provision limiting the liability of an insurer to a return of net premiums paid if an insured commits suicide within a stipulated period." See http://dictionary.lp.findlaw.com/scripts/results.pl?co=caselaw.lp.findlaw.com&topic=3c/3cee44c224663110e05e8a0cac7c12fd.

14. Alvin Poussaint and Amy Alexander, *Lay My Burden Down* (Boston: Beacon Press, 2000), 49.

15. I am emphatically *not* suggesting that the overuse of deadly force by law enforcement officers can be explained away as provoked by overstressed citizens too frightened or proud to eat their own guns; I am only attempting to describe how the facts of a situation can be legitimately confusing.

16. For example, in their 1986 study, "Delayed Effects of the Military Draft on Mortality," Hearst et al. hoped to get a more accurate picture of the extent of Vietnam veterans' self-destructive behaviors by combining statistics for post-service suicides and deaths from motor vehicle accidents. See also Tim A. Bullman and Han K. Kang, "Posttraumatic Stress Disorder and the Risk of Traumatic Deaths Among Vietnam Veterans," *Journal of Nervous and Mental Disease* 182 (1994): 604–610, and H. Hendin and A. P. Haas, "Suicide and Guilt as Manifestations of PTSD in Vietnam Combat Veterans," *American Journal of Psychiatry* 148 (1991): 586–591.

17. L. E. Davidson et al., "Current Trends in Operational Criteria for Determining Suicide," *Morbidity and Mortality Weekly Report* 37, no. 50 (Washington,

D.C.: Centers for Disease Control and Prevention, December 23, 1988): 773–774 and 779–780.

18. Jeremy Laurance, "Suicide is killing as many as murder and war, says WHO," *The Independent* online, October 3, 2002, available at http://fact.on.ca/news/news0210/id021003.htm.

19. David Satcher, "The Surgeon General's Call to Action to Prevent Suicide" (Washington, D.C.: U.S. Public Health Service, 1999), available online at www.surgeongeneral.gov/library/calltoaction/calltoaction.htm.

20. Ibid.

21. Kay R. Jamison, *Night Falls Fast* (New York: Vintage, 2000), 22–24.

22. The literature and history of the ancient Greeks is filled with suicides. The act was condoned as an appropriate avenue of escape from an intolerable situation; illness, sorrow, and disgrace were all considered reasonable grounds for choosing death. Jocasta, the first recorded suicide in Greek literature, killed herself in shame when she discovered she had married her son, Oedipus. Aegeus threw himself into the sea when he thought his son Theseus had died. In the Greek colony of Ceos, citizens over sixty were encouraged to crown their brows with garlands of flowers and take their own lives. Any taboos against the act derived primarily from prohibitions against murder in general, but especially that of a family member—and the suicide was considered to be such a member—and a fear of the unquiet spirits left behind by violent and untimely deaths of any kind. The hands of a suicide were therefore severed and buried far outside the city, so that the spirit could not again do violence (Colt, *The Enigma of Suicide,* 141).

23. Plato, *Phaedo,* Harvard Classics, vol. 2, part 1 (New York: P. F. Collier & Son Company, 1909–14), 46, available online at www.bartleby.com/2/1/.

24. Plato, *Laws* IX 873c–d, Benjamin Jowett, trans., available online at http://comp.uark.edu/ffimpianal/platolaws_sui.htm.

25. Seneca, *Epistulae,* Epistles 70.4 and 70.14, Richard M. Gummere, trans. (Cambridge, Mass.: Harvard University Press, Loeb Classical Library, 1996), 59.

Another Stoic, Cato, introduced the notion of the "reasonable exit" that has become the model for what is today known as a "rational suicide." Rational suicide assumes that the decision when, where, and how to die is a fundamental human right. It assumes that there are times when life becomes unbearably painful. Whether that pain is moral or spiritual, physical, mental, or political, if it feels as if it cannot be borne, or cannot be borne with dignity, those who believe in rational suicide hold that a person should have the right to choose death.

26. Colt, *The Enigma of Suicide,* 155–156.

27. Ironically, although Augustine makes a weak attempt to base his arguments on biblical authority, aside from the sixth commandment, "Thou shalt not kill," he found the Bible to be less helpful than the Greek philosophers. The Old Testament includes several suicides: Samson caused the temple to fall on his own head (Judges 29–30); Saul, following the death of his three sons, fell on his own sword, as did his armor bearer (Samuel 31:4–6; Chronicles 10:3–7); Ahithophel hanged himself when his son was chosen over him to lead the armies of Israel against King David; and Zimri, king of Tirzah, burned his house down around himself in sorrow over his sins (Kings 16:15–20). In the New Testament, there is, of course, Judas, who hanged himself in Matthew 27:5 (although in Acts 1:18, he "burst asunder in the midst, and all of his bowels gushed out"). And then, of course, there was the original prophet of the faith who invited and went willingly to his death. In no instance is disapproval stated or implied. The deaths are reported in a factual manner, without judgment. Augustine based his arguments finally, not on the Bible, but on the work of three pagan philosophers, Socrates (who took his own life), Aristotle (who is rumored to have done likewise), and Plato, none of whom, as we have seen, was convinced that suicide was invariably wrong.

28. Thomas Aquinas, *Summa Theologica,* Part II.2, Question 64, Article 5: "Whether it is lawful to kill oneself?" available online at http://praxeology.net/summa6.htm.

29. Dante, *The Inferno,* Canto XIII, 100–101.

30. A. Scott, *Criminal Law in Colonial Virginia* (Chicago: University of Chicago Press, 1930), 108 and n. 93, 198 and n. 15. See www.euthanasia.com/history.html.

31. J. Cushing, ed., *The Earliest Acts and Laws of the Colony of Rhode Island and Providence Plantations 1647–1719* (1977), 19. See www.euthanasia.com/history.html.

32. The religions of Asia and Southeast Asia tend to a bit less strident. Vietnamese Buddhists accepted the self-immolation of monks with less sadness or more tolerance, because of their religious beliefs. The media images of those political suicides were profoundly moving to some Americans, but for others, I suspect, they only fed into the "yellow horde" racism that characterized much American rhetoric around the Korean and the Vietnamese conflicts.

33. Many modern Orthodox Jews have taken issue with such practices, and as Rabbi Isaac Klein says, "We also take into consideration the fact that any humiliation of the dead adds to the anguish of the living, and the punishment of suicide affects them rather than the victim. This is a valid consideration, since even the early authorities permit anything that is done out of respect for the living."

Isaac Klein, *A Guide to Jewish Religious Practice* (New York: Ktav Publishing, 1979), 282–3.

34. SAW, that is, *sallallahu alayhi wa sallam,* or "We ask Allah to send His blessings on him (Muhammed)," is a necessary honorific used by Muslims when referring to the Prophet.

35. Sahih Bukhari, *The Hadith of Muhammed,* Volume 2, Book 23, Number 445, M. Muhsin Khan, trans., available online atwww.balaams-ass.com/alhaj/bukhar23.htm.

36. Further complicating the issue, according to Jamison, is "the contagious quality of suicide, or the tendency of suicides to occur in clusters." That tendency "has been observed for centuries and is at least partially responsible for some of the ancient sanctions against the act of suicide" (Jamison, *Night Falls Fast,* 276). *The Admonitions of a Sage,* a story popular in the Egyptian Middle Kingdom (2000 BCE), tells of crocodiles glutted with despairing people who had thrown themselves into the river (Colt, *The Enigma of Suicide,* 130–1). In sixth-century BCE Rome, in response to an epidemic of suicides in the army, the king found it necessary to threaten soldiers who took their own lives with post-mortem public crucifixion, in order to maintain troop strength. A fourth-century BCE Greek response to an epidemic of young female suicides decreed that their bodies would be "dragged naked through the streets with the same rope with which (they) committed the deed" (Jamison, 277). Cluster suicides occurred and continue to occur in families and in communities as diverse as psychiatric inpatients, high-school and college students, Native Americans, Marine troops, prison inmates, and religious sects. In the twentieth century, the phenomenon has become known as the Werther effect, after Goethe's story *The Sorrows of Young Werther,* and is becoming more frequent, according to Madelyn S. Gould, a Columbia University professor who has written extensively on the subject (Madelyn Gould, "Suicide Contagion," reprinted from *Lifesavers,* newsletter of the American Foundation for Suicide Prevention, available online at www.afsp.org/research/articles/gould.html). The 914 people who drank poison with Jim Jones at the People's Temple in 1978, the 80 Branch Davidians who died with David Koresh at Ranch Apocalypse in 1993, and the 39 members of the Heaven's Gate Temple who poisoned themselves together in 1997 are but a few of the most publicized examples. It seems that suicide can either be deterred or encouraged by a group, and that, depending on the group, its embrace can be comforting for some and lethal for others. Statistically, one suicide in a family makes other family members eight times more likely to take their own lives (Colt, 42). That is not a figure that is lost on the women whose stories are included in this book. Fear for the lives of their children is omnipresent. As Carla Fine says,

"When a person you love kills himself, suicide is put on your menu. It becomes a permanent part of your life." See Carla Fine, *No Time to Say Goodbye: Surviving the Suicide of a Loved One* (New York: Main Street Books, 1999), 68.

37. Jonathan Shay, "About Medications for Combat PTSD," October 1, 1995, www.dr-bob.org/tips/ptsd.html.

38. Ronald Duman, "PTSD and the Brain: What's New in Basic Research," an August 2002 interview with Janet Bailey, available online at the National Center for PTSD Web site, www.ncptsd.org/facts/specific/duman.html.

39. *Agent Orange Review* 2, no. 2 (June 1983): 1, available online at www.va.gov/agentorange/docs/Jun83v2-2.PDF.

40. Admiral Elmo Zumwalt (testimony), *Report to the Secretary of the Department of Veterans Affairs on the Association Between Adverse Health Effects and Exposure to Agent Orange,* May 5, 1990, available online at www.gulfwarvets.com/ao.html.

41. Ibid.

42. *Nehmer v. U.S. Veterans Administration.*

43. *The Centers for Disease Control Vietnam Experience Study,* "Health status of Vietnam veterans: I. Psychosocial characteristics," *Journal of the American Medical Association* 259 (1988): 2701–2707; *The Centers for Disease Control Vietnam Experience Study,* "Health status of Vietnam veterans: II. Physical health," *Journal of the American Medical Association* 259 (1988): 2708–2714; *The Centers for Disease Control Vietnam Experience Study,* "Health status of Vietnam veterans: III. Reproductive outcomes and child health," *Journal of the American Medical Association* 259 (1988): 2715–2719.

44. The Selected Cancers Cooperative Study Group, "The association of selected cancers with service in the US military in Vietnam: I. Non-Hodgkin's lymphoma," *Archives of Internal Medicine* 150 (1990): 2473–2483; The Selected Cancers Cooperative Study Group, "The association of selected cancers with service in the US military in Vietnam: II. Soft-tissue and other sarcomas," *Archives of Internal Medicine* 150 (1990): 2485–2492.

45. The Centers for Disease Control Veterans Health Studies, "Serum 2,3,7,8-tetrachlorodibenzo-p-dioxin levels in US Army Vietnam-era veterans," *Journal of the American Medical Association* 260 (1988): 1249–1254.

46. *The Centers for Disease Control Vietnam Experience Study,* "Postservice Mortality Among Vietnam Veterans," *Journal of the American Medical Association* 257, no. 6 (February 13, 1987): 790–795.

47. Zumwalt, *Report to the Secretary of the Department of Veterans Affairs on the Association Between Adverse Health Effects and Exposure to Agent Orange,* 21–22.

48. Ibid.

49. "Advocates reviving Agent Orange health issues want U.S. research in Vietnam," CNN Interactive, November 16, 1998, available online at CNN.com, www.cnn.com/HEALTH/9811/16/agent.orange.

50. Zumwalt, *Report to the Secretary of the Department of Veterans Affairs on the Association Between Adverse Health Effects and Exposure to Agent Orange,* 32.

51. See for example, Zumwalt's testimony: "Although Dow Chemical Company, the primary manufacturer of 2,45-T and 2,4-D, denied this teratogenicity, Dow's own tests confirmed that when dioxin was present in quantities exceeding production specifications, birth defects did occur." Zumwalt, *Report to the Secretary of the Department of Veterans Affairs on the Association Between Adverse Health Effects and Exposure to Agent Orange,* 8. See also J. McCullough, *Herbicides: Environmental Health Effects: Vietnam and the Geneva Protocol: Developments During 1979,* 13 (1970) (Congressional Research Report No. UG 447, 70–303SP).

52. Soft tissue and other sarcomas, Hodgkin's disease, nasal cancer, nasopharyngeal cancer, and liver cancer.

53. The military claimed that, "The greatest problem encountered in the review was a severe lack of information about the exposure of individual Vietnam veterans to herbicides. Except for particular groups, such as the individuals directly involved in spraying operations, information on the extent of herbicide exposure among veterans is practically nonexistent." Department of Veterans Affairs, "Agent Orange Brief, Fact Sheet C3," (Washington, D.C.: Environmental Agents Service (131), VA Central Office, October 2003). Available online at www1.va.gov/agentorange/docs/C3AOBRIEF72003A.doc.

54. Paul L. Sutton, "The History of Agent Orange Use in Vietnam" (presentation to the United States–Vietnam Scientific Conference on Human Health and Environmental Effects of Agent Orange/Dioxins, Hanoi, Vietnam, March 3–6, 2002), available online at www.utahcountyveterans.org/agent orange.html.

55. Richard Christian, head of the Pentagon's Environmental Support Group, testified before Congress in mid-1986 that the records of troop movements and spraying were more than adequate for a scientific study. Christian's testimony was bolstered by two other sources. Retired army major general John Murray had been asked by Defense Secretary Caspar Weinberger in early 1986 to undertake a study to determine if Pentagon records were adequate. . . . Murray also determined that the records for a comprehensive study of Agent Orange were more than adequate. In addition, the Institute of Medicine, an arm of the National Academy of Sciences, had used outside consultants to study reports of troop deployment and Agent Orange spraying to determine if they were sufficient for CDC purposes. Its conclusion: the Pentagon had the necessary records.

The Institute of Medicine also was highly critical of the CDC research methods, charging that it excluded from its study the veterans most likely to have been exposed to Agent Orange (Sutton, "The History of Agent Orange Use in Vietnam").

Christian later participated in the Stellman et al. study, "A geographic information system for characterizing exposure to agent orange and other herbicides in Vietnam," which showed not only that the amount of dioxin sprayed over Vietnam was more than double the government's estimate, but did so by disentangling government records so as to make epidemiological studies possible. See Stellman et al., "A geographic information system for characterizing exposure to agent orange and other herbicides in Vietnam," *Environmental Health Perspectives* 111 (2003): 321–328, available online at www.nature.com/nsu/030414/030414-10.html.

56. Jeanne Mager Stellman et al., "The extent and patterns of usage of Agent Orange and other herbicides in Vietnam," *Nature* 422 (April 17, 2003): 681–687.

57. *Agent Orange Act of 1991,* Public Law 102-4, 102nd Cong., 1st sess. (February 6, 1991), available online at www1.va.gov/agentorange/docs/AOIB10-49JUL03.pdf.

58. In 1984, a U.S. district court approved a global class action settlement agreement for all present and future Agent Orange victims' claims. Under the settlement, the manufacturers would pay $180 million to veterans who were exposed to Agent Orange and then died or became ill. The settlement explicitly cut off compensation for exposed veterans after 1994. On November 30, 2001, a decision by the U.S. Court of Appeals for the Second Circuit (*Stephenson v. Dow Chemical Co.,* 00-9120) allowed veterans who developed cancer after 1994 to pursue cases against more than a dozen chemical companies, including Dow Chemical Co. And it may open the door for others who got sick in recent years to sue. According to the V.A., cash payments to veterans or their survivors averaged about $3,800 each. See *Agent Orange-Herbicide Exposure: Veterans Benefits & Services,* "The Agent Orange Settlement Fund," available online at Department of Veterans Affairs, April 18, 2001, page CAP07-02: www.vba.va.gov/bln/21/Benefits/Herbicide/AOno2.htm.

59. *The Centers for Disease Control Vietnam Experience Study,* "Post Service Mortality Among Vietnam Veterans," 790–95.

60. Hearst et al., "Correspondence," *New England Journal of Medicine* 317, no. 8 (August 20, 1987): 506–507.

61. C. C. Selzer and S. Jablon, "Effects of selection on mortality," *American Journal of Epidemiology* 100 (1974):, 367–72. Cited in Hearst et al., "Correspondence," 507.

62. Hearst et al., "Correspondence," 507.

63. I wrote to all the authors of the study, specifically asking why the subject had been omitted. I got no response. I also asked the question of researchers at the National Center for PTSD Research, and in fact of every scientist I spoke to with regard to the *NVVRS* study. Those who responded at all seemed surprised at the absence, so much so that it was suggested more than once that perhaps I had not read the report with enough care. No one wanted to offer an opinion as to why the subject had been omitted.

64. In his own samples, Lindy claimed, "we have been repeatedly impressed with the frequency and severity of the problem of suicide. One hundred percent of our treatment sample . . . reported suicidal thinking in the past week." The Psychiatric Evaluation Form Lindy used in this study clustered PTSD symptoms. In "the primary cluster, most highly related to PTSD," suicide is listed first. Lindy, *Vietnam: A Casebook,* 269.

65. Maria A. Oquendo et al., "Association of Comorbid Posttraumatic Stress Disorder and Major Depression with Greater Risk for Suicidal Behavior," *American Journal of Psychiatry* 160 (March 2003): 580–582.

66. *Evatt P. Royal Commission Report on the Use and Effects of Chemical Agents on Australian Personnel in Vietnam* (Canberra: Commonwealth of Australia, 1985, study results released 1983) and M. J. Fett, M. Dunn, M. A. Adena, B. I. O'Toole, and L. Forcier, "Australian Veteran Health Studies: The mortality report. Part 1" (Canberra: Australian Government Publishing Service, 1984).

67. The results of the 1984 study were challenged for the same reason that Hearst et al. referred to in their criticism of the American CDC study—namely, the healthy worker effect. The results of the 1985 Evatt Royal Commission, which concluded that Vietnam veterans were "significantly healthier" than the rest of population, have since been entirely debunked—not least because they included "hundreds of pages copied without acknowledgement straight from the submission of one of the interested parties" (namely Monsanto Chemical Company, the manufacturer of Agent Orange).

68. It should be noted that the Australian studies since 1996 have been government reports, and results have not been published in peer-reviewed journals. Nevertheless, independent scientific committees oversaw these studies.

69. Department of Veterans Affairs (Australia), "Nominal Roll of Vietnam Veterans," 1st edition, 1996; 2nd edition, 1997. Currently out of print. For information, contact nominal.rolls@dva.gov.au.

70. P. J. Crane, D. L. Barnard, K. D. Horsley, and M. A. Adena, "Mortality of Vietnam Veterans: The Veteran Cohort Study. A Report of the 1996 Retrospective Cohort Study of Australian Vietnam Veterans" (Canberra: Department

of Veterans' Affairs, 1997), available online at www.dva.gov.au/media/publicat/mortal1.htm.

71. Australian Institute of Health and Welfare, "Morbidity of Vietnam Veterans: Suicide in Vietnam Veterans' Children (Supplementary Report 1)," AIHW Cat. No. PHE-25 (Canberra: AIHW, 2000), available online at www.aihw.gov.au/publications/health/mvv-svvc/.

Since 1997, the Australian government has commissioned a series of studies that have continued to identify illnesses, both mental and physical, related to Australian veterans' Vietnam combat experience as well as their exposure to Agent Orange. These researchers have often determined specific diseases to be service-connected years before their American colleagues. The *Australian Vietnam Veterans' Health Study,* for example, reported in 1998 that leukemia was 300 percent more prevalent among Vietnam veterans than in the general population and therefore established it as service-connected. The V.A. did not do so until 2002 (*Veterans and Agent Orange: Update 2002,* National Academies Press, 2003, available online at www.nap.edu/books/0309086167/html). Breast cancer, including male breast cancer, in Australian veterans was found to be ten times the national average and is recognized as service-connected; see Vietnam Veterans Association of Australia (VVAA) Media Release: "Vietnam Veterans' Children At Risk! Study Reveals Illness, Deformity, 700 Unnecessary Deaths Through Accident and Suicide," March 20, 1998, available online at www.vvaa.org.au/media07.htm. The V.A. has yet to include breast cancer in the list of service-connected illnesses. And though the Australians found a 6000 percent excess of motor neurone disease (amyotrophic lateral sclerosis, otherwise known in the U.S. as Lou Gehrig's disease) in 1998 (VVAA Media Release, "Vietnam Veterans' Children at Risk!"), ALS was determined to be service-connected by the V.A. in 2001, but only for veterans of the Gulf War (Anthony Principi, "Vet-erans on Timely Issues," October 16, 2003, available at Military.com, www.military.com/NewContent/0,13190,Principi_081603,00.html).

Admittedly, it took the Australians the better part of two decades to come to terms with the damage the war had done to their soldiers and citizens, and they certainly had their versions of politically corrupted studies along the way, but for years after the haunting results of the 1998 *Australian Vietnam Veterans' Health Study* were published, U.S. studies have referenced them, dismissed their findings, and continued to deny coverage to U.S. veterans. (See for example the American Cancer Society Web page, "Agent Orange and Cancer," which suggests that the Australian studies were "limited by their small size [and] by the lack of detailed exposure assessment" (www.cancer.org/docroot/PED/content/

PED_1_3x_Agent_Orange_and_Cancer.asp?sitearea=PED). However, 85 percent of almost fifty thousand veterans participated in the study and in the subsequent annual verification studies that confirmed the results of the original study (VVAA Media Release, "Vietnam Veterans' Children at Risk!").

72. Personal e-mail communication from Keith Horsley to Penny Coleman, September 20, 2005.

73. Stellman et al., "The extent and patterns of usage of Agent Orange and other herbicides in Vietnam," 681–687.

74. National Gulf War Resource Center, "NGWRC Lariam Self-Help Guide," September 4, 2004. Available online at www.ngwrc.org/?page=article&id=1874&CFID=424878&CFTOKEN=87939550.

75. James Denver, "Horror of USA's Depleted Uranium in Iraq Threatens World," April 29, 2005. Available online at www.truthout.org/cgi-bin/artman/exec/view.cgi/37/11023.

76. Kent D. Drescher et al., "Causes of Death Among Male Veterans Who Received Residential Treatment for PTSD," *Journal of Traumatic Stress* 16, no. 6 (December 2003): 541.

77. "Falkland veterans claim suicide toll," bbc.co.uk, BBC News, January 13, 2002, available at http://news.bbc.co.uk/1/hi/uk/1758301.stm.

78. Alison Benjamin, "Fatal fallout," *The Guardian,* April 23, 2003, available online at Guardian Unlimited, http://society.guardian.co.uk/mentalhealth/story/0,8150,941306,00.html.

79. Organization for Security and Cooperation in Europe (OSCE), "Report on Community Trauma in Eastern Croatia" (Vukovar, Croatia, August, 2002), available online at www.cwwpp.org/Documents.htm.

80. Siri Thoresen and Lars Mehlum, "Suicide prevention in veterans from peace-keeping" *Suicidologi* 3 (1998), available online at the University of Oslo Suicide Research and Prevention Unit Web site, www.med.uio.no/ipsy/ssff/engelsk/menuprevention/Thoresen.htm.

81. Lars Weisaeth, Lars Mehlum, and Mauritz S. Mortensen, "Peacekeeper Stress: New and Different?" *National Center for PTSD Clinical Quarterly* 6, no. 1 (Winter 1996), available online at www.ncptsd.org/publications/cq/v6/n1/weisaeth.html.

82. Matt Kelley, "US soldier suicide rate up in Iraq" Associated Press, January 15, 2004, available online at www.heraldsun.news.com.au/common/story_page/0,5478,8397337%255E401,00.html.

83. See, for example, The Suicide Wall Home Page, at www.suicidewall.com/, or the "The Vietnam Veteran Suicide Study Project," at http://members.aol.com/forvets/vvssp2.htm.

CONCLUSION

1. William Safire, "Syndrome Returns" *New York Times*, April 30, 2001, A19, column 5.

2. Joel Osler Brende and Erwin Randolph Parsons, "Vietnam Veterans: The Road to Recovery," 1985, available online at www.ncfc.net/ptsdrec.txt.

3. In June, the British journal *Lancet* estimated that 100,000 Iraqis had died since the U.S. invasion began. See Rob Stein, "100,000 Civilian Deaths Estimated in Iraq," *Washington Post,* October 29, 2004, A16.

4. Mark Benjamin, "How many have gone to war?" Salon.com, April 12, 2005, http://archive.salon.com/news/feature/2005/04/12/troops_numbers/index_np.html.

5. U.S. Army War College, *Study on Military Professionalism* (Carlisle Barracks, Pennsylvania: U.S. Army War College, 1970).

6. Major Donald E. Vandergriff, "The Culture Wars," in *Digital War: A View from the Front Line,* Robert L. Bateman III, ed. (New York: Presidio Press, 1999), 197–256 (endnote 64).

7. Dan Baum, "The Price of Valor," *The New Yorker*, October 13, 2004, 49.

8. Mark Benjamin, "Wave of mental problems follows GIs home," UPI, May 13, 2004, available online at Veterans for Peace, www.veteransforpeace.org/Wave_of_mental_051304.htm.

9. Jeanne Marie Laskas, "The Coward," *GQ,* July 2004, available online at www.lariaminfo.org/information/military.shtml.

10. The charge was later dropped to "dereliction of duty," which in itself is punishable by up to six months in a military prison and a less than honorable discharge. Those charges were also later dropped. See E. Kelley. E. and Emery, "GI faces shame of cowardice accusation," *The Denver Post,* November 23, 2003, 1, and A. Gumbel, "US sergeant branded a coward mounts furious fightback" *Independent* (UK), January 12, 2004, available online at http://archives.econ.utah.edu/archives/marxism/2004w02/msg00012.htm and http://psychoanalystsopposewar.org/resources_files/US_sergeant_branded_a_coward_mounts_furious_fightback.html.

11. Laskas, Jeanne Marie, "The Coward."

12. *Department of Defense Dictionary of Military and Associated Terms,* as amended through May 9, 2005, online at www.dtic.mil/doctrine/jel/doddict/.

13. "Iraq Coalition Casualty Statistics," Center for Media and Democracy, May 2005, online at www.sourcewatch.org/index.php?title=Iraq_Coalition_Casualty_Statistics#Fragging.

14. Rick Anderson, "Home Front Casualties," *Seattle Weekly,* August 31 to September 6, 2005, available online at www.seattleweekly.com/features/0535/050831_news_soldiers.php.

15. Ibid.

16. Paul Krugman, "Design for Confusion" *New York Times,* Op Ed, 5 August 2005.

17. For example: Sally Satel, "Saving Our Vets Once They're Home: The right kind of mental health treatment is vital," *Los Angeles Times,* June 13, 2005, B.11; Sally Satel, "Talk About Trauma," the *Wall Street Journal,* May 2, 2003; George F. Will, "Therapeutic culture fanning flames of national enfeeblement," *San Gabriel Valley Tribune,* April 21, 2005, available online at www.sallysatelmd.com/html/on_sgvt.html; House Committee on Veterans' Affairs, Subcommittee on Health, *Hearing on the Status of the Department of Veterans' Affairs Post-Traumatic Stress Disorder (PTSD) Programs,* 108th Cong., testimony of Sally Satel, March 11, 2004. Available online at http://veterans.house.gov/hearings/schedule108/mar04/3-11-04/ssatel.html.

18. Mark Benjamin, "Sticker Shock over Shell Shock," Salon.com, August 9, 2005, www.salon.com/news/feature/2005/08/09/vets/print.html.

19. Sandra L. Bloom, "Our Hearts and Our Hopes Are Turned to Peace: Origins of The International Society for Traumatic Stress Studies," in *International Handbook of Human Response to Trauma,* Arieh Y. Shalev, Rachel Yehuda, and Alexander C. McFarlane, eds. (New York: Kluwer Academic/Plenum Publishers, 2000). Available online at www.istss.org/what/history.htm.

20. Baum, "The Price of Valor," 50.

21. Lars Weisaeth, Lars Mehlum, and Mauritz S. Mortensen, "Peacekeeper Stress: New and Different?" *National Center for PTSD Clinical Quarterly* 6, no. 1 (Winter 1996), available online at www.ncptsd.org/publications/cq/v6/n1/weisaeth.html.

22. Baum, "The Price of Valor," 52.

23. James Brooke "On Farthest U.S. Shores, Iraq Is a Way to a Dream," *New York Times,* July 31, 2005, 18.

24. Damien Cave, "For Recruiters, a Hard Toll from a Hard Sell," *New York Times,* March 26, 2005, available online at www.michaelmoore.com/words/index.php?id=1981.

ADDITIONAL SOURCES

Anderson, R. S., A. J. Glass, and R. J. Bernucci, eds. *Neuropsychiatry in World War II*. Washington, D.C.: Office of the Surgeon General, Department of the Army, 1966.

Barker, Pat. *The Eye in the Door*. New York: Plume, 1995.

———. *The Ghost Road*. New York: Plume, 1996.

———. *Regeneration*. New York: Plume, 1993.

Committee to Review the Health Effects in Vietnam Veterans of Exposure to Herbicides, Institute of Medicine. *Veterans and Agent Orange: Health Effects of Herbicides Used in Vietnam*. Washington, D.C.: National Academy Press, 1994.

———. *Veterans and Agent Orange: Update 1996*. Washington, D.C.: National Academy Press, 1996

———. *Veterans and Agent Orange: Update 1996: Summary and Research Highlights*. Washington, D.C.: National Academy Press, 1997.

———. *Veterans and Agent Orange: Update 1998*. Washington, D.C.: National Academy Press, 1999.

———. *Veterans and Agent Orange: Update 2000*. Washington, D.C.: National Academy Press, 2001

———. *Veterans and Agent Orange: Herbicide/Dioxin Exposure and Acute Myelogenous Leukemia in the Children of Vietnam Veterans*. Washington, D.C.: National Academy Press, 2002.

———. *Veterans and Agent Orange: Update 2002*. Washington, D.C.: National Academy Press, 2003.

———. *Veterans and Agent Orange: Update 2004*. Washington, D.C.: National Academy Press, 2005.

Ellsberg, Daniel. *Secrets: A Memoir of Vietnam and the Pentagon Papers*. New York: Viking, 2002.

Figley, Charles R., ed. *Stress Disorders among Vietnam Veterans: Theory, Research and Treatment*. New York: Brunner/Mazel, 1980.

———. *Trauma and Its Wake: The Study and Treatment of Post-Traumatic Stress Disorder*. New York: Brunner/Mazel, 1985.

———. *Trauma and Its Wake: Traumatic Stress, Theory, Research, and Intervention*. New York: Brunner/Mazel, 1986.

Figley, Charles R., and Seymour Levantman, eds. *Strangers at Home.* New York: Brunner/Mazel, 1980.

Freud, Sigmund. *Beyond the Pleasure Principle.* New York: W. W. Norton & Co., 1961.

Gitlin, Todd. *The Whole World Is Watching: Mass Media in the Making and Unmaking of the New Left.* Berkeley: University of California Press, 1980.

Glass, Albert J. "History and Organization of a Theater Psychiatric Service Before and After 30 June 1951: Volume II." In *Medical Science Publication No. 4: Recent Advances in Medicine And Surgery.* Washington, D.C.: U. S. Army Medical Service Graduate School, 1954.

———. "Introduction." In *The Psychology and Physiology of Stress: With reference to special studies of the Vietnam War,* edited by P. G. Bourne. New York: Academic Press, 1969.

———. "Lessons Learned." In *The History of Neuropsychiatry in World War II,* edited by W. Mullins and A. J. Glass. Washington, D.C.: Government Printing Office, 1973.

Hackworth, Colonel David H. and Julie Sherman. *About Face: The Odyssey of an American Warrior.* New York: Simon & Schuster, 1989.

Hendin, Herbert. *Suicide in America.* New York: W. W. Norton & Co., 1995.

Herr, Michael. *Dispatches.* New York: Knopf, 1977.

Kerry, John, and Vietnam Veterans Against the War. *The New Soldier.* New York: Macmillan, 1971.

Lewy, Guenter. *America in Vietnam.* New York: Oxford University Press, 1983.

Mailer, Norman. *The Armies of the Night.* New York: New American Library, 1968.

———. *Miami and the Siege of Chicago: An Informal History of the Republican and Democratic Conventions of 1968.* New York: New American Library, 1968

Mason, Patience H. *Recovering from the War: A Woman's Guide to Helping Your Vietnam Vet, Your Family, and Yourself.* New York: Penguin, 1990.

Matsakis, Aphrodite. *Vietnam Wives: Women and Children Surviving Life with Veterans Suffering from Post-Traumatic Stress Disorder.* Washington, D.C.: Woodbine, 1988.

———. *Trust after Trauma.* Oakland, California: New Harbinger, 1998.

Minow, Martha. *Between Vengeance and Forgiveness: Facing History after Genocide and Mass Violence.* Boston: Beacon Press, 1998.

Moser, Richard R. *The New Winter Soldiers: GI and Veteran Dissent During the Vietnam Era* (Perspectives on the Sixties series). New Brunswick: Rutgers, 1996.

Nicosia, Gerald. *Home to War: A History of the Vietnam Veterans' Movement.* New York: Crown, 2001.

Niehoff, Debra. *The Biology of Violence: How Understanding the Brain, Behavior, and Environment Can Break the Vicious Circle of Aggression.* New York: The Free Press, 1999.

Ninh Bao. *The Sorrow of War: A Novel of North Vietnam.* Translated from the Vietnamese by Phan Thanh Hao. Hanoi: Writers Association Publishing House, 1991; New York: Pantheon, 1995.

O'Brien, Tim. *Going after Cacciato.* New York: Broadway Books, 1999.

———. *The Things They Carried.* Boston: Houghton Mifflin, 1990.

Sassoon, Siegfried. *Collected Poems 1908–1956.* New York: Faber and Faber, 1984.

———. *Sherston's Progress.* Rochester, New York: Simon Publications, 2004.

Shapiro, Francine, and Margot Silk Forrest. *EMDR: Eye Movement Desensitization and Reprocessing.* New York: Perseus, 1997.

von Clausewitz, C. *On War.* Princeton, New Jersey: Princeton University Press, 1989.

Williams, Candis M., and Tom Williams. "Family therapy for Viet Nam veterans." In *The Trauma of War: Stress and Recovery in Viet Nam Veterans,* edited by Stephen Sonnenberg, Arthur S. Blank Jr., and John A. Talbott. Washington, D.C.: American Psychiatric Press, 1985.

Williams, Tom, ed. *Post-Traumatic Stress Disorders: A Handbook for Clinicians.* Cincinnati, Ohio: Disabled American Veterans, 1987.

Winterson, Jeanette. *The Passion.* New York: Vintage Press, 1989.

Zinn, Howard. *You Can't Be Neutral on a Moving Train: A Personal History of Our Times.* Boston: Beacon Press, 1994.

INDEX